Jua Kali
Kenya

Change & Development
in an Informal Economy
1970–95

Jua Kali in Swahili means 'hot sun'. But over the course of the 1980s, and perhaps a little earlier, it came to be used of the informal sector artisans, such as car mechanics and metalworkers who were particularly noticeable for working under the hot sun because of the absence of premises. People began to talk of taking their cars to jua kali mechanics. Gradually the term was extended to refer to anyone in self-employment, whether in the open air or in permanent premises. On 28 May 1988 *The Standard* reported that the Minister of Technical Training and Applied Technology wished to encourage the use of the term jua kali rather than informal sector, and had therefore announced that the small-scale industry which had come to be known as the informal sector would henceforth assume the name Jua Kali Development Programme.

The term 'informal sector' was first used of Ghana by Keith Hart in 1971. But it was in Kenya that it was first widely applied in 1971 and 1972.

This photograph was used on the front cover of The African Artisan *by Kenneth King (1977). John Nene was one of the original group of informal sector workers interviewed by Kenneth King in the early seventies. See page 63 for photographs of him, his son and his work today.*

Front cover. *A view of part of Kamukunji in Nairobi, one of the oldest sites of jua kali activity in the city; it was visited by President Moi in 1985 and it was on this spot where he delivered his promise to provide sheds to shade jua kali workers from the hot sun. One of these sheds can be seen in the picture.*

Eastern African Studies

Jua Kali
Kenya

Change & Development
in an Informal Economy
1970–95

KENNETH KING
Professor of
International & Comparative Education
& Director of the Centre of African Studies
University of Edinburgh

James Currey
LONDON

EAEP
NAIROBI

Ohio University Press
ATHENS

James Currey Ltd
54b Thornhill Square
London N1 1BE

East African Educational Publishers
Kijabe Street, P.O. Box 45314
Nairobi, Kenya

Ohio University Press
Scott Quadrangle
Athens, Ohio 45701, USA

First published 1996

1 2 3 4 5 00 99 98 97 96

British Library Cataloguing in Publication Data
King, Kenneth, 1940–
    Jua Kali Kenya : change and development in an informal
economy, 1970–95
    1. Informal sector (economics) – Africa
    I. Title
    331.1'25'096

ISBN 0-85255-240-8 (James Currey Cloth)
ISBN 0-85255-239-4 (James Currey Paper)

Library of Congress Cataloging-in-Publication Data available

ISBN 0-8214-1156-X (Ohio University Press Cloth)
ISBN 0-8214-1157-8 (Ohio University Press Paper)

Typeset in 10/11pt Baskerville
Long House Publishing Services, Cumbria, UK
Printed in Great Britain
by Villiers Publications, London N3

To
Pravina

Contents

List of Tables

Acknowledgements

I owe a special debt to the Presidential Commission on Education and Training to the Year 2000 and Beyond, since it was their invitation to me to return to Kenya and participate in one of their seminars in Eldoret in May 1987 that rekindled my interest in revisiting the informal sector, which I had last worked on in 1974. Also at that seminar, I was impressed by the very strong policy support for the informal sector coming from Professor Terry Ryan, Director of Planning in the Ministry of National Development and Planning. At that same seminar John Bunde Owigar, Assistant Director of Technical Training in the Ministry of Technical Training and Applied Technology (MTTAT) also strongly encouraged me to undertake this work. Once the research had been agreed, I was given considerable assistance by many different individuals in different ministries. I would particularly wish to single out Dr I. Onyango and Dr R. Gachira, at that time in the Ministry of Finance and Planning, who were very supportive, as well as being ready to provide the latest information as the *Sessional Paper no. 2 of 1992 on small enterprise and jua kali development in Kenya* took shape. Within MTTAT, I had very valuable discussions with the head of the Jua Kali Development Programme, Mr Mutiso, and was given generous access to materials relating to the informal sector, and particularly valuable were the files on the individual jua kali associations.

My period of research planning and then the research itself spanned three directors of the Institute for Development Studies (IDS) at the University of Nairobi, to which I was attached. First, Kabiru Kinyanjui, then Njuguna Ng'ethe, and finally Patrick Alila all gave generously of their time in support of the project. Also within the IDS, I am extremely grateful to Dorothy McCormick, first for suggesting that Charles Abuodha might assist with the research, and later for involving me in her own international seminar on micro-enterprise.

Many individuals in donor agencies were extremely helpful, and also in NGOs that were concerned with micro-enterprise development, there were particularly helpful directors and researchers. I would want, amongst many others, to single out Chris Aleke-Dondo of K-REP, Aidan Broderick of the British Council, David Wright, Small Enterprise Adviser with ODA in London, Hugh Scott of the ODA in Kenya, and David Court of the Rockefeller Foundation.

Research in a foreign country is greatly assisted by certain colleagues and associates who are prepared to go out of their way to provide insight into the wider context of Kenyan and East African developments. Very generous help in these areas was afforded by Nick and Bridget Evans, Neils and Inger Jorgensen, Ben and Leah Kipkorir, Anna Obura, James and Sarah Foster, Fitz and Romila De Souza.

I owe a particular debt of gratitude to my research associate, Charles Abuodha. He had extremely good skills in interviewing, as well as being able to make a very valuable contribution to the conceptualization of the work as it progressed. I was also helped by Maya De Souza in the later stages of the work.

The bulk of the work was supported by the Economic and Social Research Council (ESCOR) of the Overseas Development Administration (ODA). Additional support was provided by the Gatsby Trust for Charles Abuodha to visit Edinburgh in 1991. The Rockefeller Foundation in Nairobi was also supportive of Charles Abuodha. Clearly, none of these bodies bears any responsibility for the contents of this book.

As to completing the writing on the book, I owe a particular obligation to Natasha Gray and Janet McMillan who ensured that three consecutive family holidays at Menton were organized around its completion rather than on more trivial pursuits.

A last word of gratitude must be awarded to my close associates within the informal sector itself. As last time in the early 1970s, I owe a particular debt of gratitude to Andrew Gachangiu, James Giathi, Gacuiri Kagotho, Kimotho, and Mutang'ang'i. Three individuals deserve very special mention. James Kamande, candlemaker in Starehe, was unfailingly helpful in conversations over a five year period. Paul Thairu made his office and workshop available to me for meetings and discussions in Gikomba. But my largest debt, as last time, must be to John Nene Ihugo. He would go out of his way to meet me and discuss the progress of the research despite being a full-time plumbing sub-contractor. As last time, it is just a small acknowledgement of my gratitude to him that he and his son appear in the photographs on pp. iv and 63.

Kenneth King
Edinburgh

Introduction

In 1972 I started research in Kenya which would go on for several years and finally be published as *The African Artisan* in 1977. A full ten years later, in 1986/7, I found myself being drawn back into commenting on the informal sector, as governments and donor agencies began to give it renewed attention. The reasons for this fresh agency interest in the informal sector have been more fully discussed elsewhere (King, 1991a), but they are directly connected with the perceived crisis of the state and of the formal public sector of the economy, especially in Africa. They were also linked to a new realization about the crisis in formal sector employment, and to a recognition that even if the formal sector of the economy in Africa had continued to expand – which it manifestly had not in these past years of job-shedding associated with structural adjustment – the sheer number of new aspirants to that once preferred job sector could not conceivably have been absorbed.

But by the late 1980s there were several other differences in attitude towards the informal sector beyond this employment dimension. For some agencies one attraction of the informal sector was that it could be conceptualized as a small-scale but very important part of the private sector of the economy. In contrast to the public sector, both government and parastatal, which had been judged so unsuccessful in so many developing countries, the informal economy from Peru, to Ghana and to Kenya could be characterized as dynamic. It did not suffer from the bloated numbers so often alleged of the public enterprises. It illustrated the virtue of high levels of competitiveness as compared to the widely criticized monopolies associated with the state sector. And, perhaps as important as anything else, it operated quite without subsidy in respect of its inputs or its products. In a word it exemplified for many of its admirers the benefits of the market.

Not only was the informal sector not subsidized in any way but traditionally it had either been neglected or even actively harassed by the national government or the municipal authorities. Unlike the higher echelons of the private sector where, in several countries, select numbers of incipient small-scale entrepreneurs were installed, through joint schemes of donors and governments, in highly subsidized mini-industrial estates, and then protected and allegedly featherbedded to an excessive degree (World Bank, 1987), the regular informal sector operators have had little or no transactions with government. They have not been the recipients of credit; they have had no help with access to land, and no assistance with marketing their products. To many outsiders disenchanted with the role of the state in Africa, the informal sector demonstrated a very different kind of Africa.

Finally, unlike so many of the formal sector training schemes, with their emphasis on certification, training in the micro-enterprise sector was judged to be highly efficient. Indeed it corresponded to many of the criteria that were becoming associated with appropriate training for less developed countries. It was entirely local and unsubsidized; it was carried out in very close proximity to the workplace and hence did not suffer from the alleged irrelevance of so much conventional vocational training (World Bank, 1991; Birks *et al.*, 1992); and, typically, the beneficiaries or trainees contributed to the costs of their own training.

This book is concerned with two dimensions of this increasingly admired informal sector in the late 1980s and early 1990s. First, it recognizes that the admiration of the informal sector began to lead to a change both in external donor and non-governmental organization (NGO) policies on the one hand and to shifts in attitudes of national governments on the other. Quite suddenly from a situation where there had been almost no informal sector projects, it became commonplace for external donors and NGOs to be supporting schemes that touched the informal sector in many different ways, from micro-enterprise credit, to entrepreneurship training, and from income-generation schemes for women, to appropriate technology development programmes for informal sector artisans. On the government side, too, there was new interest, and especially in the re-orientation of national schooling systems towards self-employment, and in a recognition of the potential of job creation in the micro-enterprise sector.

The second dimension of the changes traced in this book is whether the informal sector entrepreneurs themselves see their situation differently in the early 1990s than they did in the early 1970s.

In respect of both sides of these changes Kenya is a very appropriate research site. First, as the country where the concept of the informal sector was originally developed in 1972 as part of the recommendations of a World Employment Programme mission, there has been a tradition of research and policy discussion on the informal sector almost continuously for 20 years.[1] It is perhaps, therefore, no accident that it should have been in Kenya first that the idea of an informal sector policy emerged as part of central government thinking. The same thing was almost certainly true of many of the development assistance agencies – that they selected Kenya as the first site in Africa for some of their earliest programmes of support to micro-enterprise development.

As far as the informal sector artisans themselves are concerned, a number of them were interviewed intensively in the early 1970s as part of the research that was reported in *The African Artisan*. It was possible almost 20 years later to revisit both the artisans and the main worksites in which they had earlier worked. This suggested the possibility that it might be feasible to compare some dimensions of change over time within the informal sector.

Research method

Initially, an attempt was made to trace the main body of those informal sector operators who had been interviewed in the early 1970s. The bulk of these had been in two very different trades, metalwork and candlemaking (creating small tin lamps out of scrap). But it proved relatively easy to find most of them again, since many of them were known to each other through being in the same extended family, trade or village. In addition to this core group, a larger number were contacted in the same two trades, as well as in the trades of carpentry and tailoring, bringing the total interviewed to 100 in all. In most cases these additional numbers were drawn from the same two areas as the original artisans – from Gikomba, one of the earliest sites of informal sector activity within Nairobi, and Githiga, a small village some 40 km north of Nairobi in the Kiambu District of Central Province.

Beyond these 100 artisans, recourse was also had to the Ministry of Technical Training and Applied Technology (MTTAT) which in the late 1980s had been made responsible for some support to informal sector development. As part of that activity it had followed President Moi's prompting and had encouraged artisans to form associations and register themselves to acquire identification cards. This had the effect of large numbers of artisans registering with the Ministry, including, by good fortune, associations of artisans from Gikomba and Githiga. This meant that many of the individuals who had been interviewed personally had also given the essential information about their enterprise on a standard form to the Ministry. It was possible to have access to all these forms.

In our own interviewing, in 1989, 1990 and early 1991, I was greatly helped by Charles Abuodha, a fellow of Nairobi University's Institute for Development Studies. One of our principal preoccupations in the interview checklist was with change over time, not only because we were particularly interested in a group who had been initially interviewed some 17 or 18 years earlier, but also because we wished to achieve something of this same historical depth with our additional interviewees. Accordingly, we deliberately sought in our interviews to identify such processes as the move into self-employment (both in the case of those who had earlier been employed and those who had only known self-employment). How had tools been acquired? How had savings been utilized? Had the entrepreneur actually started by taking small sub-contracts while remaining basically employed? Our interest in this often lengthy and hesitant transition to self-employment was sharpened by the very loose and optimistic discussions about how all training institutions in Kenya – and indeed all primary schools – could be asked to re-orient their trainees and pupils to self-employment.

We tried also to create for each of our interviewees a history of their production over time. What had they started with manufacturing and why had they moved on to other products? We were also interested in their aspirations to try and make particular tools, even if these had not succeeded. We created, therefore, inventories of their stock of machines, and sought to distinguish between those that had been bought and those that had been devised and constructed personally. And along with the machinery, we made inventories of what had been produced, and in some cases, who these products had been sold to.

As we interviewed around these kinds of issues, we became aware of the importance of rather a slippery concept which we termed 'technological confidence'. Although it was difficult to define, it could be summed up as a kind of 'can-do' attitude to be found in several of the more innovative entrepreneurs. It was not particularly based on schooling, nor on access to specialized vocational training. Rather it was an attitude of mind that was ready to figure out how something could be made. It was clearly not a scientific confidence – in fact some of the innovators had little or no formal science education. But it was a confidence in their own capacity to understand and mould materials for particular purposes.

For some of these artisans, therefore, we developed interview texts that were many pages long. Others were much shorter. But, initially, we sought to examine some of the more obvious contrasts within our sample of four trades, and in a first report on this research, we laid out some of these differences, especially in the areas of education, capital stock and estimated income (Abuodha & King, 1991). It became clear from this preliminary analysis that a more in-depth, qualitative account would be needed if we were to understand some of the developments over time with which we were concerned. Accordingly, this present text looks into the life histories, and seeks to achieve a balance between the history and development of particular individuals and the larger picture of the informal sector in Kenya as a whole.

Snapshot versus multiple visits

Although the initial research report was made to the sponsor, the Overseas Development Administration (ODA), in 1991 as planned, there were some advantages to the completion of this monograph taking place over a longer period. The initial field work was carried out in the British summers of 1989 and 1990, and thus took place before November 1990 when there was some of the most serious harassment of the urban informal sector ever to take place in Kenya. A further small grant (from the Gatsby Foundation) allowed Abuodha to visit Edinburgh and report on further developments in both our sample and in government policies during 1991. Then in 1992, the ODA supported a brief updating visit to Kenya. These three separate visits to Kenya allowed contact to be maintained with the key informants over a three-year period. But it also made it possible to trace the changes in government, donor and NGO policies towards the sector much more effectively than in a single intensive visit.

By good fortune, it was possible to connect this present research with

Fig. 2.6: Paul Kairu's office in one of the Gikomba streets. Above the factory floor.

Fig. 2.7: Part of the large order for window-stays being completed by Paul Kairu (left). Seven or eight different hand-operated machines with customized tools and dies are needed for this one item.

Figs. 2.9 and 2.10: One of John Nene's early plumbing jobs in a science laboratory (Nene on left); a later job, in 1992, involving all the plumbing, septic tanks and drainage for a large mansion outside Nairobi.

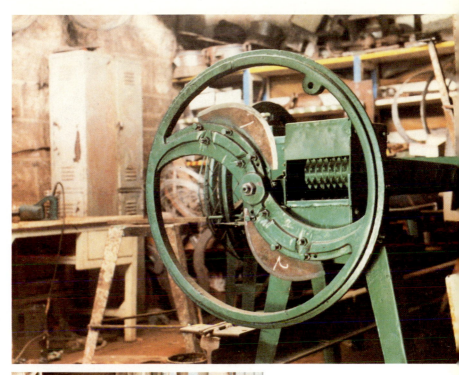

Figs. 2.13 and 2.14: The 'zero-grazer' with its heavy flywheel and its blades for cutting maize stalks and napier grass into very short pieces, in Peter Kagotho's Gikomba workshop. And being prepared for sale and transport outside his workshop (Kagotho on right).

Figs. 2.19 and 2.20: James Giathi (with formal sector type work-coat) welding digging tools (jembes) in the workshop in California, Nairobi, shared with Gacuiri. Apart from one old electrically powered punch machine and welding equipment, the workshop has a forest of hand-operated machine tools.

Figs. 2.22 and 2.23: Gacuiri (middle) building a bus body onto a vehicle frame in his shared Nairobi workshop. Also Gacuiri (on right) checking the welding on a nearly completed maize mill.

Fig. 2.25: Njenga still operating under the hot sun in both Shauri Moyo and in nearby Kamukunji. Note the supply of digging tools (jembes) *made on his hand operated shears.*

Fig. 2.27: Gachangiu (left) operating a hand-grinder, still in the open air in Kamukunji, Nairobi.

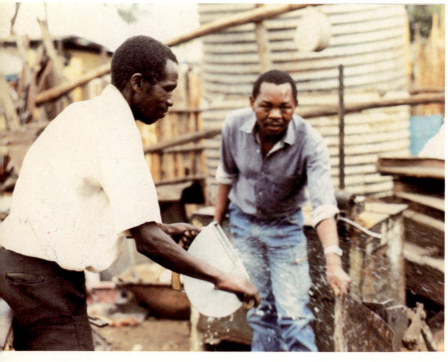

Fig. 2.30: Njagi at Starehe, surrounded by a sea of candles, prepared in strings of 20 for sale.

Fig. 2.31: Joseph Kamande (in green jersey), tin-lampmaker, operating in Starehe, Nairobi in very temporary premises with a group, including his Form IV educated son.

Fig. 2.33: Kimotho, one of the longest serving tin-lampmakers. Now operating in Jerusalem, Nairobi, and an office bearer of the Kimathi Ward Jua Kali Society.

Fig. 4.6: Mutang'ang'i (right) in part of his large, partly open-air yard in Githiga village

a wide range of associated micro-enterprise research being conducted in Kenya and more generally in Africa, since there was a major seminar held in Nairobi on the micro-enterprise sector in January 1993 organized jointly between Dorothy McCormick of IDS Nairobi and Poul Pedersen of the Centre for Development Research in Copenhagen,[2] and the following autumn it was possible to participate in an international seminar organized by ILO in Turin which focused very specifically on the extent to which vocational training centres, including those in Kenya, should orient their clienteles towards self-employment.

This effectively widened the context of Kenya's own innovations in vocational training for self-employment. But more generally the educational dimension of our research on Kenya was further extended by the ODA's Education Division commissioning Roy Carr-Hill and myself in 1993–4 to carry out a comprehensive review of education and training for self-employment. There was scope within this review for a case study from Kenya and other countries to be included. Which in turn meant that the Kenya Rural Enterprise Programme (K-REP) made an important contribution to the ODA study. Both the wider review and the case studies, however, have fed into the education and training chapter of this present book.[3]

Effectively this has meant that in addition to maintaining contact with certain key informants in Kenya over the period from July 1989 to December 1994, it has also been possible to try and make connections between the particularity of this Kenya study and the wider international thinking about education, training and micro-enterprise as it has developed in this same period.

Notes

1. The term 'informal sector' was first used of Ghana by Keith Hart, but only became commonplace after the ILO Kenya Mission in 1972.
2. See further McCormick, D. and Pedersen, P. (eds), 1996 Small Enterprises: Flexibility and Networking in an African Context, Longhorn Kenya, Nairobi.
3. McGrath, S. and King, K. with Leach, F. and Carr-Hill, R., 1995, Education and Training for the Informal Sector, ODA Occasional Publication, Serial No. 11, vol. I, ODA, London.

Abbreviations

ApT	ApT Design and Development (Moreton-in-Marsh, Gloucs.)
ARTCA	Association of Round Tables of Central Africa (Salisbury/Harare)
BMZ	Federal Ministry for Economic Cooperation (Bonn)
CESO	Centre for the Study of Education in Developing Countries (The Hague)
COTU	Central Organization of Trade Unions (Kenya)
CZI	The Confederation of Zimbabwe Industries (Harare)
DSE	German Foundation for International Development (Bonn)
EARC	East Africa Royal Commission
FIT	Farm Implements and Tools (Amsterdam)
GEMINI	Growth and Equity through Micro-enterprise Investments and Institutions (USA)
GTZ	German Agency for Technical Cooperation (Eschborn)
ICDC	Industrial and Commercial Development Corporation (Nairobi)
ICED	International Council for Educational Development (New York)
IDRC	International Development Research Centre (Ottawa)
IDS	Institute for Development Studies (Nairobi)
IIE	Institute of International Education (Stockholm)
IIEP	International Institute for Educational Planning (Paris)
ILO	International Labour Office (Geneva)
KIE	Kenya Industrial Estates (Nairobi)
K-MAP	Kenya Management Assistance Programme (Nairobi)
KNFJKA	Kenya National Federation of Jua Kali Associations (Nairobi)
KNJKF	Kenya National Jua Kali Federation (Nairobi)
KNJKO	Kenya National Jua Kali Organization (Nairobi)
K-REP	Kenya Rural Enterprise Programme (Nairobi)
KYTEC	Kenya Youth Training and Employment Creation
MEDI	Malawian Entrepreneurs Development Institute
MRTT&T	Ministry of Research, Technical Training and Technology (Kenya)
MTTAT	Ministry of Technical Training and Applied Technology (Kenya)
NEPI	National Education Policy Initiative (South Africa)
ODA	Overseas Development Administration (London)
OECD	Organization for Economic Cooperation and Development (Paris)
PRIDE	Programme of Rural Initiatives and Development Enterprises Ltd (Kenya)
RPED	Regional Programme on Enterprise Development (World Bank)
SDSR	Skills Development for Self-Reliance (Nairobi)
TADREG	Tanzania Development Research Group (Dar es Salaam)
TOOL	NGO for the Transfer of Technology to Developing Countries (Amsterdam)
UNDP	United Nations Development Programme (New York)
VET	Vocational Education and Training
VSO/IT	Voluntary Service Overseas (London)/Intermediate Technology (Rugby)

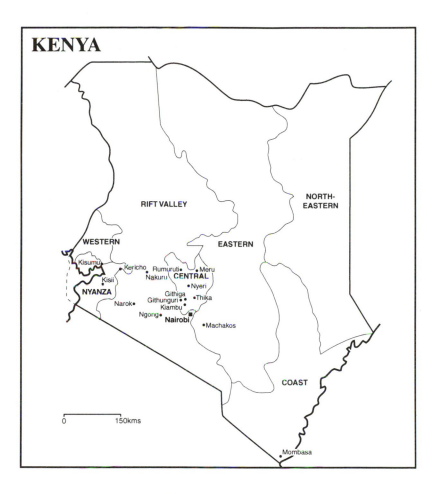

KENYA

RIFT VALLEY

NORTH-EASTERN

WESTERN

EASTERN

Kisumu

Kericho• •Rumuruti• •Meru
Nakuru• CENTRAL
Kisii
NYANZA
•Nyeri
Githiga •Thika
Githunguri•
Narok• Kiambu•
Ngong• Nairobi
•Machakos

COAST

0   150kms

Mombasa•

Frequently used Swahili words

harambee	self-help, local community fund-raising
jiko	charcoal brazier
jembe	digging instrument
matatu	local taxi
askari	municipal police
magendo	stolen goods
fundi	skilled worker
jua kali	informal sector worker (literally 'hot sun')

Note: Several of these are locally used in East Africa
with an English plural
(e.g. askaris, fundis, matatus, and jikos).

xix

City of Nairobi

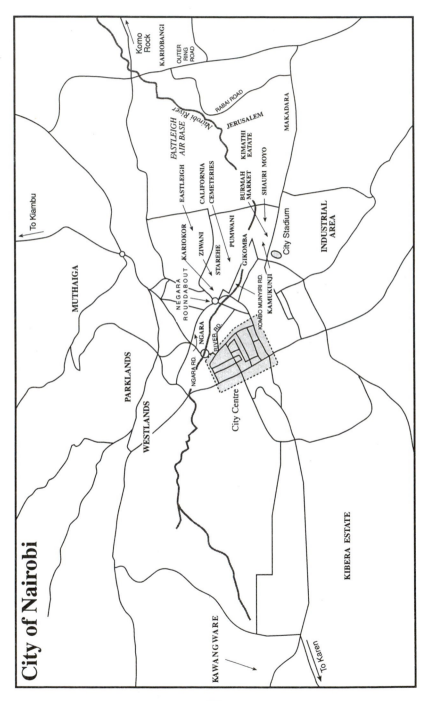

One

From Informal Sector to Jua Kali

The Kenyanization of Micro-enterprise Development

One afternoon in November 1985, President Moi stopped off at the area called Kamukunji on the way back from visiting the nearby City Stadium in Nairobi. On the surface it would seem that he had been drawn by the incessant hammering and clatter of the metalworkers who for many years have clustered there, and have transformed the heavy metal of the secondhand oil drums into cooking vessels, and the lighter tin sheets from the adjacent formal industrial area into a whole variety of domestic goods. It seemed that he had stopped by chance, and in a highly symbolic act he promised sheds to shade these 'hot sun' (*jua kali*) workers from the weather (see figures 1.1 and 1.2). Would this be a turning point at last in the official recognition of what had been called the informal sector since the early 1970s? (See Map 2)

What was intriguing about the events of late 1985 was that the President was back in the area just two weeks later, visiting both the tinsmith/blacksmith concentration in Kamukunji and also the agglomeration of automobile and lorry mechanics in nearby Gikomba and Ziwani. This time the headline in the *Kenya Times* read that he was organizing a Christmas party for the mechanics. Furthermore, the building of sheds for them would be the beginning of their fuller incorporation into the national economy:

> Once the sheds are completed, the mechanics would be properly organized so that their skills could be harnessed to the mainstream of the country's industrial development. (*Kenya Times*, 20 November 1985)

President Moi was back visiting the same area in early December. Then again early in January 1986 he revisited the Gikomba jua kali garages, and in February, to thunderous applause from the mechanics, he was promising free sheds and title deeds to go to those allotted spaces (*Kenya*

1

Figs. 1.1 and 1.2: The first sheds, built in 1986 at Kamukunji, Nairobi, at the request of President Moi, to shade some of the jua kali metalworkers from the hot sun. The stoves, kitchen utensils, trunks, cans and bicycle carriers are mostly made from scrap metal.

Times, 5 December 1985; 9 January 1986; 6 February 1986). Five Presidential visits to one small area in just four months is an indication of something very special.

Ten years later, it may be appropriate to try and make some judgement about just how special the informal (jua kali) sector has become in Kenya and to what extent it has become an integral part of the national economy.[1] But it would also be useful to sketch the historical process whereby in the years before the open Presidential approval in 1985 an awareness grew about the importance of the informal economy in Kenya. We may then judge whether it was really by chance that the President stopped to visit the informal sector in November 1985, or whether it was rather the culmination of a series of other developments.

* * *

But there are at least three dimensions of what may be called the Kenyanization of the informal sector. One is the issue of incorporating the informal economy fully into the national economy, and giving due recognition to its importance. Another is the development of a specifically Kenyan contribution to the continuing academic and policy debates about the role of these micro-enterprises, in a situation where traditionally both the academic and policy discussions of the informal sector had been dominated by foreign scholars. Then there is a third dimension which has often been absent in discussions of the informal economy and that is the voice of the jua kali themselves.

In *The African Artisan* (King, 1977) particular importance was attached to 'peopling' the analysis of the informal sector with individuals who were in the early 1970s at the cutting edge of technologies that were becoming important to these small groups of self-employed. Out of the pages of that book came individuals who were identified as the first Africans in Kenya to use hand-operated machine tools. These included both urban and rural operators, such as Mutang'ang'i, Nene, Gacuiri, Gachangiu and Njenga; and in the production of low-cost light, they included Kimotho, Njiru and Njagi. Equally now, in returning to examine change and development in the informal sector over the period of the last 20 years, it has been important to maintain this personal dimension. Hence, the cover of this book captures 20 years later the same person, John Nene, who was photographed in the early 1970s and who was on the cover of *The African Artisan*. What has happened over more than 20 years to someone who was cynical enough to say in 1974:

> Anyway, I will come to my point; young boys are becoming very rich due to nepotism, loans and connections. The only thing I want ... is a loan of about four to five thousand shillings, since I have seen that without a loan or robbery, you can't improve. With robbery I have never attempted yet. But with a loan, I will be able to master it till I get what I want – 'up from the slavery of poverty'? (Nene in King, 1977: 189)

3

And what of the many others apart from Nene? Has any one of the informal operators from those early days 'made it' to the Industrial Area of Nairobi? Has anyone crossed over from the informal to the formal sector of the economy? Is there any evidence that, like many of the East African Indians before them, there would be a move over time from the *duka* (small trading store) to the factory? And what of the technology? At the end of *The African Artisan* we made the point that relatively low-level informal sector technologies were fanning out horizontally across Kenya at great speed, but what was much less evident was any vertical integration into more skill-intensive or capital-intensive modes of production.

History and research on the informal sector

As we address these questions, it will be necessary to go back a little earlier so that the sweep of the last 30 or 40 years can be seen as a whole.

The 'prehistory' of the informal sector in Kenya

Two of the essential elements of the prehistory of the informal sector in Kenya are the *East Africa Royal Commission* of 1953–5 and the Report of the 1966 Kericho Conference in Kenya, published as *Education, Employment and Rural Development* (Sheffield, 1967). The first of these is particularly important because it addressed for the region as a whole one of the issues that was so frequently later on to be considered an obstacle to informal sector development. It drew up a very powerful indictment of the restrictions and regulations that affected so many areas of colonial African life – from marketing, to provision of credit and licences, to the use and sale of land itself. On many topics, the Commission was exceedingly perceptive. It noted, for example, that the clusters of settlements just outside the boundaries of all the main towns were not so much eyesores as they were 'important as centres of African trade' (EARC, 1955: 208). Anticipating the spirit of the International Labour Office's (ILO's) Kenya Employment Mission some 15 years later when the term informal sector was first publicly applied to these kinds of clusters, it argued that

> Their [African traders'] activities are on a very small scale and, lacking security of tenure, they have no incentive to improve their premises. Yet to clear these areas of their inhabitants would be to destroy what in some urban areas, constitutes the only development of African commercial enterprise. (EARC, 1955: 208)

The Commission also argued for the individualizing of land tenure, an initiative that was rapidly put into place in parts of rural Kenya, and which would soon have a powerful influence on the development of cash crops and on farm incomes more generally. In a rather forward-looking comment, the Commission affirmed its belief that African enterprise development was inseparable from urban land reform:

4

> ... experience elsewhere in Africa suggests that private ownership of land in the towns makes possible large-scale indigenous development in the form of well-equipped factories, workshops and stores. (EARC, 1955: 222)

A second important milestone in the prehistory of the informal sector in Kenya came in 1966, just three years after Independence, in the major Kericho Conference. The meeting was the result of the growing awareness of the scale of Kenya's primary school leaver crisis, and what was conceived of as the stark arithmetic of unemployment that faced the dramatically rising numbers of young people. For our present purposes it is interesting to note that what would shortly be termed the urban informal sector was still being characterized by Frederick Harbison, of manpower planning fame, as a sector where the unemployed can 'eke out an existence as casual labourers, stall-holders, beggars or petty thieves' and whose activities also included a 'wide variety of petty barter trade and traditional crafts' (Harbison, 1967: 175, 177). He was aware however that the challenge to this 'traditional sector' in the urban areas was how to 'utilise them somehow in small-scale service industries such as automobile and machinery repair, maintenance, construction and other activities for which demand is constantly rising in urban areas'; there was little point when the traditional sector was either unemployed or 'under-employed in petty trade, primitive crafts, begging and other low productivity activities' in just promoting the expansion of 'the services of stall-holders, casual labourers, artisans and beggars' (Harbison, 1967: 191). This contrast between Harbison's negative description and what would later be termed the productive and service sides of the informal sector is an interesting one, but it does not appear to have been based on a field knowledge of petty production in Nairobi and other towns. [ILO] International Labor Organ.

A third important source of insight into micro-enterprise became available in the very year, 1971, that the ILO Employment Mission were out doing their analysis of Kenya, and that was the publication of *African Businessmen* by Marris and Somerset. The field work for this book had been carried out in 1966–7, and had consisted of some 90 small businesses supported by the Industrial and Commercial Development Corporation (ICDC) in Kenya and some 850 small African enterprises whose owners had been interviewed in market centres across the country. What was unusual about this book was that in facing the fact that 'in 1967 there were scarcely 200 African businesses in Kenya larger than a country store or a craftsman's workshop', the authors still sought seriously to understand the 100 years of continuities and discontinuities between pre-colonial trading patterns and the emergence of African business in the post-Independence period. They also put their finger on something that was becoming unfashionable in the swirl of nation-building, and that was the fact that there was a distinctive trading culture and a business ethic amongst the Kikuyu in parts of Central Province. They did not seek to examine the traditions of business in other indigenous communities, but their

5

acknowledgement of this enterprise culture amongst the Kikuyu might well prove to have been a significant milestone in trying to explain the differential involvement of Kenya's various communities in both formal and informal sectors.

In their own sample of ICDC loan recipients, no less than 64 per cent of the industry loans went to Kikuyu businessmen and 44 per cent of the commercial loans. No other ethnic community was at all close to the Kikuyu in the extent of their participation with this particular scheme. The authors also noted in their market survey that some 5–10 per cent of the shops in the Luo, Luhya, Kisii and Kamba markets around different parts of the country were owned by Kikuyu but that no other people had set up businesses in another tribal area (Marris & Somerset, 1971: 70–1).

Marris and Somerset's book is a landmark at the very start of the period under review because it looks not only at the pre-independence base of African business, and focuses on the particular group who had acquired ICDC loans, but it is able to examine this special group against the background of the ordinary, very small-scale trader or producer in the market squares across Kenya. The ordinariness of these little beginnings of African business are well captured in the following passage, where the lack of differentiation amongst the enterprises is very marked:

> The shops, perhaps 50 or 100, are mostly retail stores selling the same scanty stock of cigarettes, cloth and general groceries, ranged on rough wooden shelves behind a counter. But there may be, too, several bicycle repairers and blacksmiths, hotels and bars, tailors and butchers, a barber, a photographer, a hides and skins dealer, a posho mill, a furniture maker or watch repairer, and two petrol pumps in front of the most prosperous store. Some of the shops are always closed, or open sporadically when the owner has no work on his farm, and others seem more a way of passing the time congenially in the bustle of the market place than a serious enterprise. (Marris & Somerset, 1971: 16)

Marris and Somerset were also unusual in acquiring data on Asian businessmen in order to contrast their attitudes and creed as the group who were located immediately above the aspiring African entrepreneurs. They picked up a very significant level of African animosity towards Asian business practice, which, the authors note, cannot be understood simply as a reaction to ill-treatment. 'It was also a rationalisation of hostility towards their principal competitors' (Marris & Somerset, 1971: 96–7). This question of the relations between African and Asian businessmen we shall return to from time to time in subsequent chapters, and we shall note that in several key trades, the African entrepreneurs have directly acquired many of their skills from their years of employment in the small-scale Indian factory sector.

The 'discovery' of the informal sector in Kenya

The Comprehensive Employment Strategy Mission came to Kenya in 1971 at the request of the ILO and it was responsible for dramatizing the concept of the informal sector. It is intriguing that this concept was

6

disseminated as a result of the Kenya Mission and published in 1972 in the report *Employment, Incomes and Equality: A Strategy for Increasing Productive Employment in Kenya* (ILO, 1972). In point of fact the term 'informal sector' had come from Keith Hart's work among the Frafra migrants from Northern Ghana working in Accra, and a first paper using the term informal sector had been read in a Conference on Urban Unemployment in Africa in Sussex in September 1971. Hart's paper on 'Informal income opportunities and the structure of urban employment in Ghana' crystallized exactly the kind of worry that scholars had been having with the previous emphasis on the unemployment crisis and a sharp urban–rural and modern–traditional divide. In a retrospective reflection on this episode, Hart sketched out the distinctiveness of this unorthodox point of view he had absorbed from Ghana:

> In my paper (Hart, 1973) ... I argued that the new urban poor were certainly employed, if not always for wages. Their incomes were qualitatively more irregular and uncertain; but in quantitative terms they covered a wide range above and below the unskilled wage rate at which the majority of uneducated migrants found jobs. The goal of most people was to combine wages and self-employed incomes. I talked about an 'informal economy' or sector of urban opportunities, drawing on Max Weber's theory of rationalisation to contrast the stable wage employment offered by corporate organisations with the more unpredictable commercial activities I had studied in Accra. (Hart, 1992: 216–17)

The Kenya Mission, a few weeks later, offered the first opportunity to test this unorthodox view (that the allegedly traditional urban sector was actually quite innovative and productive), and the result was that the unorthodox became the new orthodoxy within a year. It is not perhaps surprising, however, that it should have been in Kenya rather than in Ghana or Nigeria that this research idea became adopted as a policy priority of the Employment Mission. What favoured its application in Kenya was that petty enterprise and services had quite rapidly, since Independence, attached themselves to Nairobi and other towns that had been colonial and racially segregated creations. These African beginnings of micro-enterprise were therefore suddenly becoming quite visible. In West Africa, by contrast, with its longstanding local traditions of urban living and trading, the informal economy was so much more a part of the fabric of life it was harder to recognize its policy importance.

What also made it likely that the informal sector concept would take root more readily in Kenyan soil was that there had been a good deal of relevant work done in the Institute for Development Studies of the University of Nairobi on many of the key sectors, such as Education, Housing, Technology, and, in that very same year, African business (with Marris and Somerset). But even before the concept of the informal sector had been openly disseminated in late 1972 by the ILO, parallel ideas such as the 'intermediate sector' had been promoted by scholars such as David Steele who had also been working in Kenya (Steele, 1972: 208).

In other words the climate was right in Kenya for the discovery of the informal sector. It was reinforced also by the fascination with non-formal education, the processes of education and training that were going on outside the formal education system, and which had also just been noted for their policy implications (King, 1991b). It was these latter interests that brought me back to do research in Kenya in July 1972, in blissful ignorance of the Employment Mission visiting Kenya that same year, or of its report that would soon be published. Within a week or two of arriving, I was interviewing young men who had constructed their own rough and ready machines for cutting metal, and had mounted them on wooden poles, just a few yards from the site that President Moi would visit 13 years later. My own interest in the informal sector had been born.

Researching the informal sector: the first phase

The Kenya Mission had drawn upon some 50 expatriate researchers and consultants, and had made a point about the importance of local expertise shortly after it had started its work:

> ... there emerged a clear need to draw more fully on local expertise. Obvious though this need may seem, its recognition on the part of an international mission was something of an innovation... The full involvement of local residents of the country in the work of the mission added greatly to the report and, judging from this experience, would be a valuable innovation for other international missions. (ILO, 1972: xiii)

There have been substantial numbers of papers written on Kenya's informal sector (or intermediate sector) since 1972 when it first swam into public recognition with the publication of the ILO's Employment Mission. But it could be argued that the concept of the informal sector remained relatively remote from ordinary Kenyans, and was really only a technical term restricted to academics, planners and consultants. Indeed, the ILO Report (with its very important chapter 7 on the informal sector in Kenya) had almost certainly much more influence on the development and research community internationally than on Kenya. Undoubtedly, there was a discernible impact on subsequent Kenyan development plans (for example, 1974–8, and 1979–83), and there was no shortage of academic papers on the informal sector with explicit policy implications, produced principally by the University of Nairobi's Institute for Development Studies. But at this stage during the 1970s, the writing and debates on the informal sector were predominantly carried on by foreign academics and planners attached to Kenya. Many of these were well known, and they played an important role in internationalizing debate about the informal sector that was derived from Kenyan data. They would include: Frank Child, Walter Elkan, Peter Henning, Dharam Ghai, Frances Stewart, Ichiro Inukai, Malcolm Harper, Peter Kilby, William House, Raphael Kaplinsky, Tony Killick, Kenneth King, Per Kongstad, David Steele, Steve Langdon, Colin Leys, Ian Livingstone, and Glen Norcliffe – to mention only some of those who wrote at that time on the informal sector (K-REP, 1993a; Abuodha & King, 1991).

There were local scholars such as Philip Mbithi contributing to some of these debates in the 1970s, but it was not really until the 1980s and early 1990s that Kenyans were taking lead roles in research and writing about the informal sector. These would include G. Ndua, Njuguna Ng'ethe, B. Makau, Robert Gichira, Chris Aleke-Dondo, Kinuthia Macharia, Patrick Alila, I. A. Onyango, Charles Abuodha, Mauri Yambo, G. Ikiara, and Henry Oketch (K-REP, 1993a). In many cases such research was still sponsored by external agencies. Indeed there were many fewer local research funds in universities in Sub-Saharan Africa in the 1980s than in the previous two decades; hence external research funding and research priorities were in some ways even more dominant in the 1980s and early 1990s than in the 1960s and 1970s. Even if there were many more Kenyans writing on the informal sector in the 1980s and 1990s, this could also be a pointer to the topic remaining important in agency agendas. This is certainly the case, as we shall see shortly. But a more worrying trend had begun to affect the academic community in Kenya at the very point that a substantial Kenyanization of research on the informal sector had become a possibility.

Researching the informal and micro-enterprise sector: the second phase
What had become vividly clear by the 1980s was that the research environment in developing countries in general had dramatically changed (Nkinyangi and Shaeffer, eds, 1983), and this included research in Kenya on the informal sector. In the late 1960s and early 1970s, expatriates and Kenyans had been attached to the Institute for Development Studies, and even the expatriates had been on relatively long-term contracts to the University of Nairobi. But at the very point when the younger Kenyans could have been expected increasingly to build up substantive research careers in the university, the financial crisis struck. Kenyan university salaries – and indeed the salaries in many of the other universities in Sub-Saharan Africa – failed to provide a living wage. Academic research, unless funded by an external body, became a luxury that few could afford to maintain whatever their dedication to a particular field of study. There were two consequences. Many academics began progressively to rely on consultancy research to supplement their meagre salaries. Others left the Kenyan university sector completely in order to work outside the country or for the donor agencies.

Those who remained in the country, in the university world, were increasingly dependent on consultancy funds for their research, but they were also squeezed by the massive and unprecedented rise in student numbers, and by a change in the very character of the university. The University of Nairobi, for example, shifted from being an elite, research-oriented institution to one that had to face the rise in student numbers along with savage reductions in the resourcing of the library and other research collections. The consequence for many of its staff, including for those interested in developing and maintaining their work on the informal sector, was that they could not be certain of working steadfastly on this

9

topic for a significant portion of their professional lives. The exigencies of the consultancy mode of research are that it is not possible to work on the same field year after year (Court, 1991). In a situation where two months of consultancy may be equivalent to a substantial portion of annual salary it is not surprising that local academics have found it difficult to focus consistently over time on the same academic field.

One result of this contract research mode within a wider context of a deteriorating academic environment is that a rather large number of Kenya scholars have written just a handful of articles on the informal sector over the past 10 to 15 years. In the very useful review of *Jua Kali Literature: An annotated bibliography* (K-REP, 1993a), it is noticeable that there are many Kenyan names with just a single entry relating to the informal sector. By contrast the two or three scholars with the longest list of publications directly relating to the informal and micro-enterprise sector in the recent period are either working outside the local university world (e.g. Chris Aleke-Dondo and Henry Oketch in the Kenya Rural Enterprise Programme; Kinuthia Macharia in Harvard, and Robert Gichira in ILO) or they are in the University of Nairobi but in special circumstances (e.g. Dorothy McCormick, an American scholar working in the Institute for Development Studies, Nairobi on a local salary, but attached to an American religious order).

The growth of a Kenyan capacity to monitor and analyse developments in the sector has been affected consequently by this broader malaise affecting higher education research environments across Sub-Saharan Africa. One result has been the absence of major academic monographs by Kenyan scholars on micro-enterprises, small-scale industry or the informal and jua kali sector in these last 20 years. This is not to say that there have not been a large number of very valuable, shorter policy studies, consultancy papers, occasional papers and edited collections, examining all manner of specific dimensions, from loans, to buildings, to policy development, and particular trades. The range of work associated with Kenya Rural Enterprise Programme has been particularly important in this respect. But there has not been an enabling higher education research environment for a Kenyan scholar to focus on the academic study of the informal sector for a substantial period and author a major monograph.

The policy development process: from the ILO Mission (1972) to *Economic Management for Renewed Growth* (1986)

The reason for selecting these two documents is that the first, as we have already noted, is very much the starting point for major policy attention to the informal sector in Kenya, even if there had been a series of other less dramatic developments in the previous 15 years. And the second marks the point at which we can really talk about a local ownership – almost a rediscovery of the importance of the informal sector.

It is worth analysing, however, whether there has been a notable development in the Kenyanization of informal sector policy over the period from the early 1970s to the late 1980s and mid-1990s. At the beginning of this period, we have said, there was a very powerful, generative theme – the new potential of the informal sector – identified by an international employment mission which happened, partly by coincidence, to illustrate this theme in a Kenyan setting. By the end of the period under review, almost 25 years later, it will be useful to discuss to what extent this informal sector theme has become localized as a component of employment or labour market policies in Kenya.

The character of the informal sector according to the ILO

What was notable about the ILO's analysis of the informal sector in 1972 was that, in contrast to prevailing attitudes towards the large numbers of Africans not working in regular, modern sector jobs, the Employment Mission was extremely positive. Unlike the images of shiftless, under- or unemployed Africans, engaged in living off the towns and off the wage and salary workers, the ILO Mission made the simple assertion that most of those outside the modern sector were actually also working. Not only were they working, but working very hard, with resources they had saved by themselves, with labour-intensive and adapted technologies, with skills acquired outside the formal system, and most important of all, it seemed relatively easy to enter this mode of work, even though it was clearly unregulated and highly competitive (ILO, 1972: 6).

The ILO advice to the Kenya Government was in some way parallel to the liberalization that the East Africa Royal Commission had urged Kenya to adopt in the late colonial period. In particular, they urged the abandonment of the shanty demolition and harassment policies and their substitution by site-and-service schemes, and greater security of tenure. They also recommended the simplification of the trade licensing system, and suggested that there should be much closer ties between formal and informal sectors through subcontracting.

Conceptually, the ILO recognized that the informal sector was not just an urban phenomenon, but was a very important part of rural life. More interestingly, they characterized the development of the sector and of the activities associated with it as illustrating the spirit of self-reliance that had been so obvious in other spheres of Kenyan life:

> In a striking way it is a parallel to the Harambee, or self-help, movement which has been such a fundamental part of Kenyan social and economic development in the period since the attainment of national independence: in both cases the recognition of unfilled needs generated by social change is followed by individual or group action on a local basis. (ILO, 1972: 225)

The ILO Mission acknowledged that the informal sector's development had, like *harambee*, been independent of government support, but they felt that there must be a close relationship between the policies adopted by

11

government in all major spheres – fiscal, employment, education, agriculture, technology and exchange rate – and the impact on the informal sector. Significantly, they recognized that the informal sector was here to stay and to expand, whatever policies the government did or did not adopt. It also was the provider of employment, goods and services for lower-income groups, for which there was no alternative source of supply.

The analogy with the *harambee* movement touches, however, on the dilemma of much informal sector policy: that if what is special and positive about the informal sector has been developed despite total neglect and even active discouragement by the state, then would it not be valuable for government to continue a hands-off approach? This was the origin of the view that on the whole the sector should be left well alone; that there was nothing to be gained by government interference. Any attempt to 'formalize the informal sector' could well undermine its robust independence. Surely, it was said, if the sector were made more secure in respect of work sites, housing, and subcontracts from the modern sector, there was a danger of damaging its creativity and rugged self-reliance?

In many ways, this tension between doing nothing and intervention characterizes a good deal of the next ten and more years of government thinking in Kenya. True, there were references in the Development Plans to the informal sector, and there was even a Sessional Paper on Employment issued shortly after the ILO Mission. In the Kenya Government Development Plans that followed the ILO Mission, figures for the urban and rural informal sectors were duly produced, and it is interesting to note that 10 years after the Mission had estimated the size of the urban informal sector as at least 100,000, it was said to be just over 150,000 (Kenya, 1983: 7). Equally, at this same time, the Development Plan was distinguishing in a highly artificial manner between different categories of small and cottage industry, as if the more flexible approaches to enterprise associated with the ILO Employment Mission had been forgotten:

> The following definitions of Small and Cottage Industries will be adopted at the national level. Small industries are units engaged in processing, manufacturing, assembling and/or servicing activities having total fixed investment ranging from K.Sh. 50,000 and K. Sh. 500,000 if the cost of land, buildings and civil works are included...; or in which employment varies between 6 and 49 persons and the plant is run partly or wholly with motive power. Cottage industries are those in which the fixed investment is less than K. Sh. 50,000 *or* employment is less than 6 if the plant is run with motive power or any number if no motive power is used. (Kenya, 1983: 199)

The informal sector moves centre stage – an element in *Economic Management for Renewed Growth* (1986)

Quite suddenly, within two years, the mood had changed. In 1985 the government had introduced a major restructuring of education and training, with much greater emphasis on vocational, scientific and technological development. This was followed almost immediately (in August 1985) by the commissioning of a 'Presidential working party on education and manpower training for the next decade and beyond' which was very concerned about the skill base of the expanding population. By this time also in late 1985 the core thinking about the macro-economic changes necessary in Kenya and the crucial role of the informal sector in these policies had already been discussed by cabinet, in anticipation of the publication of the Sessional Paper No. 1 of 1986 *Economic Management for Renewed Growth* (Kenya,1986). Consequently when in November 1985, President Moi stopped off in Kamukunji as if by chance to investigate the informal sector, he was in all likelihood pursuing a priority that had already been fully discussed and agreed by cabinet.

This first show of interest by the President was followed, as was said above, by several other visits from him between late November 1985 and early 1986. In these he had suggested that sheds would be provided free by government to offer shade against the hot sun; he had urged the jua kali also to organize into sizeable groups in order that they could be more easily helped by government. He had even encouraged the jua kali mechanics in the nearby Ziwani workshops to think that government vehicles would be repaired in the informal sector. In declaring that government would subcontract work to the jua kali sector, he was not only fulfilling the spirit of the recommendation by the ILO Mission 13 years earlier, but he was clearly drawing on the idea of the not yet published Sessional Paper No. 1 of 1986, which said amongst much else:

> Government will issue new regulations on tendering to require central ministries and district authorities to favour small-scale producers. (Kenya, 1986: 56)

What is intriguing about these Presidential pronouncements is that they actually preceded the formal publication of policy in 1986, and clearly constituted government initiative in terms of our contrast between government intervention and the minimalist hands-off approach consistent with maintaining the self-reliant character of the sector. We shall note shortly that one of the President's suggestions – the encouragement to the jua kali themselves to form groups as a way of qualifying for assistance – was one of the first to be implemented.

However, in the Sessional Paper, *Economic Management for Renewed Growth*, the informal sector was once again brought centre stage, as it had been so much earlier in the ILO Mission. There were several rationales for its reappearance as a main actor. As important as any other was the stark reality of the cost of creating jobs. In the modern sector, it was costing approximately £16,000 sterling to create a single job – a calculation that would leave 6 million without work in the year 2000, if that was the route to be followed:

> Obviously, the modern, urban, industrial sector cannot be depended on to employ much of the growing work force. To employ people on small farms, in very small-scale industry and services, or in self-employment takes only a

fraction of the £16,000 per worker required in the modern sector. Clearly the bulk of the work force will have to be productively employed in these activities. (Kenya, 1986: 2)

What made the 1986 analysis different from the desultory discussions of previous years was that the stimulation of the informal sector was to come from macro-economic policies·aimed at the economy as a whole, such as the strategy to raise farm productivity and income, lower tariffs and encourage the substitution of labour for machinery (Kenya, 1986: 55). But these macro-economic measures were to be complemented by direct assistance to individuals and small-scale businesses. These latter measures were not so much the time-honoured ones of reducing harassment and restrictions, but the rather more positive lines of devising much more flexible credit schemes, encouragement of technical graduates to start up their own businesses, and of the informal sector generally to produce cheap alternatives to expensive imported items. There was also the suggestion that informal sector firms and individuals should form co-operatives, 'through which they can obtain information and assistance on new technologies, access to credit, the purchase of inputs and the marketing of outputs' (Kenya, 1986: 57). This latter item would have been the one which encouraged the President to speak out in favour of forming associations and sizeable groups, when he visited Kamukunji some months earlier.

As important as any other move proposed in 1986 was the establishment of a task force to review all policies to promote the informal sector. Its aim would be to recommend ways to create 'a healthy regulatory climate' for informal sector activities (Kenya, 1986: 110). In addition, the Sessional Paper discussed the variety of ways that a culture of enterprise could be encouraged, and training institutions be re-oriented to produce entrepreneurs and risk takers (Kenya, 1986: 33; Ryan, 1987: 12–13).

Two years later, in the *Development Plan 1989–1993*, the term 'jua kali' is finally accepted into a major planning document, and a whole section of the chapter on Industrial and Commercial Development is dedicated to 'Development of Small-Scale and Jua Kali Enterprises' (Kenya, 1988a: 162). In other ways, this Sixth Plan might have appeared less innovative in respect of the informal sector; indeed, it reproduced in almost identical language as had been used 16 years earlier by the ILO Mission the characteristics of the jua kali sector. This may in fact be quite significant, for at the time, in 1972, the thinking about the informal sector was certainly not part of Kenyan national policy. Now, since the 1986 Sessional Paper, there was a real sense in which the informal sector was being re-discovered by the Kenya government. Not just in a section of Development Plans but in many of the other institutions of society.

The achievement of a Sessional Paper on *Small Enterprise and Jua Kali Development in Kenya* (1992)

The momentum was maintained after the 1986 Sessional Paper, and in

1987, in collaboration with the ILO and UNDP, a project on entrepreneurship was started. This soon broadened, in 1989, into a small enterprise development policy project, and was organized in a highly participatory manner, involving all the relevant ministries, the aid agencies, representatives of industry and commerce, and with targeted seminars and workshops focused on small-scale exporters, the banking sector, NGOs and many other interested parties. A very effective management strategy held together a strong Core Committee throughout the project, and duly in 1989, three volumes were produced:

- *A Strategy for Small Enterprise Development in Kenya: Towards the Year 2000 Part One* (Kenya, 1989a; hereafter, Strategy Paper)
- *Small Enterprise Development in Kenya: Programme of action Part Two* (Kenya, 1989b)
- *Small Enterprise Development in Kenya: Project ideas Part Three* (Kenya, 1989c).

This is probably one of the most thoroughgoing attempts in Africa to date to put into place a set of strategies that would privilege the small enterprise and jua kali world (Assunçao, 1993: 5). It may, therefore, be useful to indicate what was special about the apparently wide ranging consensus achieved by these reports.

The scope of what was attempted covered three main domains; the first of these looked at what was called the enabling environment. This examined many of the macro-economic, legal, technological and fiscal obstacles to small enterprise. Central to this part of the strategy was the argument that the role of government should be changed from being interventionist to being facilitative of efforts by the private sector itself. The judgement is made, not only of Kenya but of other developing countries, that:

> Programmes to sponsor private sector growth through direct Government interventions have been very costly and only a small number of enterprises have been assisted. The results have not been up to expectations and few government programmes would continue to exist without regular infusions of relatively large sums of money. (Kenya, 1989a: 10)

Evidence for this position on small-scale enterprises is not of course derived from the jua kali sector where the great majority of firms have never received any government assistance at all; it seems rather to have been confirmed by the poor showing of Kenya Industrial Estates (KIE) which was alleged to have undermined entrepreneurial capacity by featherbedding and over-subsidizing (World Bank, 1987: 269; and Ikiara, 1991a). But the importance of the position taken up by the 1989 Strategy Paper was that government should not presumably try and do for the microenterprise sector what they had sought to do so unsuccessfully for the next largest sector, those with 10–50 employees. Indeed, the Strategy Paper, following World Bank and other data, argued that Kenya was particularly poorly served by this type of small enterprise. It became commonplace to suggest that above the jua kali and micro-enterprises but below the large-scale modern firms there was a 'missing middle' – an absence of modern (non jua kali) small enterprises (Kenya, 1989a). Liedholm and Mead (1986) compared several developing countries and showed that in contrast with Nigeria (60 per cent) and Sierra Leone (50 per cent), Kenya had only 12 per cent of of its total employment in this type of modern small-scale manufacturing, though Zambia had even less (6 per cent).

If this analysis about the missing middle can be sustained, it suggests that Kenya's small and micro-enterprise strategy as a whole has had a very idiosyncratic character. At the lowest level of micro and jua kali enterprise, there had generally been no government intervention (except negative intervention in the form of harassment), and yet most accounts (from the ILO Mission to the 1986 Sessional Paper) reported very dynamic growth. At the next level, however, there had been rather major government subvention, principally through KIE, and yet there had only been a net addition of 800 firms in the category of 10–50 employees in 20 years (Kenya, 1989a: 12-13; Burisch, 1991). But it is important not to dichotomize micro from small enterprise too sharply; the problem of the missing middle could also be seen as a problem of the micro-enterprise sector, if indeed there was little or no tradition of 'graduation' from micro to small enterprise status (Liedholm, 1990).

The Strategy Paper addressed this question of the bottleneck to dynamic entrepreneurship through what it termed its Non-Financial Promotion Programmes. A central feature of this part of the strategy was the development of an Enterprise Culture, and a whole series of recommendations were made that would seek to ensure that 'students at all educational/ training levels in Kenya should receive instruction in content relating to self-employment and entrepreneurship' (Kenya, 1989a: 85). Some of the assumptions associated with entrepreneurship development appear to have been derived in part from North American experience, but it should be noted that Kenya had already moved rather forcefully in its own educational reform of 1985, and had installed compulsory Business Education even down at the level of primary schools. And it had followed this up with the strong recommendation (in the *Report of the Presidential Working Party on Education and Manpower Training*) that 'formal training programmes be oriented to take into account the special training needs of the informal sector with particular emphasis on providing entrepreneurship skills' (Kenya, 1988b: 91). The Strategy Paper was therefore building on an existing foundation.

A third element in the Strategy was concerned with the many obstacles to credit experienced by the small and micro-enterprise sectors. Here again there was a whole battery of compelling changes proposed, involving shifts in collateral policies, the change in bank incentives to lend to small-scale enterprises, and much else.

16

Within three years, these three reports with their three key recommendations on the enabling environment, on entrepreneurship and on credit, had been translated into Kenya's first Sessional Paper on *Small Enterprise and Jua Kali Development in Kenya* (Kenya, 1992a). Thus, just exactly 20 years after the ILO Employment Mission, Kenya had finally got its own policy paper on the informal sector. Support from the ILO had been important on both occasions, but in the later policy, there had been very little expatriate technical assistance of the sort that had been so very visible in 1972.

One advantage of the participatory process that had been adopted for developing the three 1989 reports on small enterprise in Kenya is that they had disseminated a consensus about the nature of the challenge across many different sectors of the policy community. As a consequence, when the Presidential Committee on Employment reported in January 1991, in its findings *Development and Employment in Kenya*, it very much confirmed several of the main lines of discussion which had been becoming commonplace through the small enterprise development process (Kenya, 1991c).

The Sessional Paper on *Small Enterprise and Jua Kali Development in Kenya* (Kenya, 1992a) did in fact condense a good deal of the insights that had been gained in the development of the Strategy Paper and its Programme of Action (Kenya, 1989a, 1989b). It confirmed the lack of any significant 'graduation' from micro to small-scale formal enterprise. It strongly underlined the 'missing middle' problem in Kenya compared to other developing countries, and it pointed to the lack of powerful indigenous role models for entrepreneurship in the country. It then proceeded to make a very wide ranging set of summary recommendations for almost every ministry, financial institution, and non-governmental organization in Kenya. This followed the three volumes of the Strategy Paper but unlike much of the earlier policy recommendation, the accent was now on very specific actions by very particular constituencies. These reflected the participatory process described above, and covered a huge swathe of institutions from the Women's Bureau and the Public Law Institute on the one hand to the Commercial Banks, District Development Committees, and Electricity Development Fund, on the other.

Apart from the large number of policy recommendations, the Sessional Paper also in a last chapter, 'Agenda for Action' laid down a summary of those 38 items that 'require significant speeding up or other changes in implemention... They are taken as an agenda for priority action within a time-span of 12–24 months after the adoption of this Paper' (Kenya, 1992a: 31–2).

A whole further study could be undertaken on what elements in this very ambitious – indeed comprehensive – plan have been implemented in full or in part over the two years since it was adopted. There certainly has been some action taken, for example, in introducing entrepreneurship education and Small Business Centres in some technical training institutions. But probably the greatest positive impact on the informal sector has

17

flowed from the macro-economic reforms of the Kenyan economy, such as the import liberalization, relaxation of price controls, or the deregulation of interest rates. Even these have been far from wholly positive, of course. The liberalization of certain imports, e.g. secondhand garments, has had direct knock-on effects on informal sector workers (tailors and dressmakers).

It would seem to be the case not only that it has been the reforms not specifically aimed at the informal sector that have been put into place, but also that these macro-economic reforms have been as much implemented through external conditionalities imposed on the government as they have been through government policy initiative on its own account. It is perhaps the case that the changes that have been implemented most rapidly in areas that are explicitly concerned with the informal sector have also derived from the availability of external funding. This would be true of the Entrepreneurship Education and Small Business Centre developments, for example. A similar point could be made about the availability of credit for the jua kali sector; a good deal of the new credit lines from commercial banks that have targeted the informal sector has been the result of subsidized funds from the donor agencies which have had almost no risk to the banks, as opposed to funds that are the result of policy changes in the banks themselves.

More detailed work would need to be carried out to explore this contrast between externally conditioned or funded initiatives and changes initiated locally, but at least one commentator since the publication of the Sessional Paper of 1992 has argued that not a great deal has changed:

> While reform of the macro-economic framework, like exchange rate and interest rate policy, were actually implemented, most of the reforms in the policy towards the urban informal sector failed to go beyond intention. (Assunçao, 1993: 14)

The external dimensions of the national policy development process

Our focus on policy development, from the early debates about African trade in the East Africa Royal Commission to the emergence of a Kenyan Sessional Paper on small enterprise almost 40 years later, is not meant to give the impression that there is a rational and linear relationship between policy and implementation. Rather, it is intended to underline the importance of a particular, originally foreign, discourse and approach gradually becoming locally owned. The ownership of this set of ideas about an enabling policy and financial environment, and about the potential of the jua kali has grown slowly, but by the early 1990s they would be relatively well known to policy people in many different ministries in Kenya.

However, it must be emphasized that the achievement of some such consensus as we have suggested has not been carried out only within the government ministries. We have underlined the view that the recent

18

consensus about the informal sector has been much more locally owned than the original discovery in the ILO Kenya Mission. Nevertheless, throughout the 1980s and 1990s, there has been a very powerful sub-text of influence from the donor community on this policy development process. Indeed, despite all that we have said about the gradual Kenyanization of informal sector policy, it would not be difficult to write a different script for the last 20 years in which all the main dates would be those associated with key projects, programmes or policy papers of donors already committed to small and micro-enterprise in Kenya.

Such a text would point to the United States Agency for International Development (USAID)/Kenya private enterprise programme which had run from 1983 in support of a large range of both small and larger enterprise related activities (Young, 1989; Ernst & Young, 1989), including the support of the Kenya Rural Enterprise Programme (K-REP) from 1984. As early as 1983 and 1985, there would be key documents which led to these complex projects, such as *Rural Private Enterprise* (USAID, 1983) and USAID/Kenya *Private Enterprise Strategy Statement* (September 1985). Equally such an alternative approach could point to the ILO/SIDA-supported Skill Development for Self Reliance (SDSR) project and its *Strategy for Self-employment Creation* (Chaturvedi, 1989), or the German (GTZ)-funded informal sector programme attached to Kenya Industrial Estates from 1987. There is a wealth of other donor material that could be referred to, and some of it has doubtless been influential not only within the donor community, but also within government. This would include the World Bank's *Kenya Industrial Sector: Policies for Investment and Export Growth* (1987), or the Bank's jointly-sponsored 'Africa. Regional programme on enterprise development' (World Bank, 1990), David Wright's 'Proposals for British aid to small-scale enterprise development in Kenya' (ODA, 1989), Mauri Yambo's 'Reconnaissance of jua kali support activities in Kenya' (Yambo, 1988, for DANIDA), and Robert Gichira's 'Problems facing entrepreneurs in Kenya' (Gichira, 1987, for Ford Foundation). The list could very easily be extended both further back and into the early and mid-1990s, but certainly by the time that the Kenya Government had its Strategy Paper available in 1989, it was correct to say in the words of one analyst: 'Almost all the official donor agencies represented in Kenya are currently involved in projects in the small-scale enterprise (SSE) sector' (Wright, 1989).

In other words, at a point before the 1992 Sessional Paper had been written, the donor community was very widely involved in micro-enterprise development work, projects and programmes in Kenya. And, arguably, since the Sessional Paper it has been the donor community reports on small enterprise development that have broken the most new ground. These would include the very influential USAID-sponsored report on 'Micro and small enterprise in Kenya: results of the 1993 national baseline survey' (Parker & Torres, 1994) which amongst other things fundamentally revised upwards the size of the informal sector in Kenya to 900,000 enterprises employing some two million people. A second major source of policy analysis on the sector in Kenya would be the various reports of the small enterprise policy and implementation (SEPIP) mission (e.g. Dolman, 1994; Gachugi, 1994), along with its five supporting papers. This was carried out by British Aid to Small Enterprise, through the ODA, in conjunction with the Netherlands Government and the United Nations Development Programme (UNDP).

It would similarly not be difficult to construct a map of the major non-governmental organizations involved in supporting the informal sector or what may be termed by NGOs income-generating projects (Gichira & Aleke-Dondo, 1988). Again, many of these, whether international NGOs such as ActionAid, Technoserve or Oxfam, or national NGOs such as the Undugu Society of Kenya, Partnership for Productivity, the National Christian Council of Kenya (NCCK), or Kenya Management Assistance Programme, would often have been involved in support to various forms of micro and small enterprise long before even the 1986 Sessional Paper on *Economic Management for Renewed Growth*. For example, Undugu's *Annual Report for 1986* may not be far out of line with several other NGOs in seeing that Sessional Paper as legitimating what they were already doing rather than setting a new direction for their activities with the informal sector:

> This document has defined the informal sector as having the greatest growth potential for employment creation and as such, proposes to support and diversify the sector. Undugu is pleased with the general direction since it justifies part of the thrust of our operations during the year under review. (Undugu, 1986: 6)

Although a number of the NGO projects go quite far back – two of the better known being the NCCK's Small-scale Business Enterprises which started in 1975 and Partnership for Productivity which supported small business work even earlier – many of them are clustered around the late 1980s and, thus, they too precede at least the Sessional Paper of 1992 on small enterprise. This is not to say that new work was not encouraged and old work further affirmed by this policy development process. But there was certainly no clear line between the elaboration of government policy and the emergence of projects around the country. What was clear, however, by the early 1990s was the sheer range and diversity of small-scale initiatives amongst NGOs in Kenya in support of the jua kali, documented through the publication of an *Inventory of Projects and Programmes for Small and Jua Kali Development in Kenya* (K-REP, 1993b).

The jua kali contribution to jua kali development

One of the issues that has not yet been touched on in this chapter is the jua kalis' own role in determining policy towards the micro-enterprise sector. What is intriguing about the Sessional Paper on *Small Enterprise and Jua Kali Development in Kenya* is that while every conceivable organization and government department is charged with doing something about the informal sector, there is not a single recommendation in which the jua kali themselves have to take the initiative. It might appear that the jua kali are very much seen as the recipients of actions taken by others.

Thus, the District Development Committees are encouraged to take a lead in stimulating local groups of artisans to form associations 'to make easier the administration of assistance programmes' (Kenya, 1992a: 7). This language gives the impression that one of the prime purposes of a jua kali association would be to assist government to implement its plans for the jua kali rather than for the jua kali to set its own goals. This is given further support by the recommendation that 'The Ministries of Industry, Technical Training and Applied Technology, and Culture and Social Services will initiate the formation of SSE [small-scale enterprise] sectoral assocations' (Kenya, 1992a: 39).

What makes this even more surprising is that this particular recommendation (No. 36 out of 38 that were meant to be acted upon within a two-year period of the Sessional Paper being approved) was urging that something be done (the formation of associations) which had already been happening for seven years.

The Sessional Paper of 1992 was also very categorical about the existing large array of women's self-help groups, and amongst these the women's income-generating groups were accorded particularly critical attention:

> Group approaches in SED [small enterprise development] have, however, revealed major problems arising from the original concept of women's groups activities as social welfare projects rather than business ventures. Most of the so-called income-generating activities are non-starters while the groups themselves do not lend themselves to the spirit of entrepreneurship ... there is an urgent need to rethink and redefine their role. (Kenya, 1992a: 15–16)

There is certainly research that would support these qualifications about women's income-generating projects (Buvinic, 1986; Moser, 1989), but what is striking is that the problems of women's groups are not related to the proposals about forming associations, and neither are connected to what had been happening in Kenya since the President's visits to Kamukunji and Gikomba.

Associational activity: the informal sector begins to find its voice
The most astonishing dimension of informal sector history in Kenya is the silence of its principal actors. There has been no shortage of papers about the informal sector, but it has had no voice of its own, until almost the end of the period under review. This is unlike the artisan trades in several other countries, especially parts of West and Central Africa, where there has been a strong sense of craft membership within particular associations, each having its rules of apprenticeship, society meetings etc. In East Africa, by contrast, with few exceptions, there has not been a longstanding craft tradition, fenced about with rules and obligations, and there has been little corresponding organizational history.

In Kenya, there were some hints of associational activity in the mid-1970s, but not until the informal sector taxis (matatus) flexed their muscles in the early 1980s was there much evidence of the importance of organization. What is intriguing about the really major development in the formation of informal sector associations is that the President appears personally to have encouraged it, as we have seen, in late 1985, by suggesting a valuable connection between artisans organizing themselves into groups and their then getting free access to sheds, and even getting title deeds. Outside the trade and craft area, there had been plenty of experience of forming self-help groups, cooperatives, and companies to build schools, to market cash crops and to purchase land; and so it did not take much prompting once the President had led the way.

Some of the earliest to register themselves did so as local self-help (*harambee* groups) with the Ministry of Culture and Social Services; and it is interesting to note that they did so as location-cum-trade groups: the Kamukunji Blacksmith and General Metal Works, or the Jua Kali Nyayo Garages Association (this latter was later amended to Ziwani, a particular location rather than using the President's keyword, *Nyayo*). It is perhaps worth noting that these first associations were in the trades associated with the original meaning of jua kali – blacksmith, metalwork and mechanics. But as associations began to be formed upcountry, they were much more likely to emphasize the town and not the trade. Thus the Nakuru Jua Kali Cooperative Society was reportedly being formed in 1986, with no trades specified, and similarly many others from Narok to Nyahururu, and from Mombasa to Kisii. Nairobi was the only city where perhaps because of the specific sites of the President's visit and his gift of sheds to those areas, there was a tendency for all subsequent societies and associations to be very restricted in their constituency. Thus, there emerged the Rabai Road Jua Kali Society, or the Makadara Engineering Workers Cooperative Society (see figs. 1.3 and 1.4). But most other provincial and district centres, and even smaller towns, and some villages, simply used the place name.

The preference for location-specific rather than trade-specific associations seems now to have become the pattern in Kenya, even though the first two or three associations to be founded in the country included the Kamukunji Blacksmiths and the Ziwani Garages. There are clearly some advantages to geographical versus trade associations, especially where there are small concentrations of artisans as for example in villages. On the other hand, the Ghanaian example where there have emerged national associations or federations of Traditional Caterers, Traditional Healers, Tailors and Dressmakers, Market Women, and Garages – to mention just a few – offers an opportunity for individual trades even in small villages to become part of a national association (McGrath & King, 1995: 74). In addition, there is some possibility when a single trade is represented in a national association or chapter that there will be greater cohesion amongst the membership.

Once the Ministry of Technical Training and Applied Technology

22

Figs. 1.3 and 1.4: From 1986, Jua Kali associations and societies started forming, some linking with the Ministry of Cooperatives, Culture and Social Services, and some with the Ministry of Technical Training and Applied Technology (MTTAT). Gikomba and Kimathi Ward cover just small parts of Nairobi.

(MTTAT) had been formed in early 1988, with particular responsibility for Jua Kali Development, it became commonplace for emerging groups seeking advice about registration as a jua kali association to be told to gather a list of interested members, and to fill out a ministry questionnaire for each member with a photograph and registration fee of K.Sh.20. In this way a Jua Kali Artisan Identification card could be acquired by individuals which was initially thought to ensure some security of tenure, and also some rights over whatever good things might later be allocated – whether sheds, land, title deeds, or loans. The significance of this issuing of jua kali identity cards should not be underestimated. Here was a formal sector ministry solemnly collecting data on individual artisans within associations and providing them with what was seen as some kind of recognition. It seemed a far cry from the harassment of earlier days.

Defining the jua kali in Kenya

There was accordingly some considerable interest in knowing how wide the definition of jua kali might be, and, since spaces in any sheds would be limited, who might qualify as a jua kali. As late as 1990, the Meru Jua Kali were still seeking to discover from the government as 'we are not very clear on who actually is a jua kali artisan … whether we should continue to register our women artisans engaged in various jua kali activities like knitting, ciondo (basket) making, dressmaking and weaving'. They were told that of course women are an integral part of the sector; but that the definition of jua kali artisan was deferred for some period.

Another dimension of the definitional question was whether only the owners of micro-enterprises were jua kali, and the employees were not eligible to register and be members of the new associations. In practice it was owners rather than employees who probably made up the bulk of the early registrations. And in addition the standard jua kali questionnaire from MTTAT asked about the number of other artisans or trainees working for the individual, but did not seem to allow the possibility of the respondent being an employee.

A further aspect of the ongoing debate about who is a jua kali relates to the rapidly expanding meanings of the term. There is in fact probably an interesting piece of sociolinguistic research to be done on the layers of meaning added to the term, jua kali, over the last decade and more. Originally from its meaning of hot sun, it had first come to refer to hard work done predominantly by male blacksmiths and metalworkers out of doors, in the open air. It seems to have been extended to car and lorry mechanics next and it became commonplace for many lower middle and middle income clients to talk of appreciating jua kali skills and very competitive prices. The term took on overtones of creativity and improvisation; and stories abound of how jua kali mechanics saved the day when a car broke down far from a regular formal sector garage. Finally, the term broadened to stand not just for a particular form of micro-enterprise, but for a Kenyan African version of capital accumulation to be contrasted with that of the multinationals or Kenya Asians. It came to be associated with Kenyan (African) technological capacity, and with a moving frontier of products that the jua kali had succeeded in making. In 1989 and 1990 MTTAT, for example, took pride in explaining that indigenous jua kali industry had been responsible for putting an Asian-owned formal sector factory out of business, through the sheer competitiveness of their products. It is in this spirit also that the headline would declare: 'Jua kali man branches into wheel rims in Kariobangi garage' (*Daily Nation*, 24 October 1986). Or the sign in front of a jua kali stand at the Nairobi Show would claim: 'It was jua kali type people who helped rebuild Germany after the last war' (Kagotho, interview, July 1989).

For a nation struggling with structural adjustment and with the need to fight its way out of crisis by hard work, there is a sense also in which people can and do say, only half-jokingly, 'We're all jua kali nowadays'. The term, therefore, has been important not just in Kenyanizing the concept of informal sector but in communicating a feeling that it is the informal sector that is the ordinary economy in which the bulk of Kenyans gain their livelihood. It is not the informal sector that is somehow special and extraordinary, but the formal sector, which encompasses such a small portion of the economically active population. Increasingly it has been felt that it is the jua kali economy that provides people with their work, health, law, housing, and their training (King, 1987). A similar point is made in Undugu's 1992–3 Biennial Report:

> In 1993 the informal sector accounted for a remarkable 50 per cent of the country's employment. In this light, the jua kali sector can be considered the saving grace for hundreds of thousands of Kenyans, for whom life is a constant struggle to earn daily bread, for themselves or their families. (Undugu, 1994: 39)

This all-embracing interpretation of jua kali to cover anyone wishing to identify with a particular town and its possible development opportunities can go too far, so that the original notion of productive artisan trades gets quite lost. This clearly appears to have happened in Meru:

> When, for instance, a Jua Kali Association was started in Meru town (Kenya), membership consisted only of artisans. But after the association was opened to doctors, lawyers and teachers, and artisans made up only 20 per cent of total membership (of 3,000 members), the artisans decided to leave and form their own (sectoral) association. (Haan, 1994a: 13)

The process of association formation initiated a form of communication between the association and the local administration as well as with one or other ministry in Nairobi. In a number of cases, the local MP or a minister from the area took a personal interest in his or her constituency getting sheds and other facilities. Inevitably in a new ministry with no fieldstaff initially, it was not easy to push ahead with a national programme of building sheds for the jua kali. But by June 1988, there were some 13 groups of sheds built. A year later the number was 27, and it continued growing to some 300 shed sites by 1993. It is interesting to note that here too in one of the first visible examples of government support to the informal sector, there were significant donor (USAID) funds involved. And this would continue from 1993 with German support to the Nyayo Sheds Project (K-REP, 1993b: 76).

But from the perspective of the ordinary reader of the Kenya press between 1988 and 1990, the various announcements about support to sheds almost always promised one million or half a million shillings towards these facilities in particular districts, towns, or sections of towns. One of the more typical linkages of sheds to numbers of firms was made by the President himself who was reported on 1 August 1990 to have released one million to build jua kali sheds in Kariobangi. Phase one would accommodate 3,500 firms, and Phase Two no less than 5,000 (*Daily Nation*, 1 August 1990). But at a certain point this kind of support for sheds was only a small part of what must have seemed like a stream of generous allocations by private firms, embassies and donor agencies, as well as the government itself to the informal (jua kali) sector. Thus, the US ambassador was reported to have allocated K.Sh. 92 million to the jua kali programme on the same day that the Minister of MTTAT launched a jua kali fund of up to K.Sh. 50 million (*Daily Nation*, 7 January 1989). And there were many smaller amounts.

The jua kali as a form of harambee *(local, community self-reliance)*
But the very insistence by government that due procedures be followed in forming associations, appointing officers, and registering members put new pressures on the 'Jua Kali Ministry', as some called MTTAT. In the manner of *harambee* self-help groups most of the societies had fixed certain levels of contribution and membership charges (quite apart from the registration fee with government), and in the case of some associations, there were possibilities of buying shares. In this situation it became important for jua kali association chairmen to be able to deliver some return on these investments. But from the early provision of sheds in Ziwani and Kamukunji, at apparently little or no cost to the members, it seemed that it was not going to be necessary (as in other *harambee* fund-raising activities, such as building secondary schools) first to raise substantial funds as a society or an association, and then apply for supplementary government aid. It looked, instead, as if government might have good things to give out almost immediately. The response to the President's initial encouragement to form associations, in any event, was dramatic, and by mid-1990, there were well over 100 registered jua kali societies and associations, and many others, such as that in our study village of Githiga, were already under the process of formation (see further Chapter 4). It is estimated that by 1994 there were some 400 associations (World Bank, 1993c).

This early pattern of a certain dependency on government may well have meant that there was a good deal less interest in organizing major local fund-raising events, with MPs as guest celebrities, than was the case with other *harambee* activities. The priority issue instead seemed to be the possibility that government might allocate plots, linked to sheds, and, given the pressures on land, especially in Nairobi, it should not perhaps be surprising that in these early years some association chairmen spent a lot of time in the corridors of the Ministry seeking to put pressure on the government to act.

While there was clearly potential for jua kali associational development to turn into the newest phase of very local *harambee* fundraising, there was also scope for this mushrooming of societies to take on more of a national dimension, which had never happened with the other *harambee* fund-raising activities. This nationwide jua kali idea had been discussed by various individual chairmen of jua kali societies from relatively early on. Indeed it may have occurred to some of them, particularly in Nairobi, where there were no less than 25 very local associations, that the division of jua kalis into these small groups militated against the emergence of what could have been otherwise a very large urban movement. One of these Nairobi jua kali association chairmen in fact wrote to MTTAT in June 1989 specifically about the proposal to form a National Jua Kali Association:

> It was the wish of all attendants (at the seminar) that we be advised by the Ministry of how to form a national body to bring together all the established jua kalis countrywide. (Makadara Jua Kali Cooperative Society files, June 1989)

The Ministry in the longer term was not necessarily opposed to the idea of an apex body for jua kali, with representation built up from district to province to the national level, and closely linked to the Ministry itself. But a national jua kali association with possibly mass membership in all the main towns, and setting its own agenda publicly on all the controversial issues that had been repeated since the 1972 ILO report was a very different matter. Furthermore, as these associations were forming at the very time that multi-party politics and grassroots representation were gaining widespread popularity in many African countries, including Kenya, it may well have been thought by government that a new countrywide movement was not yet opportune. It would be almost three more years before the notion of a National Jua Kali Federation would be accepted.

Image, visibility and the market

Unlike the many different reports and policy papers on the informal sector which we have discussed, one of the most direct consequences of the President's historic visit in 1985 is that informal activities were popularly named and given legitimacy, and these particular markets and locations for goods and services were much more visibly put on the political and business map. The term jua kali to refer to the informal sector almost certainly dates from somewhat earlier than 1985, but this official use of a Swahili term rather than the nebulous 'informal sector' and the identification of the jua kali as covering a particular set of activities were crucially important for the new image. Mr Ongeri, the MTTAT minister at the time, sought to formalize the local use of the term by stating in May 1988 that the small-scale industry which came to be known as the informal sector would hitherto assume the name of Jua Kali Development Programme (*Standard*, 28 May 1988).

Of course, very large numbers of customers from Nairobi and up-country had known of these sites of jua kali goods and services, such as Kamukunji, for a long time, but the provision of a limited number of shelters, and the appearance of name signs for the Society, and for some of the leading firms within the location, have certainly affected the marketing and public face of Kamukunji. It has almost certainly also increased the range and even the quality of the goods on offer. The publicity for jua kali has put sites like Kamukunji, Ziwani and Gikomba on the map for key civil servants, foreign visitors, and of course for those donors and NGOs that did not already know of them. Indeed, in 1989 and early 1990, it was not uncommon to see groups of official visitors being conducted around some of the jua kali sites of Nairobi, to be shown illustrations of Kenya's dynamic micro-enterprise economy, almost as if the Government had been responsible for creating it.

Before this period many leading Kenyan politicians clearly did not appreciate the product diversity in the informal sector workshops, but in recent years and in conjunction with the media they have probably contributed in a small way to more people becoming jua kali customers. It has been not uncommon to hear better-off Kenyans claiming to have ordered something in the informal sector that was a fraction of the price for the same article in the main streets of Nairobi. The view of a number of the owners is that the demand for their products has grown since 1986. There is a difference, however, between a Kamukunji or Ziwani where the new sheds and publicity have simply been added to their existing relatively well known operations, and other Nairobi and up-country associations which may have a name, a committee, a membership list, and not much more, after several years of being in the business of associational development. Indeed, some of their chairmen would argue that their personal businesses have taken losses because of the amount of time dedicated to lobbying and negotiating with government.

There is a different case again where the provision of sheds turns out to be the occasion to move artisans away from some central area with large numbers of consumers to a location which, however new, has no access to the market.

Technological transfer into and within jua kali associations

In the first flush of enthusiasm the Jua Kali Development Programme in MTTAT did try to have a discernible impact on the dissemination of knowledge about jua kali technical capacity within the country. It did so by encouraging greater jua kali participation in the regular agricultural and trade shows, but more particularly by sponsored exhibitions dedicated to jua kali products, of which there have been examples from as early as November 1989 and 1990. Typical of this emphasis on creativity in the months after the 1986 Sessional Paper underlined the potential of the informal sector was Minister Ongeri's claim that the government would develop an award scheme for 'jua kali innovators/inventors who come with useful spare parts, tools and working gadgets' (*Daily Nation*, 28 Sepember 1986).

More intriguing, however, in the whole process of technological dissemination was the MTTAT support of visits of jua kali groups from one part of the country to some of the more advanced centres. It is not clear how much of this actually happened but certainly one very dramatic example of this was the visit of the relatively remote Rumuruti Jua Kali Self Help Group in mid-1989 to Gikomba and Kamukunji. In the domain of technological intervention, it is rare to have such explicit accounts of what a group of artisans from a small rural centre like Rumuruti could gain by a visit to the more technologically advanced jua kali areas of Nairobi. Some excerpts from their report are worth reproducing here:

> We learnt how to make metal boxes ... as many as 6–8 a day. Why? This is because they [in Kamukunji] had Jua Kali machinery which made work easier...

> Forge machines:.. Our artisans have already started making one which will save time and money...

> [In Gikomba] ... Cutting machines ... the hand-operated ones were better than those in Kamukunji and simple to make. Our artisans have started to make one.

> Wood furniture: These were of very high quality. The machines involved were very expensive. (Jua Kali files, MTTAT)

There were surprises of a different sort also in store for these rural artisans. In particular they were astonished to discover that the urban artisans did not seem to pay trade licenses. They commented:

> In our area there are many artisans who are just at home doing nothing because the licenses are too high for them to pay in order to operate. (Jua Kali files, MTTAT)

They also judged, interestingly in view of what we have just said about *harambee* and dependency, that one of the urban associations seemed to have 'no plans to assist themselves but were looking forward for assistance from the ministry' (Jua Kali files, MTTAT).

There are a number of questions to be asked about these kinds of technological exposure visits. They apply perhaps equally to the more formal courses mounted by some of the NGOs (such as Undugu, ActionAid, and ApT) and the planned intervention by UNIDO in relevant machinery development in a pilot site near Kamukunji. All of them are predicated on the view that the more people there are who have machine-making capability the better. For instance in the apparently very successful

ApT courses run in the Karen Centre in Nairobi in 1991 (funded by ODA), it is actually stated as one of the course objectives:

> By the end of the course, each participant must be able to replicate his chosen design, and be able to teach other artisans from his local area how to make it. (Apt, 1991b)

We are not arguing here against the spread of machine-making capability – by any measure there are far too few labour-saving technologies readily and cheaply available in Kenya. Our concern is rather with how these new technological initiatives being introduced into the informal sector from outside may impact on the already very high levels of competitiveness and low profits in the sector, and how they may affect the existing systems and procedures for technological change. It is certainly going to be important for policy makers to have a longer term vision of where Kenya's informal sector can expect to proceed technologically, and what are the principal mechanisms that can connect the jua kali technologies to a trajectory of increased growth. But, ideally, any such jua kali policy framework should be connected to an overall technology and industry policy, as Ikiara has recently argued:

> The government's optimistic focus on the informal sector risks underrating the need for comprehensive planning for industrialization. (Ikiara, 1991a: 318)

However, this larger vision of industrialization is difficult for smaller donors and NGOs to target. Consequently, at one point it seemed possible that the jua kali associations might become the focus of a number of donor projects and of international and national NGO attempts to do something about enlarging the current technology frontier in the informal sector. Thus, ODA was initially interested in exposing jua kali association leaders to technological developments in India and Ghana, and was exploring a technology support project with a particular group, the Mombasa Jua Kali Association (Stevens, 1990). The same was true of DANIDA (Kahiga & Lauridsen, 1993). The very existence and apparent leadership structure of these jua kali associations have made it suddenly much easier for external organizations to approach the informal sector and explore new ways of thinking about technology and other support. In this respect, one NGO linked to the ILO has argued that associations are the obvious vehicle:

> There are few other effective [ways in] which to reach small producers, who constitute a sector which is very fluid, diverse, fragmented and ever-changing. (Haan, 1994a: 27)

and a project for a bilateral donor has made the same point:

> It is necessary to have access to the Jua Kali Artisans, and the most natural 'gateway' seems to be the Jua Kali Associations. (Kahiga & Lauridsen, 1993: 5)

And on the other hand, it seems equally likely that the leadership of the associations will take the initiative increasingly to approach donors and international NGOs direct, in the manner that has been followed already by many national NGOs.

From Informal Sector to Jua Kali

Associations, Jua Kali differentiation, and institutional incorporation

What is still unclear after almost ten years of associational activity is the direction these new groupings will take. At one level, they could become the leading edge of a new *harambee* fund-raising frontier, once it had become clear what were the priority actions for which funding should be secured. At another level, they constitute a massive if highly internally differentiated sector of the population. They could emerge as a pressure group like local chambers of commerce, to put pressure on local government and town councils for equitable treatment, allocation of space, and for representation.

The sub-sectoral difference amongst trades may suggest that it will prove difficult to find common ground amongst entrepreneurs who are at very different levels of technology, capital stock, and ownership of permanent premises. We suspect there may emerge a two-fold differentiation in respect of jua kali association membership. On the one hand, there may well be a tendency only for the owners to seek to become association members, which we have already noted. On the other, there may also be a tendency for the distinction between what may be called the subsistence self-employed and the entrepreneurial self-employed to be reflected in jua kali association membership. This division, which we have elaborated more fully elsewhere, between the micro-entrepreneurs in the upper echelons of the informal sector and those in the lower reaches or lower tiers of the self-employed who are surviving rather than developing through self-employment, could be reproduced in jua kali associations (McGrath & King, 1995). A great deal will depend on what kind of membership associations these turn out to be, and what sources of support become available beyond their own resources. If, for example, associations can become the direct recipients of the rather large amounts of aid for micro-enterprise that are in the hands of NGOs and other donors, then a certain pattern of development could emerge. Many NGOs are ideologically more committed to assisting the lower reaches of the informal sector through income-generating and other projects than they are with support to individual micro-entrepreneurs who are already established. Equally, some of the donors are more likely to be interested in aiding what are sometimes called the entrepreneurial group who are business owners by choice rather than those who are trying self-employment by necessity (Ashe, 1985: 23–4).

It is still too early to be certain what is happening to the membership side of associational development. But the more urgent and critical question must be the emerging relationship of the jua kali associations to the state in Kenya. Thus far, they have scarcely been considered important players in the whole policy development process that we have sketched in the first part of this chapter. It is worth noting that the leadership of jua kali associations were not involved in the main working groups for the Small Enterprise Development Strategy even though this was a highly consultative and participatory process. This is perhaps understandable since jua kali associations had only begun to be formed, and there had not yet emerged any national apex body by the time the Strategy Paper

31

was completed in 1989.² However, as the national and local governments proceed to examine the needs of the informal sector in different towns, they are increasingly likely to pay some attention to the local jua kali association. In one recent report for the Ministry, it is clear that the lack of consultation between the jua kali association and some local authorities (town councils) has been a problem, but in others there is evidence of an evolving relationship, especially where the artisans are clear about their priorities (Matrix, May 1990).

The changing politics of harassment and security of tenure
One of the themes running through the 40 years from the East Africa Royal Commission in 1955 to 1995 has been the threat to micro-enterprises of the slum and shanty demolition policies of the national, and more commonly municipal governments. In a country where sequestration of land by the stronger had been an organizing theme of politics throughout the colonial period, there is still today no issue that is more contentious than access to land, plots and building development opportunities. The Royal Commission warned, as we saw earlier, that there was a direct relationship between the lack of security of tenure and the quality of the built environment, and that to clear the slum areas would be to destroy 'the only development of African commercial enterprise'. The ILO Mission urged in their chapter on the Informal Sector that 'the policy of slum demolition should be abandoned, except where it is a necessary part of a positive housing and town planning policy (ILO, 1972: 229). Finally the Strategy Paper on *Small Enterprise Development in Kenya* noted that small-scale enterprises 'are squatting on government or other empty land and therefore they do not hold title and hence cannot put up a permanent building from which to operate. From this also follows that the temporary structures do not meet the standards required both by local bye-laws or under the Public Health Act' (Kenya, 1989a: 25).

It is not being argued that any temporary structure, wherever it is located, should somehow be sacrosanct. Rather there needs to be a policy both in urban and rural areas, in small towns and large, for the allocation of plots for micro-enterprise, just as there has been for markets. But it is vitally important that the development of micro-industrial estates not be restricted to major towns, for there is plenty of evidence that there is a large and unfulfilled demand for similar premises in much smaller towns and villages. The fact that there are more than 400 jua kali associations around Kenya is itself testimony to the very widespread demand for recognition and greater security of tenure. And it should not be forgotten that possibly the single most influential reason for the organization of these associations were the President's words as reported in the press on 6 February 1986:

> President Moi said the sheds would be provided free and title deeds given to the allottee. (*Kenya Times*)

Yet in the very year (1989) that the three volumes of the Strategy Paper for Small Enterprise Development with all its multifaceted recommendations were being accepted by the Kenya Government, the business of harassment was going on as usual in the urban, jua kali areas around the country:

> In Nairobi's Eastlands Jua Kali plots had their structures pulled down. The land had previously been allocated to them. (*Daily Nation*, 2 February 1989)

> 530 Jua Kali artisans evicted by Thika Municipal Council. (*Daily Nation*, 6 February 1989)

> Jua Kali sheds in Sixth Avenue Parklands in Nairobi pulled down. (*Daily Nation*, 20 April 1989)

> Jua kali artisans in Kisumu Estate given 3 days' notice to leave by Assistant Housing Manager. (*Daily Nation*, 5 July 1989)

> Meru District Commissioner tells Jua-Kali artisans operating in KANU plot to quit. (*Daily Nation*, 24 September 1989)

However, it was in 1990 that in Nairobi and a number of other towns the new and more positive strategies towards the jua kali were most dramatically put to the test. The troubles started in Muoroto in Nairobi on 25 May 1990 when earth moving equipment moved in to demolish housing around the Machakos bus stop. Over the next several days skirmishes involving the City Commission askaris, hawkers, jua kali operators and squatters continued, with Church leaders denouncing City Hall's 'demonic' brutality. The following week President Moi was criticizing a cabinet minister for making adverse statements on the brutal eviction of Muoroto villagers by City Commission askaris. (*Standard*, 2 June 1990)

The situation did not settle down, and by later in the year it had reached crisis proportions, intensified by the widespread demands for political reform. One long term analyst of government industrial policy, Gerrishon Ikiara, assessed what happened next in the following words:

> The authorities feared the danger posed by the hawkers and slum dwellers and responded, in the last quarter of 1990, with the most brutal demolition of slum areas and informal sector business ever witnessed in the country. Up to 50,000 people were made homeless and destitute. Bulldozers razed their homes and tiny businesses. Household names of informal sector – Muoroto village, Kibarage, Machakos bus-stop area in Nairobi, and many others – now inspire sad memories and anger. For many, the magnitude of the brutality and the style of demolition discredited the declared government policy of making the informal sector play an enhanced role in the economy. (Ikiara, 1991a: 316)

It is still too early to say whether the events of November 1990 (with the wholesale destruction of jua kali areas) both in Nairobi and in several other towns have undone a great deal of the cooperation between local authorities and the informal sector that had been emerging, nor whether it has altered the informal role of patron of the sector that had been taken by the Head of State since November 1985. But what can be said is that the politics of demolition and clearance have been made a great deal less acceptable by the widespread corruption and illegal land transactions, the most notorious being those in Nairobi in which councillors and politicians have allegedly allocated to themselves whole sections of public land. In relation to the particular clearances mentioned above, it is ironic that the allegations indicate that the area of public land around the Machakos country bus-stop in Nairobi were secretly sold to leading figures, including the Machakos branch KANU chairman just four years after the demolitions (*Kenya Weekly Review*, 2 December 1994).

What is less well known in this same area of Nairobi which the President visited to launch his programme of interest in the jua kali in 1985 is that the very stone buildings with their one, two and more storeys, which are now the centre of the busiest part of Gikomba, were in the early 1970s given out by an earlier mayor of Nairobi to jua kali for almost nothing. That was probably also an irregular deal, but it was crucial in creating one of the most dynamic small business areas in Nairobi.

In this connection, also, the tin-lampmakers in Nairobi who we shall be analysing later in this book, felt particularly vulnerable. They had traditionally had no permanent premises; they had not become members of any of the jua kali associations. Those within our sample all registered in August 1990, and received their identification cards a month or so later, but in a communication of November 1990, just a few days after the clearances, there was a distinct sense of uncertainty about the future:

> Another thing is the authority here has given an order to demolish all non-planned buildings and shanties, and they have cleared most parts of the city; so although we are not cleared, they may come at any time and we have no idea where to go. (26 November 1990)

Four years later, in December 1994, they were still operating from the same site, but the process of hitherto open land being fenced off and allegedly sold to individuals was evident just two hundred yards from their temporary site.

The development of national jua kali organizations

We have already referred above to an interest among some jua kali in forming a national apex body, but it was not until early in 1992 that a Kenya National Jua Kali Federation (KNJKF) was formed. One of its leading lights, and indeed its first national chairman was James Bwatuti, who had been the chairman of the Mombasa Jua Kali Association. The latter had relatively early on gained visibility by obtaining apparently secure locations for jua kali members, and by negotiations with several donor agencies about support to institutional and technological development for the Mombasa Jua Kali.

We have, however, deliberately referred to more than one national organization under this sub-heading to make the point that the emergence of the Kenya National Jua Kali Federation has not been trouble-free nor uncontested. According to the leadership of one of the Nairobi-based jua kali associations, there has been in existence since at least May 1991 a different national grouping, called the Kenya National Jua Kali Organization (KNJKO). This has been headquartered in Eldoret, and as early as October 1991 it was seeking an interview with the President. It duly was registered with the Attorney General's Chambers in February 1992. Evidence from some early research on these embryonic national groupings would suggest that there has been some considerable rivalry, and that several jua kali associations in Nairobi including the Rabai Road, Makadara and Kamukunji Jua Kali Associations have all been linked to KNJKO (Macharia, 1995; King, interviews, 1992).

What is clear is that early in 1992, the KNJKO was outmanoeuvred by the KNJKF. The latter had managed to get the support of the German Friedrich Ebert Stiftung (FES) which has had a long tradition of support to political and civic education and to 'social democratic' processes in developing countries, including in Kenya. This body helped the Federation to put on an allegedly fair election in the Kenya Polytechnic on 26 February 1992, though it is said that many members of the opposing KNJKO boycotted this crucial election. Be that as it may, the occasion gave the Federation a measure of legitimacy which came from having two delegates elected from all but one of the eight provinces of Kenya. The Federation also managed to get the official support of MTTAT, and within a short period after the election a formal letter had been circulated from the Ministry, affirming that the election had been supervised by the officials of the Ministry and that the named members of the Federation should be afforded 'all necessary assistance during the discharge of their duties across the country while serving their Jua Kali members' (Mutiso, 10 April 1992).

The FES apparently covered the cost of holding these important elections as well as a first Board of Directors' management workshop, and is also said, on good authority, to be providing the Federation with expensive offices in Nairobi (Macharia, 1995: 20). What may concern some observers of this process is that almost before the Federation could possibly have made itself known and respected amongst its own prime constituency of jua kali associations and of jua kali members, it had become dependent on sources of external finance. This state of external dependency prior to any possibility of the Federation achieving a sense of local ownership is probably unfortunate, but is a condition shared by a number of non-government organizations in Africa. This lack of what has been termed 'rootedness' of such bodies in African patterns of local support (Kajese, 1991) is intimately connected with their sustainability. In a situation where a foreign foundation was covering the cost of offices, operating expenses and staff salaries for the first two years, it might well prove difficult to become self-sustaining through association and individual membership fees.

An additional problem in the Kenyan political system in particular has been the way in which national bodies representing e.g. trade unions or women's organizations have become too closely associated with the state or the ruling party and have compromised their obligations to be autonomous. The notion which is reflected in the strategic plan of the Federation that they should 'seek and ensure better recognition of the Jua Kali sector by Government and local authority' may be put at risk through this very proximity. Macharia, for instance, has argued that 'when the Federation is so closely linked with the government, one wonders when it will stand out against some of the government's oppressive regulations towards the jua kali sector' (Macharia, 1995: 20). The original idea of the FES that the Federation would be in a position to lobby for the rights of the ordinary jua kali operator could well be undermined if they come to be seen merely as another spokesman for MTTAT.

There has in fact been a third national grouping of jua kali in existence, termed the Jua Kali and Kazi Cooperative Union (Kenya) Ltd. When the national chairman of this was interviewed in 1992, it was stressed that this Union drew together those jua kali groupings which could be regarded as primary societies in a cooperative sense, and which were registered with the Ministry of Cooperative Development or the Ministry of Culture and Social Services. Explaining the use of the Swahili word *kazi* (work), he emphasized that nobody could be a member of a primary society who was not a working artisan. At that point, also, he claimed that some 100 relevant societies were grouped under the organization.

From the constitution of the Federation, it would appear that only jua kali associations registered with MTTAT can become members of the Federation. This suggests that apart from the differences amongst the three national bodies on other grounds, there may be pressures within the different ministries that are encouraging a degree of competition for emergent jua kali societies.

Quite how this differentiation has worked out in the most recent period is not yet clear, but at a relatively early stage in the Federation's history it certainly had rather ambitious plans for itself on the national stage. For example, it foresaw a role for the jua kali control of certain manufacturing and a possibility that the Federation would be able to secure bulk purchases of essential materials such as welding rods. Amongst other ideas discussed with the author in the summer of 1992 were access to duty free machinery, the creation of a Jua Kali Bank, and the development of a major showroom for jua kali products in Nairobi. By contrast with some of these plans, what actually has taken place in the period since 1992 has been the Federation's identification with the Annual Jua Kali Exhibition of products, sponsored by British American Tobacco in association with MTTAT.

The linkage between the Kenya National Jua Kali Federation and the World Bank
By far the most important development, however, that has happened with the Federation has been the cementing of a relationship with the World Bank in a set of linked projects that are intended, through the Government

of Kenya, a) to provide skill upgrading and improved training for the benefit of jua kali; b) to increase access to appropriate technology, marketing information, and better infrastructure; and c) to improve the policy and institutional environment, in part through addressing the management capacity of the National Federation. These components are part of an approximately US$20 million loan from the Bank outlined in the Staff Appraisal Report of November 1993 on the *Micro- and Small Enterprise Training and Technology Project* (World Bank, 1993b). The anticipated schedule of the seven-year project, subject to preliminary conditions being met, was from July 1994 to the year 2001.

The main elements concerned specifically with jua kali training within the loan are dealt with later in this book (Chapter 5), but here it should be noted that already in the second year of this National Federation's existence, it was being identified as one of the primary executing agencies of a relatively large and complex initiative. Even though the bulk of the loan is targeted at training, technology and infrastructural developments, our interest in this chapter is particularly in the policy development side of the loan. In this respect it is clear that the loan is seen as an opportunity to leverage change in respect of the legal framework under which many jua kali work at a disadvantage. Conditionalities to improve the legal side of this operating environment for jua kali operators are specifically built into the loan:

> As a condition of Disbursement on the civil works and building materials procurement categories of the infrastructure component, the Government of Kenya would amend the Registration of Business Names Act, Trade Licensing Act, Local Government Adoptive Bye-Laws (building standards), and the Electric Power Act, as well as the Vagrancy, Nuisance, and Chief's Authority Acts, according to the Letter of Informal Sector Policy and Action Plan. (World Bank, 1993b: 23)

The Bank is also anxious to use the occasion of the loan to leverage change in the very longstanding problem of secure work-sites and access to appropriate infrastructure. In seeking to address this issue of security of tenure, the Bank is entering one of the single most politicized areas in Kenya life – access to title. The Bank is certainly aware of the challenge of using its influence to secure clear land titles for jua kali associations or individual enterprises, and has sought to build this into the agreement:

> As a condition of negotiation the Government of Kenya would provide evidence of (i) bonafide membership (registration list) in the Jua Kali Association; (ii) clear individual or Association ownership (copies of letter of allotment purchase receipt, and leasehold title) of sites (Kisumu and Mombasa) designated for infrastructure provision under the project. (World Bank, 1993b: 29–30).

More broadly this micro- and small enterprise training and technology project is designed to fit in with all of the key areas of the Bank's involvement in Kenya. First, the planned adjustment of the public sector, including divestiture and rationalization, is certain to lead to large scale lay-offs, and Kenya, along with many other countries in Africa and Latin America, is looking to the informal sector as one route to take up some of the increased requirement for self-employment. Second, the Bank is seeking to develop the private sector in Kenya, through encouraging reform of the regulatory environment, as well as the usual range of liberalization measures. In respect of this aim, the informal sector can be conceptualized as a dynamic element, and particularly in relation to its upper levels of more entrepreneurial self-employment it can be seen as a natural target for a private sector policy. However, the informal sector can also because of its very diversity and the low incomes of many of its incumbents, and especially women, be the object of the third Bank policy in Kenya – one that seeks to alleviate poverty (World Bank, 1993b: 3–4).

It should be noted that this particular Bank project probably has a much greater emphasis on training and staff development because it has been negotiated from within what was called the Population and Human Resources Division of the Eastern Africa Department of the Bank, but even with this proviso, it is instructive to see how the very diversity of what falls under the informal and jua kali constituency can allow the Bank to meet multiple goals.

The wider lessons learned by the Bank in small enterprise support:
implications for Kenya

This pioneering jua kali training project of the Bank is starting up at the very time that the World Bank has sought to review what it has learned from 20 years (1973–93) of support to small and medium enterprises. This has been summarized in a useful report, *World Bank Lending for Small Enterprises 1989–93* (Webster *et al.*, 1994). There are indeed a number of lessons learned that may well prove relevant to the Kenya project, and since the review of lending comes out of the Private Sector Development Department of the Bank, it may well provide a valuable backdrop against which the micro-enterprise training project may be assessed.

First, it must be said that according to this review, 'Lending for SMEs [small and medium enterprises] has failed notably in Africa'. Partly this has been as a result of non-repayment of loans, partly because few jobs have been created and those few at high cost. Partly there has been too much reliance on public development finance institutions as loan inter-mediaries. But it should also be noted that SME promotional projects have not fared well either: 'Programmes to strengthen institutions that provide services for SMEs generally have had little impact on the institutions or on the level and quality of services offered' (Webster *et al.*, 1994: 7–8).

Second, and more specific to Africa, there have been according to the review a series of additional factors (political instability, lack of competition in banking, inadequate infrastructure, institutional under-development, and interest rate ceilings) which have allegedly made SME project imple-mentation more problematic. Indeed, one of the lessons for Africa of the above catalogue of difficulties is worth underlining for current or future project design:

> SME lending in Africa should be approached with extra care. If the preconditions listed above are not in place, experience shows that projects undoubtedly will fail. Lessons learned about how to maximise success should be applied rigorously. This means designing projects with only a few, highly focused components; recruiting the strongest financial institutions available and using strict eligibility criteria to ensure that their operations remain sound... (Webster *et al.*, 1994: 8)

A third level of concern was raised by the review, and especially in the very recent period for those projects that sought to address poverty via micro-enterprise support. These loans were themselves a recognition that in earlier years Bank lending for so-called small-scale in Africa had reached nowhere near the jua kali sector. As a result micro-enterprise development began to be packaged within poverty alleviation loans with social welfare components. However, on reflection, the review judged that this mixing up of enterprise messages with welfare services could communicate quite the wrong signals about business-like approaches to micro-enterprise. Instead, these mixed programmes risked giving quite contradictory messages about access to credit, repayment and fiscal rigour.

Some of these lessons of experience do perhaps have implications for the current World Bank loan to Kenya for micro- and small enterprise training and technology. This is not least because the Kenya project is dependent on the institutional capacity of a relatively young Ministry (the Ministry of Technical Training and Applied Technology – MTTAT – was only formed in 1988), and since then (in 1993) has been merged with the Ministry of Research, Science and Technology to produce a new body: The Ministry of Research, Technical Training and Technology (MRTT&T). Only since 1988, therefore, has MTTAT been charged with responsibility for informal sector development, and although this has continued since the merger, there is scarcely much of an institutional memory or tradition of dealing with micro-enterprise. The same is even more glaringly true of the Kenya National Jua Kali Federation which has no experience of project implementation of any kind.

In other words, right at the end of the period under review in this book, there is, in one sense, finally evidence that the jua kali sector, through some of its representatives,[3] are thought to have come sufficiently centre stage to be recipients and, in part, implementers of a US$21.8 million project from the World Bank. On the other hand, the experience we have reviewed from the World Bank itself would suggest that project implementation for this loan might be a high risk endeavour. At this stage in the project's implementation it is simply too early to know how the National Federation will react to these new levels of responsibility, nor how supportive the Kenya Government will be in an exercise that is designed rapidly to build jua kali leadership capacity.

Some tendencies in jua kali policy at the end of the review period 1955–95

Ten years after the seminal government paper of 1986 on *Economic Management for Renewed Growth* which had been a significant impetus towards jua kali recognition, there have been no less than three major reports which allow some tentative judgements to be made about the status of Kenya's micro-enterprise sector half way through the 1990s. One is the World Bank Staff Appraisal Report on *Micro-enterprise Training and Technology* just referred to, and the others are the USAID-sponsored report on *Micro and Small Enterprise in Kenya: Results of the 1993 Baseline Survey* (Parker & Torres, 1994) and the *Report of the Small Enterprise Policy Implementation Programme (SEPIP) Mission* (ODA, 1994b), with its five supporting papers. In combination, these documents, but particularly the latter two, communicate a good sense of where policy on the informal sector has reached at the end of our review period.

One of the first lessons apparent from the USAID survey is the need massively to revise upwards the number of those employed in micro-enterprises. As opposed to previous estimates of jua kali employment in Kenya of some 600,000, the new survey suggests over 2 million individuals are working in some 900,000 enterprises. A change of this magnitude finally acknowledges that there had been previously a major urban bias in the micro-enterprise figures; consequently a great deal of the revised estimate can be accounted for by a new awareness of micro-enterprises in rural areas (no less than 78 per cent are now said to be located there). It should be noted that enterprises were not counted in rural areas if they were in 'primary agricultural or mineral production' (Parker & Torres, 1994: 4). This recent acknowledgement of the sheer scale of the rural jua kali sector makes it all the more important for us to look carefully at the rural enterprise world (in Chapter 4).

A second finding from the USAID survey is helpful in correcting some of the worries about the alleged missing middle that we have already referred to. Instead of continuing to focus on the supposed absence of businesses in the size 11–50 workers, the survey spends much more time commenting favourably on the dynamism of Kenya's micro-enterprise sector in general, and it locates the key graduation issues in the transformation of one-person firms into 3–5 worker enterprises, and 3–5 worker enterprises into those with 6–10, or more (Parker & Torres, 1994: 63–4).

A third set of findings revises opinion about the role of women in Kenya's micro-enterprise sector and notes that women make up 46 per cent of the sector's entrepreneurs, and that they outnumber men in commercial, agriculture-based, forest-based, and in textile sub-sectors. The notion, probably widely held still in Kenya, that the typical jua kali is a man in the urban areas making metal products can clearly no longer be upheld. But in some respects it may still be the case that female entrepreneurs are more clustered within subsistence self-employment, working more frequently from home, using less skilled labour, and relying on informal rather than formal credit (Parker & Torres, 1994: 64).

By contrast, the Small Enterprise Policy Implementation Programme (SEPIP) report is less concerned with the scale of the sector, and more with the continuing barriers to its development. It concludes that at one level the problem continues to be the lack of availability of land, adequate infrastucture and access to credit. However, equally important is SEPIP's view that the SME sector continues 'to be regarded as an isolated sector that can be planned for in isolation' (ODA, 1994b: 17). Despite the fact that the sheer size of the sector means that it impinges on the lives of all Kenyans and on all policies related to rural development, industrialization and urbanization, it still gets thought of as a convenient sponge for surplus labour. Even more damagingly, the report argues that high-level policy makers in Kenya regard self-employment, jua kali and micro-enterprises as 'manifestations' of underdevelopment, and not as a sector to which Kenya's future is inextricably linked (ODA, 1994b: 18).

As evidence of this continuing low priority of jua kali is the fact that the three small enterprise development units in different ministries are all relatively weak, and the one with the highest policy making status (in the Ministry of Planning and National Development) has only three individuals concerned with the area, and not all of these have SME as their only principal responsibility (ODA, 1994b: 73). In reality, the report argues that there is no apex body in government with capacity to coordinate and carry on strategic thinking on behalf of the myriad of smaller bodies which have been identified as having some role in SME. In parallel with the government institutions, it judges that many of the newly formed private sector organizations are weak, politically motivated, and 'like some jua kali associations, may not be equipped to engage in effective advocacy or to represent the interests of their members' (ODA, 1994b: 73).

Beyond these cautionary statements about the policy environment, the SEPIP report argues strongly for a 'Debt-for-Jobs' swap, in which some of the debt repayment could be converted into land, credit and infrastructure. This is an interesting enough idea, but there is no evidence in the report of there having been any discussion in government about it.

A concluding word on the Kenyanization of jua kali policy

It would be inappropriate to leave this account of more than 25 years of history with the impression that the local policy development process is in disarray, and that the single most significant reports at the end of this period were three predominantly externally financed and expatriate led missions and surveys on micro-enterprise (ODA, USAID and World Bank).[1]

A great deal has been learnt locally about the informal and jua kali sectors of Kenya's economy over the past two decades. This may not have translated into a series of major single-authored monographs for the reasons given earlier in this chapter but there are now a substantial number of younger Kenyans, including women, who have done masters and doctoral theses on the jua kali sector and on its connections with other urban industrial or rural development issues. These would include Grace Ongile, Joyce Malombe, Geoffrey Njeru, Mary Njeri Kinyanjui, Charles Abuodha, Peter Ondiege, Irene Keino, Peter Ngau, and Catherine Masinde.

But though a focus on the informal sector in Kenya has been retained in the Institute for Development Studies of the Univerity of Nairobi, much assisted by the present director, Patrick Alila, and his predecessor, Njuguna Ng'ethe, and by the presence of Dorothy McCormick as a fellow of the Institute, it would need to be acknowledged that the major focus of academic and particularly policy analysis of the micro-enterprise world has moved out from universities, and is now located in consultancy centres, in major NGOs, illustrating the argument made by David Court that 'a large proportion of the research and scholarship previously housed in universities [in Kenya] has moved out, and now occurs across a variegated host of institutions, activities and networks' (Court, 1995: 11).

Fortunately for Kenya, one major focus of this expertise resides now in the Kenya-Rural Enterprise Programme (K-REP). Their series of studies have sought to enhance understanding of the small and micro-enterprise development problems. They have pioneered the introduction to Kenya of Grameen Bank style very small loans in which the group stands guarantor for its members, and they have been picked out in the World Bank review of micro-enterprise learning as one of just four organizations from around the developing world that have been successful in reaching out to a large number of micro-enterprises (15,000 in the case of K-REP). In World Bank terms they have been successful in achieving substantial impact and in attaining a measure of financial viability. But K-REP has not only been identified with innovative programmes of micro-credit, and training for other NGOs, it has also become the information centre for jua kali and small-scale enterprise in Kenya. Witness to this focus on synthesis and review are some of the essential state of the art reviews, reviews of project and lending experience, bibliographies, and inventories of activity being undertaken for the jua kali.

This latter is the single greatest evidence of the shift between 1970 and 1995. At the beginning of our period, and even a little later in the 1970s, the amount of material available on the informal sector in Kenya was relatively small. In the bibliography of *The African Artisan* (King, 1977), for example, the literature on small-scale enterprise and petty production in Kenya could be contained in less than one page. Now in the early 1990s K-REP's *Inventory of Projects and Programmes for Small and Jua Kali Development in Kenya* (K-REP, 1993b) is 81 pages, and contains over 130 separate projects. And its parallel volume, *Jua Kali Literature: An annotated bibliography* (K-REP, 1993a) carefully breaks down by 12 different sub-sectors the very substantial literature that has been accumulated over 20 years. No less than 468 items are annotated, and a further 176 are listed without annotation – a total of almost 650 items analysing different aspects of the jua kali in Kenya.

The evidence from K-REP's studies and synthesis, and from their successful attempt to draw together the institutional memory on informal, jua kali and micro-enterprise development in Kenya, underlines the fact that there is now a critical mass of expertise on this sector in Kenya, scattered across NGOs, consultancy companies, higher education institutions, and in government ministries. That expertise is still not utilized sufficiently by policy makers, and, we have shown, even the government's own policy development process still awaits a much stronger coordinating and implementing hand. But there is certainly no shortage of debate about the options for policy.

The weakest link in this history of the Kenyanization of the jua kali sector remains the voice of the jua kali themselves. We have noted the formation of primary associations since the President's encouragement in 1985, and in 1992 we witnessed the emergence of a series of more national voices claiming to represent the jua kali. But we still know relatively little about how life has changed for the ordinary jua kali over these 20 years. How have the 'recipients', 'objects' and 'targets' of this protracted policy process actually fared?

The jua kali themselves are unlikely to have heard of their 'missing middle', or of their problems of graduating from one size of micro-enterprise to another. They almost certainly do not discuss the impediments to an enabling environment for SME. There is however a very important story to be told about their own perceptions of development and change over these past many years. The following chapters seek to communicate a flavour of this jua kali history, in urban and in rural areas, and in some of those fields, such as education, training and technology, that affect them so directly.

Notes

1. Just two years later this issue of integration of the informal sector was the subject of a conference, *The Informal Sector as an Integral Part of the National Economy. Research needs and aid requirements*, Danish Association of Development Researchers, 1987.
2. It is worth noting in this regard that Wilson Muchiri, national chairman of the Kenya Small Traders' Society, was included in one of the main Small Enterprise Development committees.
3. The Bank report makes no mention of the other contenders for national representative status amongst the jua kali associations and societies.
4. This is not to say that these missions and surveys did not draw a great deal on local consultants and local institutions.
5. A bi-monthly, *Jua Kali News*, started publication in 1995, and carried many topical items on jua kali developments.

Two

The
'Jua-Kalification'
of Nairobi

This chapter is about the 'jua-kalification' of Nairobi – the processes whereby the jua kali modality has spread from a small number of concentrations 40 years ago when the East Africa Royal Commission noted the development of small groups of African traders to a point in the mid-1990s when the City in the Sun (of the tourist brochures) could also be described as appropriately as Hot Sun (Jua Kali) City. Of course, it is still possible to take a drive that would cover some 30 km from the suburbs of Karen and Langata, looking out towards the Ngong Hills and Maasailand, via the great boulevards and central parks, fringing the city-centre skyscrapers, up through Westlands to the embassies and great houses around Muthaiga and beyond that to the newer estates extending for miles around the UNEP headquarters – and never see a jua kali settlement. A route could be chosen without much difficulty that would only reveal at the most a handful of informal enterprises – perhaps an urban woodlot, a very enticing nursery of trees and shrubs by the roadside, or a few sites for acquiring mangoes, papayas and passion fruit, all handy for cars to pull in to on their way home. Most of these small sites appear to have been sanctioned by tradition; they have been there for 20 or 30 years, and they would not be particularly offensive in London or Paris.

The jua kali character of Nairobi

But you could come into quite a different central Nairobi, on one of the thousands of fully packed matatus (taxi-cars and transit vans) or on the huge number of predominantly privately owned buses. These tend to avoid the formerly white suburbs for the economic reason that there are very few potential passengers to be picked up there. Instead they come

44

Fig. 2.1: One site of the hugely popular second-hand clothes (Mitumbi) *business in Gikomba, run by jua kali workers right next to the headquarters of the Central Organization of Trade Unions (COTU) which has no policy for the jua kali.*

racing in, on the roads from Kiambu, Thika, Machakos, Ngong, Mombasa, the Rift Valley and beyond, as if they were daily all on a gigantic national safari, in which there were additional marks awarded for scooping up the maximum number of passengers in the most competitive manner, and depositing them, in the very busiest and densest part of Nairobi, in the area between Ngara, Kariokor Market, Gikomba and the middle of River and Government Roads. The notion that transport, population density, trade and production should be integrated is powerfully illustrated in this square mile of Nairobi. Originally, as a predominantly Indian part of colonial Nairobi, its streets and buildings were on a smaller scale than white Nairobi, as befitted the Indians' status as the second grouping in the economic and social hierarchy of the time. The area combined streets of small workshops with regular Indian trading stores, with their fronts of stone, asserting already in their inscriptions from the 1930s, 1940s or early 1950s the successful accumulation of capital by the second generation of the particular migrant Indian family.

The temples, graveyards and schools sites for Nairobi's very diverse Indian colonial community are still landmarks from this earlier pattern of occupational and residential segregation. The Sikh temple is now a kind of religious roundabout in a racetrack of matatus, buses and handcart pullers. Similarly the Hindu temple at the end of Ngara Road looks out on to the competing transport careering in from Thika and Kiambu. And the once peaceful and relatively expansive graveyards and crematoria for different Indian communities abut now at one side on to one of the densest informal car and lorry repair operations in Kenya. Almost no vehicle ever dies there, but is kept alive through every kind of informal refit. This site of urban informal sector activity, we noted in the previous chapter, was one of the earliest to become organized with the Ziwani Jua Kali Association, after it had been visited by President Moi, and been allocated a series of jua kali sheds to shield some of its enterprises from the fierce sun. On the other side of the graveyard complex, the elaborate stone-carved gate of one particular Gujarati community's crematorium, with its tree of life, provides a convenient backdrop for the lean-tos of assorted African tinsmiths, charcoal stovemakers and other metalworkers, most of whom may not know that this entrance was in use just 20 years ago, and not have noted its significance any more than Indian informal workers in old Delhi today may realize that they are incorporating into their businesses some 300 or 400-year-old fragment of a Mughal tomb.

Indian buildings are not the only ones to have been surrounded by the rising flood waters of African jua kali development. Just down the road from the Gujarati stone gateway stands the headquarters of the Confederation of Trade Unions (COTU). Doubtless, when it was built, not far from where there would have been whole streets of Indian-owned electrical and mechanical engineering workshops, it was seen as a very appropriate site. Now, its compound is surrounded on the one side by a sea of secondhand clothes sellers, with their wooden stalls, and their special trade cries, and at the other side by tinsmiths, locksmiths, watch repairers, and shoemakers, all working from completely casual premises (see fig. 2.1). A third side has a pentecostal church, and the fourth has a compound bought by a developer whose purpose was not yet clear in 1994. On the pavements nearby, the most mobile segments of the informal sector have colonized every single foot of available walkway and laid out their collections of new, rather sturdy underwear, cutlery, watches, trinkets, bright enamel plates, – all ready to be scooped into the bright cloths they lie on as soon as the city policemen (askaris) race up in their big vans to try and confiscate as much as possible, and fine the hawkers.

The real paradox of COTU's location, however, is that they are now surrounded by hundreds upon hundreds of small enterprises, many of which do have employees, and these micro-enterprises cover many of the different categories of industry and commerce that COTU's affiliated trade unions claim to represent. But almost certainly there may not be a single unionized worker in the whole area now surrounding COTU headquarters, since most trade unions have not yet come to terms with the massive, and often highly exploitative, employment of people in the informal sector, and COTU itself has failed to develop any policy on informal employment. The result is that it represents only a fraction of the employed workforce, in the formal sector, and even there it is probably acutely aware that there are huge numbers of casual (*Kibarua*) un-unionized workers attached to the formal sector firms, whose terms of work are as insecure as many in the informal sector.

The unplanned transition from Indian (Asian)[1] to African

Thus far we have talked of a part of one city, in which like all cities, a portion once dominated by a particular community has changed its composition in the period of some 30 years since Independence. But there has not been anything like a full-scale substitution of Indian by African. Many, perhaps most of the retail and wholesale shops in River Road remain in Indian hands, as do many in Biashara Street. And apart from the continuing Indian domination of the upper end of the vehicle spare parts market there are still a number of key productive enterprises owned by Indians along some of the very busy streets in downtown Nairobi. These would include firms specializing in making heavy duty wood saws, some printers, some clothes factories, one or two high quality furniture producers, and a small number of firms specializing in the manufacture or repair of particular vehicle parts (engine-regrinders, manufacturers of leaf springs, vulcanizers) and specialized castings firms.

Even in residential terms, there are Indians living right in the heart of this particular stretch of the city. Most noticeably there is a part of the Ismaili (Aga Khan) community (all of whom took out the option to become Kenya citizens at Independence) living almost invisibly in a high-walled enclave right on the Ngara Roundabout, and there are other Indian housing areas not far away. But the huge area of Eastleigh that was predominantly Indian residential in the late colonial period has passed into African hands.

However, the key residential and industrial development in the last 20 years amongst the Indian communities that used to run small factories, and live in them or near them in earlier years, is to have moved the factories out to newer and much larger premises in Nairobi's formal Industrial Estate, while their domestic premises have shifted either to Parklands or out to the newer suburbs which have no particular Indian community tradition.

The characteristics of a jua kali residential or commercial area

Thus far we have talked about jua kali developments indirectly, implying perhaps that an Indian pattern of formal sector business, industry and residence was being informalized through increasing waves of African settlement. This is not the contrast we intend between African and Indian, as we shall note a little later on. What we intend to suggest is something rather different: that there are jua kali areas and non-jua kali areas of Nairobi. This is nothing as simple as there being squatter housing in one versus permanent buildings in the other, for there are plenty of jua kali areas where the majority of the buildings are permanent. Indeed, the distinction between permanent and temporary is not a helpful signpost to the presence of the informal, since there are a whole series of gradations from the most temporary structures of plastic, cardboard and wood, through solid wood, through site-and-service structures, to fully permanent

47

buildings, and it is by no means the case that the informal can only be associated with the most temporary. All over Kenya, from smallest village to the city centres of Mombasa, Kisumu and Nairobi, jua kali can, in popular usage, be found in very permanent buildings in some streets and not in others. What is there really in the distinction then of formal and informal, jua kali and non-jua kali?

In terms of whole areas or sub-areas of towns and cities, the distinction, if it is to be useful at all, would not be by type of building but rather by kinds of activities being pursued in and around the structures. Thus there are some parts of Nairobi (e.g. the main boulevards, the industrial area, the middle class shopping malls in the suburbs) where it is almost impossible to conceive of hawkers getting the opportunity to cover the whole pavement with their wares for even five minutes. There are other large expanses of Nairobi (and of many other towns) where interference with such an activity would be almost equally unthinkable, and there are grey areas where, as we illustrated above from the operations of the askaris near Gikomba, there are desultory attempts to maintain the myth that this is a regular commercial quarter.

But it is not just a question of the degree of freedom allowed to hawkers; rather it is the tolerance of a much more flexible use of buildings, whether these are temporary or permanent. Thus, what may appear to be a carpentry or furniture workshop can well have someone doing metalwork just inside the door, and there seems to be another person with access to the workshop's electricity supply who is running a grinding machine, or a wood-lathe from it. This flexible diversification is not some elaborate industrial strategy; it is more a determination to make the most of a scarce commodity, such as prime city-centre space, an electricity supply, and some connection with formal premises which would discourage the askaris from pushing the workman along. We shall illustrate this multiple utilization of industrial and commercial space later on. But there is a parallel in the residential area to this multiple activity base.

Housing and part-time commerce

Much residential building exemplifies this multiple activity. To have even a small house in a prime site, like Mathare Valley, and not exploit it to the full could be seen as being careless. Hence the little pyramids of vegetables and fruits at the door, or the sign to indicate that there is beer available for sale inside. But there are lots of services that do not even need to be advertised, such as building, tailoring, hairdressing and other personal services. Such part-time income generation does not need to be seen as the first stage on the road to full-time self-employment. In many different layers of Kenyan society, part-time home-based commerce and industry is combined with full-time paid activity in a different location.

The combinations are perhaps just more obvious in the jua kali neighbourhoods but in the intermediate suburbs also, people know perfectly well that, in this house, the menfolk use their compound as a part-time garage at the weekends and also once they come back from working as car mechanics in formal sector firms during the week. Similarly, the discreet signs in the windows or the letters after the names on the gates suggest that the professional skills used elsewhere during the day can also be purchased directly from the home. Computing, typing, accountancy, and, most common for teachers of every sort, the enormous world of private tuition – all these are regularly on the market – the informal, and usually untaxed market.

The jua kali dimension of the household economy is hard to generalize about in many locations. In the better-off households, both parents work full-time in the modern or formal sector, their children do not combine school with income generation, but they may well run from the home a source of second (jua kali) income at the weekend or during the week. These activities are often assisted by the use of full-time maids and servants (often poorer extended family members). In other households, only the man may have a so-called modern sector job, but on closer inspection the job, though in a modern firm, is completely casualized, in the sense that there are no benefits, no insurance, and no security of tenure. Other members of the household combine schooling with income raising (in the case of the children), and the mother supplements the domestic economy by some urban gardening and petty trading. Then there are other households, again, which have no link at all with the formal sector of the economy, but they have a full-time site elsewhere for one or both parents to maintain their own self-employment activity. Finally, there are those which have only some casual self-employment, and operate what is effectively a very low-level subsistence economy from their home.

All four contain some kind of jua kali activity – whether productive, commercial or service; but in the one case this jua kali work is a supplement to what are meant to be full-salaried jobs; in others it is a supplement to a completely unwaged, subsistence set of livelihoods. In the poorer neighbourhoods, the extension of the home to become a part-time bar, cycle repair site, tea shop, barber, vegetable seller, herbal medicine seller or tailor is all very obvious. Equally obvious are those homes that now have a virtually full-time enterprise operating within it or just outside. In some situations the development of a full-time productive enterprise means that the enterprise has to move from the home to where the customers are, as well as the supplies, raw materials etc. In other cases, as for example with many of the formerly Indian homes in Eastleigh, the home is now no longer a home at all but the site of a full-time factory, hotel, garage, set of offices, or rooms for renting (*Day & Night Boarding*, as the phrase goes in Kenya, to cover a multiplicity of uses over a 24-hour period).

Then, in the richer suburbs, the homes can well be the sites of a variety of more or less profitable jua kali activity, from the virtually invisible consultancy companies of the local academics, to the room for private tuitions, to the medical, financial and other professional services to which we have referred. It may generally be the case that the middle-class jua kali activities are as undeclared to the tax authorities as are the much more visible jua kali extensions of the home in the poor suburbs.

There is absolutely no difficulty in detecting acres and acres of the most visible kind of jua kali across Nairobi. In Kibera Division, which has been described as having Nairobi's largest slum, it is interesting to note that the bulk of the more than 7,000 micro-enterprises are 'found along paths and inside people's residences, with only one fifth located in market areas' (Parker & Aleke-Dondo, 1991). The same would be true of Kawangware, and Mathare, probably, and over in the eastern part of Nairobi where there is almost a whole new city growing up on the further side of the Outer Ring Road, the character of the development seems very much that of an intimately mixed residential and micro-enterprise style. Here, the familiar distinctions between residential, commercial and industrial districts seem to have broken down and jua kali, mixed mode Nairobi seems to be spreading relentlessly acre by acre. Mostly the buildings are small, and a first impression is that they are likely to be owned by those who live in them.

Meanwhile, only a few miles to the south, but still to the east of the Outer Ring Road, what might be called middle-class jua kali housing development continues. On these huge site and service schemes – several supported by the World Bank – it would appear that one of the commonest forms of housing is not that actually owned by the low or lower-middle income occupant (for whom these schemes were intended) but is rather the barrack-to-rent blocks which have been built informally, but which are organized to take 6–12 one-room renters. They didn't cost the civil servants and other formal sector employees much to buy off the original allottees but did cost quite a lot to build. They may, however, be thought of as jua kali projects, since they utilize a huge number of jua kali building firms. And, once completed, and possibly untaxed, they illustrate yet another, very different face of jua kali to be found in the city. A kind of middle-class self-help that finds expression in the phrase: 'We're all jua kali these days!'

A closer look at some of the productive jua kali heartlands of Nairobi
Because our concern is more particularly with the productive side of jua kali in urban Kenya, we shall look in much more detail at the area near the centre of Nairobi that we demarcated at the beginning of this chapter. Historically, a number of factors have contributed to this being one of the busiest jua kali sites in Kenya. Two of the oldest African urban markets are located within its square mile – Kariokor (named after the Carrier Corps of African support troops recruited to carry supplies but not arms, during the East African campaign against the Germans in the First World War) and Burmah (after the returning African soldiers who had fought in the King's African Rifles against the Japanese advance). It is also the site of the country bus station and of most of the long distance and short distance matatus, which means that purchasers can readily get their

materials up-country and vendors can find a huge additional source of customers. Within the area there are two of the better known Jua Kali Shed projects in Kamukunji and in Ziwani, where perhaps as many as 200 artisans are afforded a little shade by a jua kali project started personally by the President. However these sheds, both in Nairobi and countrywide, merely underline how many hot sun workers continue to work under the conditions that originally gave them their name.

What is perhaps principally responsible for giving the area its peculiarly industrial cast is that it is a site that had a genuinely diversified manufacturing base during the era of Indian ownership. Indeed, it would be an interesting research project to re-create an account of just exactly how industrially diverse this small area was in the period between 1930 and 1964. It would help to explain why an area like Kibera or Kawangware, just two or three miles away, has such a narrow industrial base, with the bulk of its manufacturing in just three categories: tailoring, shoemaking and carpentry (Parker & Aleke Dondo, 1991). By contrast, the densely packed streets around Gikomba hide a very rich range of industrial activity. And the area still contains, we have said above, a small but highly significant number of Indian enterprises.

The Indian origins of much African jua kali production

In the case study of the origins of the little tin oil lamps in *The African Artisan* (King, 1977), it was reported that 'Tin technology, along with much else now characterized as African informal sector production, is not the result of formal vocational training but of the presence of the Indian craft communities in East Africa' (King, 1977: 145). What was certainly true of the historical transfer of tin technology (without any special jua kali appropriate technology project) was equally true of many other industrial processes – whether in casting, furniture making, steel structures fabrication, or other sheet metalwork. This is not to say that there was not technological learning from other sources in Kenya, including from the European firms and farms. But in many ways it was the small scale, basic product mix of the Indian firms over a considerable period that allowed them to play an important role in skill development. By contrast, the larger firms with their much higher capital investment and their production of a small cluster of brand-name products, using the same manufacturing process as in Europe or North America, offered high quality industrial experience but not a technology that could be taken out of the firm by workers and readily reproduced.

This is to suggest that the continuous process plants, such as the giant East African Industries, British American Tobacco, or, in a different way, Metal Box, or the great brewing firms were not likely to be sources of entrepreneurs who could leave and set up on their own. In point of fact such firms have tended to be excellent employers, and had progressive schemes for their initially Indian, and then African, apprentices. But many of their skilled men and their engineers were experts on the production or maintenance of specific components or of huge systems that could not easily be imitated with the kinds of machinery that its African employees could expect to purchase if they left. Experienced employees from these large modern firms could draw on their high quality skills and their production or management experience eventually to go into their own businesses, and if the firms encouraged employees to become specialist sub-contractors, as, for example, in parts of the building industry, that could develop entrepreneurship. But generally speaking, employees from these larger firms could not transfer to the informal sector with a ready-made technology and a network of contacts.

The more common source of the African artisans and jua kali fundis (skilled workers) appears to have been the very much smaller firms – firms which made an entire series of products with machine tools that were relatively basic (especially in the 1950s, 1960s and 1970s. It should be stressed that such firms were in no sense on a training mission in favour of African development. Quite the opposite. Indeed, it was widely alleged that Indian firms did not favour the western European apprentice system, and tended to take on less highly educated labour and train them up very slowly on the job. And it is probably also the case that for as long as they were allowed to import new, skilled workers from South Asia, they actually preferred not to train up African skilled personnel at all. It was only when it became more problematic after Independence to get permission to acquire cheap, skilled South Asian labour that personnel policy began to change, and Africans began to get exposure to the whole range of the technology employed in the firm. Until that time there were firms in the Gikomba area where the main skilled work was done, in the words of one Indian owner 'by a sea of turbans' (i.e. Sikhs) at Independence, and where now in the early 1990s there are only two or three Indians and very large numbers of skilled African fundis.

When we look in much more detail at individual firms in this area, we shall bear in mind this 'Indian graduate' dimension of African expertise, but first we need to give a better feel of the geography and built environment of Gikomba and the surrounding areas.

The building of an industrial society in Gikomba, Nairobi: the early 1970s vs. the early 1990s

The part of Gikomba which we decided to look at much more closely was in one sense connected to the research project of 20 years earlier. On that occasion, in 1972–4, what had most caught the eye was that there were some significant numbers of young and old people who were scattered here and there in small groups, making small runs of metal goods. A very few had their Heath Robinson-style cutting and shearing and punching machines, and it was these young men that had been followed particularly closely to see what could be deduced about what looked like a first generation of Kenyan African machine-makers (King, 1975; also see chapter on

'Indigenous machine-making' in *The African Artisan* (King, 1977)). What had been obvious about their situation in Nairobi in the early 1970s was that they had been perched, somewhat precariously on the non built-up side of Kombo Munyiri Road that connects the Ngara Roundabout with Gikomba proper. On the other side of the road was still a virtually solid line of Indian-run businesses of the kind that have just been mentioned. Sometimes for reasons of security, they had uprooted their machines that were just strapped to poles and could be set up easily on other sites, and moved over to Burmah, and had set up business there amongst the other sheet metalworkers who appreciated being close to where the large, steel secondhand oil drums were cut into segments in preparation for their further transformation into various kinds of cooking containers, such as the thick metal one (*tava*) for Indian rotis and the multipurpose *kerai*.

In Burmah when they operated, just in twos and threes, there was no attempt to demarcate the little section of the ground they were occupying, whereas over in Kombo Munyiri, there was a rudimentary assertion of a compound. But like most of the little clusters of informal workers at that time, their place of work was simply cheek by jowl against the next person. It was easy accordingly to think of this handful of jua kali (they did not use that term then) from the 1970s as almost being defined by their lack of regular premises.

It was the same with the small groups of tin-lampmakers. Most of them in the 1970s were to be found in ones and twos, set back just a yard or two from one of the roads in Bahati and in Shaurimoyo. Their structures were also temporary, but at least they had a framework of bamboo poles and plastic sheets that kept the sun and rain off as they cut and soldered all the different parts of the little tin lamps.

Both groups had basically taken a small slice out of the range of Indian technologies or products, and had made a specialization from it. In the 1970s, the young machine-makers looked much more exciting to pursue. What would be the future of these kinds of rough-and-ready, hand-operated machines and their associated products, hemmed in as they were between the expensive, polished, western power tools and the majority of workers in the informal sector who really had no tools beyond the most basic? In what follows, we seek to some extent to take up the story 20 years later, both for the machine-makers of the early 1970s and also for those who were just working on a single product, the simple tin oil lamp but then in the following chapter, we look beyond these two somewhat arbitrarily defined constituencies at the wider climate of innovation and development, and consider how the reality on the ground relates to the changing policy environment we noted in Chapter 1.

Describing Gikomba

The challenge in describing jua kali is very great. Kenya is fortunate that a good deal of quantitative research has been carried out, both on particular towns and cities (Nakuru (Ndua & Ng'ethe, 1984) and Mombasa

(Walsh, 1991), for example) as well as on whole locations and divisions. As a result we have a much better sense of many dimensions of Kenyan jua kali than probably in any other country of the world. *Jua Kali Literature: An annotated bibliography* has no less than 350 pages of references and summaries of writings on Kenya's jua kali (K-REP, 1993a). So there is no difficulty in discovering for many different trades and jua kali locations some of the folowing: what the median size is of the so-called typical jua kali firm, how recently it has come into existence, what its likely staying power is, how many firms of different trade categories there are, how much labour they use, what their linkages are with the so-called formal sector, and also what investment and profits these firms claim to have made. Fortunately, we also know a great deal more than we used to about the role of women entrepreneurs. And of course, as we saw in Chapter 1, there is now a huge range of 'initiatives', 'projects', 'schemes', each addressing one or more of what the development community has determined as the needs of the sector. Thus there are jua kali technology projects, jua kali loan schemes, jua kali women's projects, jua kali training schemes, and a great deal else.

But what sometimes seems to be missing from all this literature on the characteristics of jua kali firms and of the multiple projects to assist them is some sense of their own development dynamic. Where have they come from, and where do they expect to go, and what do they think about where they currently are? Most particularly, how did they set out to get to where they currently are? We feel that in many ways what is missing from so many of the descriptions of the jua kali is their view of themselves. This is a view that has been echoed by Carl Liedholm and Donald Mead (1993) who have been personally responsible for a great deal of what we know about the jua kali sector in different African economies. They write about the need for different kinds of jua kali studies:

> Baseline surveys tell us quite a lot about what is, and where the existing structure has evolved from; to move on to what can be in the future, and how to get there, one needs an analysis that goes more deeply into a more limited set of enterprises, products and services. There is also a need for panel studies that monitor patterns of change among micro and small-scale enterprise firms over time. Such studies can throw considerable light on the forces that have brought about change, as well as the constraints to further growth of productive employment. (Liedholm & Mead, 1993: 36–7)

With this much background, we shall swing right just at the corner where the main road past Gikomba has a kink in it before it continues through the secondhand clothes sellers, past COTU, and out past the very earliest African houses built in Nairobi (at Pumwani) to California. The road we are now following has no name plate. It falls quite sharply, but it has no tarmac. It is only just wide enough for a small lorry or pick-up to fight its way through the dense crowds. Dense because on one side of the road there are women sitting, selling all the main varieties of maize and beans from enormous jute or plastic woven bags, filled to the brim. It is also busy because at the bottom the road narrows to a small pedestrian bridge

Figs. 2.2 and 2.3: Low energy stoves (jikos) at Kamukunji Market, with clay sleeves to retain heat. Kamukunji has no power supplies; hence most goods are made with handtools. There are a few hand-operated machines which are valuable for cutting or punching the heavy gauge of the oil drums.

Figs. 2.4 and 2.5: Two of the nameless streets in Gikomba. Note the evidence of powerlines, steel doors and permanent stone buildings, except for the little wooden hut for the Gikomba Jua Kali Society, front right.

over the Nairobi River – a rather grand name for this grubby stream – and then extending for a considerable distance all around are market stalls for clothes, vegetables and household products. Continue further and you reach the road again where Kamukunji's sheds cover very inadequately an expanse of mostly tin and metalworkers. Piled up in front of them are their brightly coloured products: tin trunks of every size right down to tin school-bags; every kind of brazier (*jiko*), from heavy duty commercial through low-energy ones, to toy ones for children; security bolts; and then the metal cooking pots, girdles, and plates (see figs. 2.2 and 2.3).

The heaviest duty of all, quarter to half-inch steel shallow, round plates are the awful products of the very back row of Kamukunji. Here there sit sweating smiths with huge hammers, fashioned roughly out of great lumps of metal. With these, all day they manage with what looks like massive strength to put the shallow depression into the great plates of originally flat steel, and also cut them into rounds, deftly holding the steel against steel wheel rims with their bare feet. The noise is deafening, the scene like some image of an inferno, with sinners being punished for hundreds of years. And yet it was this infernal din that stopped the presidential cavalcade several years back, and had the President declare that these archetypical jua kali, hammering metal all day in the sun, should at least get a little shade. Hence the start of the Jua Kali Shed Programme.

Back to the entrance road at the back of Gikomba. There are some four streets that run off it to the right. They too have no names, but run, not quite straight, and parallel roughly with the river. With the peripheral industries that spill out of them almost into the river, they constitute the micro-industrial jua kali heartland of Gikomba. What's different about this little section of rudely gridded streets is that they're all built in stone; they're industrial in their use, though there are a few that are stocking the steel rods or hardware supplies that the others will need (see figs. 2.4 and 2.5). Unlike Kamukunji which we have just mentioned where no one has access to electricity, and where the main night security are guards paid for by the Kamukunji Jua Kali Association, here everyone has electricity and at night steel doors and great padlocks are in evidence. In fact, not only is there electricity in these buildings, but it seems to have spilled out, perhaps under the road, to reach a dense jungle of tightly-packed wood-working shops that perch in the few yards between the river and where the pavement would be if this was a regular street. All of these wood shops are completely temporary by contrast, each one just big enough to fit some two or three wood lathes or band-saws, and a few woodworkers. Every-where the hum of wood being turned or carved by electric power tools.

Revisiting the machine-makers of the 1970s:
eight case studies of 20 years later

One reason this section of town had been selected for study was that on an earlier visit to this area in the late 1980s, during a conference in Kenya,

I had been walking round this part which had been open ground in the early 1970s. I had noticed new stone buildings going up, and had been surprised to be hailed by one of the owners. It turned out to be James Giathi whose photograph, as the proud producer of a load of bicycle carriers, had been in *The African Artisan* (King, 1977: 125). He told a somewhat complex story about how a mayor of Nairobi had sold off these plots very cheaply. But the interest in Giathi was that here was a man who had had nothing in 1972–3 but his wits and his skills in making simple cutting and punching machines, and who had just been operating on waste ground in Burmah and Gikomba. And now he appeared to be the proprietor of a large stone building. Would a pattern emerge of jua kali 'graduation' over a certain number of years from lowly beginnings to robust small enterprise owners?

On returning to Nairobi, and to Gikomba a year to two later to investigate what had happened to the various earlier machine-makers, and candlemakers, it turned out that Giathi was no longer in the same building. He had sold it in order to buy a different plot. But this time, in 1989, it was another of the early group of machine-makers that was identified. This was Paul Kairu Itinga, and, as a village mate of the other Githiga machine makers, he had learnt under one of them, just round the corner on the open ground along Kombo Munyiri Road. And now he too had a building on Third Street as I termed it since there were no road names despite the permanence of the buildings. It became an informal office during my field work, and it was especially convenient as it had a little first floor landing where he had his files, phone and a few seats (see fig. 2.6, colour section).

Paul Kairu: an early stage jua kali factory?

Kairu's building illustrated a number of features of those who had managed to make the transition from the roadside to a permanent structure. Over the course of this chapter we shall seek also to distil other features of some of these first generation factory owners in Gikomba that may be more widely generalizable within Kenya.

A PRIME FACILITY, BUT LACKING THE CAPITAL TO DEVELOP

To many jua kali, what Kairu has – a plot of 20 m by 50 m in the centre of Nairobi – would be a dream come true. But what is intriguing is how difficult it was to get it to the stage that it was in mid-1989. Like Giathi, he had actually been given the plot, virtually for nothing, by the City Council of Nairobi, through belonging to what was called the Gikomba Light Industrial Society – a kind of trade association that developed several years prior to the jua kali associations encouraged by the President. So here was the first feature – a plot of land – that could never easily be generalized for other jua kali hopefuls. And yet despite this extraordinary headstart, he was not able for years to capitalize on it; for he could not afford to develop the site, and so had to rent it to others for small amounts.

It was finally seven years after he had been given the site that he was able to build a front wall. He eventually got the other three walls built and a roof on, but it was just a few months before I met him that he got electricity – 11 years after first owning the site.

A PATTERN OF LETTING OTHER PEOPLE USE THE PREMISES RATHER THAN SINGLE OWNER EXPLOITATION

Just as he had moved in to Ngenda Metal Works with his own five manual machines in 1978 when the Kombo Munyiri site was cleared for development, and had presumably paid a nominal rent to the owner, Kamau Getau, for the privilege, so now, he, as proprietor, let other jua kali come in and complete their own jobs. This was not some interesting African form of joint enterprise; it was just the absence of sufficient machinery, materials, or orders to allow the factory to run all day on his work exclusively. It was not uncommon to see, for instance, Gachangiu (whose first 30 years of life is laid out in *The African Artisan* (King, 1977: 114–18) come past with a job that he couldn't complete with his own few hand-operated machines.

THE ACUTE SHORTAGE OF POWER TOOLS

One of the attractions of Kairu's (it had no trade name outside; no proud Kairu and Sons Ltd, in the manner of many Indian stores) was that he did have an old bench grinding machine which could also be used as a drilling machine. He also had two electric welding machines, an assortment of quite heavy duty cutting and bending machines, and the basic bellows equipment needed for smithy work or smelting of softer metals. Back in 1990, Kairu had estimated the value of his machinery as some K.Sh.23,000.[2] Though this was a huge amount more than the jua kali packed into Kamukunji and other dense concentrations, it could be argued that in relation to the real price and value of the site he was occupying, he was under-capitalized. Apart from the electric welders and the bench grinder, all the tools that he owned could as well have been used out in the open ground without any power, as indeed, they were by several groups of artisans both in Kamukunji and in Mlango Kubwa, another neighbouring jua kali concentration on the way to Eastleigh.

JOBBER, MANUFACTURER OR REPAIRER?

What many jua kalis are effectively doing is part-time production, on one-off contracts. Others are concentrating on a small number of lines, e.g. candlemakers on oil lamps, and they seem to be able to work non-stop on the same line, day-in and day-out. In some ways it would seem that the available, official categorization of activities does not really take sufficient account of this. Thus, Kairu has only taken out a repair licence as a trade category, which is only a few hundred shillings for three years. Whereas a manufacturing licence was K.Sh.3000 in 1990. And yet his general level of activity is much more in part-time manufacturing than in repair. It would probably be most accurate of all to call Kairu's operation a jobbing shop, in which he is only one of those carrying out such jobs. But this example of trade descriptions taken presumably from Western distinctions is not particularly appropriate for a jua kali world where manufacturing (in its literal meaning of hand work) is very common but any continuous, power-assisted process very rare.

THE ACQUISITION OF TECHNOLOGICAL CONFIDENCE BY STAGES

One of the issues that we shall be looking at in several of the different examples of the Gikomba jua kali is the character of the technological confidence that is betrayed in the development of the individual's growth over the last several years. In the case of Kairu, the first stage was really no stage at all. From the end of school (Standard VIII) when he was 21, in the year of Independence, for 12 years he just did casual work on the tea and coffee plantations. Stage two started like a number of other young men who were taught by his Githiga village mate, Gacuiri. At that time in 1975, Gacuiri had mastered ways of making bicycle carriers and bicycle stands, using the technology of the machine tools he had learnt in turn from Mutang'ang'i in the village (see Chapter Three). The key thing about the people who learnt from him was that although they started by just being used as labour on the machines, they rapidly learnt to make the machines themselves. By the end of stage two, Kairu had made some five machines of his own. It was at the end of this stage that he actually accepted himself as a jua kali worker, and forgot all other kinds of employment, according to his own testimony. It was for this reason that he began more seriously to acquire tools of his own. Stage three saw a further diversification of production, but now it was mostly small rough-and-ready items for the building trade, such as pipe fittings, holders and hooks. With one or two of these items, he seems to have developed slightly better designs, but still during the late 1970s and early 1980s, money was very tight: 'he couldn't afford even a pair of long trousers'. The idea of paying K.Sh.1000 for anything was unthinkable. Stage four began in 1985 when he started building his permanent premises and took some four years to complete. But by the end he was deliberately trying to find niches in the building components trade which he could make locally, either taking production away from some firm in the industrial area, or saving on imports. In 1989, for instance, he was making fuse boxes for the electricity company, and was just finalizing his own design and production of a window stay. He had an order for several thousand of them from one of the Indian hardware stores or builders (see fig. 2.7, colour section).

NO AUTOMATED PRODUCTION

As we have said, even in stage four, Kairu's small enterprise was a factory-cum-engineering workshop in which he still did not have one or two of the key machine tools which would allow him to move to a further stage. He did not have a lathe, which was not surprising given that there were only two lathes in 1990 in African hands in the whole of Gikomba. And both were old and not particularly accurate. But Kairu was well aware of what he would like. His first choice, in the event that he landed a large loan of, say, K.Sh.200,000, would be two press machines. Those would allow him dramatically to increase and raise the quality of his production.

Reflecting on the technological confidence displayed over these 15 years, in one way, what is evident is a growth that is slow, and not significantly different from others who have been looking for chances to supply the building industry. Only in the more recent period does it seem that he has been really challenged technologically, probably by his Indian contacts in the building industry saying of a particular component, 'See if you can make that locally, and we'll buy it'.

But in reacting to that challenge, Kairu was having to draw on ingenuity rather than years of engineering design and experience. In point of fact he had never been, as an employee, in what could be called a high-quality engineering workshop, such as a few of the Indians still operate in Gikomba, but which are mostly now to be found in the Industrial Area. So, apart from his apprenticeship with Gacuiri, who was certainly an inventive character, he had had no really demanding experience on the job. This is worth recording, because it has emerged in a number of reviews of the informal sector (Fluitman, 1994; McGrath & King, 1995) that the move from apprenticeship to self-employment is sometimes more effective if it can have a sandwich of employment, and more especially if that employment allows the acquisition of higher quality skills. Here then is the notion of graduating from employment to self-employment which we shall look at in other individuals also. But Kairu himself had something to say about this difficulty of having to acquire knowledge for himself:

> One reason for the slowness of my own move to self-employment was that I used to go to people who were not able to help. Now when someone is in my workshop I show them very carefully; whereas in my case, my employers or helpers used to prevent me from getting knowledge. All I did was to get the idea of looking at a particular process from the shop. I had to struggle very hard to understand. So getting training from jua kalis alone is very hard; but these boys of mine are actually getting a better training than me. (Kairu, Oral interview, July, 1989)

John Nene Ihugo, plumber with labour contracts

One of the more visible carrier makers of the *The African Artisan* (King, 1977) was John Nene Ihugo. He was on the front cover of the book (see fig. 2.8), and his knowledge of the village of Githiga was very largely responsible for the detail on that small village in Kiambu District. But although in the early 1970s he may have seemed just another element of Githiga's urban carrier-making cluster, he was really using carrier-making as a way of getting money to do something else. It is worth stressing this deliberate aspect of mobility in the informal sector, since rapid surveys can probably give the impression that a jua kali enterprise has closed down or failed, when in fact the person concerned was taking a highly instrumental attitude towards the particular trade.

His real interest was to become a plumber, and over the years from 1973, he had moved in and out of employment, but in reviewing the years from 1974 to 1992, it is obvious that he views them clearly as a series of labour contracts, which he can number off – from the first (for a science lab in a *harambee* school and all its basins), with very specific figures on what was the price for each of them, up to one of the more recent in 1992 which was for the installation of the entire plumbing, sewage system and septic tanks of a large mansion-house outside Nairobi (see figs. 2.9 and 2.10, colour section). This latter was clearly a really major contract, probably the largest Nene had ever had. Since then there have continued to be fluctuations with very small contracts of K.Sh.4000 or K.Sh.8000 to larger ones of K.Sh.18,000–22,000. And periods of several months with no contracts at all.

After these more than 20 years of work in the jua kali sector, there is not much visible evidence of success. No small office with a signboard. No permanent staff. A strong reliance on having to find the next contract. There are, however, a number of points to be made on the rather different career development path of this ex-metalworker.

POORER FAMILIES AND THE NOTION OF BUSINESS INVESTMENT
Nene's family had little established position in Kiambu District, though they had a small plot. Like earlier generations of poorer Kikuyu who had seen the Rift Valley Province of Kenya as a place to get the land they were denied by tradition or circumstance at home (Furedi, 1989), Nene had used quite a lot of his savings from jua kali, not to plough back into plumbing or his own business development, but rather to purchase land in the Rift Valley, around Narok, to establish his parents there, and build a house with them. In the mid-1980s this was entirely rational in family terms, since an acre of land around Githiga was K.Sh.200,000 whereas around Narok, Nene's two acres were just under K.Sh.20,000. And the extra land would mean that Nene's wife would have an additional source of both subsistence, and possibly cash-crop, income.

This particular investment strategy was undermined by factors far beyond the control of a single family. As part of the anti-Kikuyu killings and lootings in the run up to the multi-party elections, Nene's new home in the Rift Valley was burnt down, and the family had to flee back to Central Province. Again, this probably put renewed pressure on the principal breadwinner. Even though this was a highly unpredictable event, it was not that different from what happened to hundreds of urban jua kali around Gikomba in November 1990, when their temporary buildings were bulldozed and they were encouraged to start up again, several miles from the city centre.

SCHOOLING VERSUS SKILLING FOR THE NEXT GENERATION
Again it is at the lower end of the income range, whether in the formal or informal sectors, that the decision between more or less schooling

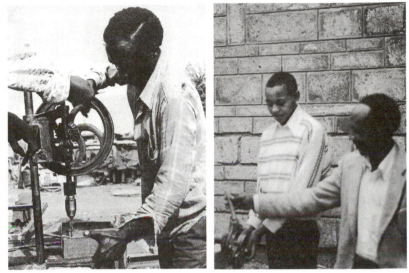

Fig. 2.8: John Nene, 1972.

Fig. 2.11: John Nene with his son, Kenneth, learning the trade of plumber.

Fig. 2.12: John Nene, 20 years after he had appeared on the cover of The African Artisan.

becomes critical. Where four years of secondary schooling for one child costs around K.Sh.28,000, it should not be surprising that with all the other problems arising, Nene's view of secondary schooling, for his son, Kenneth, should have been that unless he could get into a really good school, there was no point in spending this money, struggling through a poor school and still getting no job; his son might as well start learning plumbing. This is indeed what had begun to happen by 1992 (see fig. 2.11). For after trying to repeat Standard VII in the much less competitive Narok, as immigrants to this Maasai area had done for 20 years (see King, 1972), his son was beaten up in the anti-Kikuyu riots of November 1991, and came back, too old to continue with Standard VIII. He had therefore begun to work with his father and had learnt the skills of plumbing so that he could soon undertake a complete contract. Nene hoped that this would mean that the two of them could work together in a family unit 'like the Indians, so as to provide work for other sons'.

The son's own attitude to skill versus school was that he would like to be a *fundi*. Or in his own words, 'One's skill is one's gold. After one year, I shall be working on my own.' This last point is intriguing, for it suggests an attitude towards independence and going it alone even within the family. It points to a continuation of that process of fissure and break-up of micro-business units even amongst family members, now in the 1990s as when Marris and Somerset (1971) first forcefully remarked on this tendency back in 1971 in their *African Businessmen*. In any event in January 1995 it looked as if Nene's son, Kenneth, was going to leave plumbing and take on driving.

Nene's picture appears on the cover of this second volume as it did in 1977. And in many ways it is a remarkable contrast. The first shows part of the rough, open ground around Burmah. It is most definitely a jua kali photograph, since the sun pours down on his completely unprotected head and worksite. In the second picture, doubtless there is still a good deal of outside work, but the rough digging out of the septic tanks would certainly have been done by unskilled labour, and not by Nene. A good deal of the finishing up of the plumbing systems in the kitchen, toilets and bathrooms would have been shaded. And now, as compared to the 1975 face that looked down at the rough drill, there is a pride in the achievement of being in charge of the plumbing contract for the whole operation (see fig. 2.12).

And yet, there is still not enough money to guarantee secondary schooling, even for the first son, not to mention the other six children.

Peter Kagotho:
Traditional and modern technical skills in a new urban setting

If we now return to Gikomba from Nene with his labour contracts dispersed here and there, and go just one one street up from Kairu we come to another of the urban Githiga blacksmiths, and certainly one of the most successful. Peter Kagotho had acquired his traditional blacksmith skills as had others in his family, but he had also been exposed to some formal

Fig. 2.15: Peter Kagotho outside his larger, second workshop in the new light industrial area of Komo Rock, Nairobi.

Figs. 2.16, 2.17: Two 'invisible' jua kali premises in Nairobi, with metal gates and no indication of owner or activity.

technical training at Kabete Technical School. In addition, he had had some experience as an employee in an engineering firm before he had established himself not only in Gikomba but also in a new light industrial estate out at Komo Rock. Here, in Gikomba, it was quite clear what the most successful product had been, since its name was even written on the side of his little Peugeot pick up, *Zero-grazer by Kagothoson Machines Gikomba*. This referred of course to the development of the very basic fodder-cutting machine (of the kind that we had pictured with Mutang'ang'i in 1974 [*The African Artisan*, King, 1977: 131]). The latest orders, in a bold greeny-blue colour, were being prepared for transport after sale (see figs. 2.13 and 2.14, colour section). This particular model was adapted for either manual or power operation. The name, zero-grazer, itself derived from the practice which had become widespread in Central Province, as grazing land became short, and grade cows became very popular; families began to keep their one or two cows in a stall and they brought the feed to it rather than letting it out to graze. It was also a commentary, some 40 years after the Swynnerton Plan had encouraged the private ownership of land, on the absence of common land for grazing, and upon the need for families with little land to use it more intensively for cash and subsistence food crops. At any rate, a machine that cut maize stalks and napier grass into appropriate sizes was very handy, even if it did cost K.Sh.12,000 at 1989 prices.

The inside of Kagotho's first permanent workshop in Gikomba seemed very crowded, and smaller than Kairu's, perhaps partly because it had a nearly complete second floor in place, with the office and some of the new designs in the process of evolution. There are a number of features of this particular metalworker's stage of jua kali development that are worth picking out in order to distinguish him from the others from the 1970s who are also being mentioned.

THE PROS AND CONS OF VISIBILITY

Kagotho's products, not just the zero-grazers but the mechanized maize-mills, were just the kind of thing that the Ministry of Technical Training and Appropriate Technology (MTTAT) and its Minister of the time, Professor Ongeri, were keen to publicize. It is not known whether it was Kagotho himself who took the initiative of displaying his products at the Nairobi Show and in the Kenyatta Conference Centre. But it was certainly his decision to start advertising on TV and on Radio. This meant that demand became higher, but it also brought him to the attention of the tax system. He had apparently little or no record system at the time, and he was accordingly obliged to take on an accountant (the same that Mutang'ang'i had used from 1984–7). This man was having to work out accounts right back to 1983 – from 1988. This was the downside of publicity – a publicity that many jua kali in both the formal and informal sectors fear. But on the positive side, he can have publicity on the side of his van, with his box number and phone number, and not be afraid to try and trade his jua kali products in the most prestigious agricultural fair in Kenya. His workshop can have his name and products advertised in bold. And the same is true of his second workshop, a very much larger one (10 m by 20 m) 3 km or so away in Komo Rock, the new light industrial area (see fig. 2.15).

THE TECHNOLOGY NICHE IN THE KENYA MARKET

The jua kali engineer entrepreneur, par excellence, such as Peter Kagotho, is very aware that there are niches in the local market where products can be designed that have a comparative advantage over what can be imported. The zero-grazer is perhaps one of the best examples. But other, relatively bulky, but not complex machines such as maize-mills, and block-making machines are also obvious candidates for local fundis to take on. This seems to be precisely what Kagotho has done, concentrating on the machines rather than on their products. But at the same time, he has kept trying to develop ways of making in Kenya products that could compete with imported items. Quite some effort has been spent also in trying to make a machine for making nails, but there he has found that he couldn't develop a facility (and equally important get hold of the materials) that would allow the nails to be any cheaper than the imported ones, or those made by completely automated processes.

TECHNOLOGICAL CONFIDENCE AND THE ROLE OF THE JUA KALI

In one way, the example of Peter Kagotho raises a further question about definitions of jua kali. Here is someone who has established himself in product development and sale. His enterprises are in the public domain and are recognized. He has an accountant helping with the taxes. He has even got a big sign up in his office (perhaps taken from some exhibition of his goods): 'After World War II, the German economy was restored by the Jua Kali like people'.

But in what sense is he still a jua kali? Has he now graduated and become just a regular small businessman? It might well seem that he had. But there is still very much a feeling that he has done all that he has done without any help or any credit. He may appear to have succeeded, but compared to the industries he knows, he has done it all without really modern machine tools. He might well think that an engineering workshop without a modern lathe was itself an indication that he was still operating in the jua kali mode. It is a question that we shall need to return to.

Mr 'X': an invisible jua kali success story

The question of when is a jua kali a jua kali is also very dramatically illustrated by our next example of a metalworker who certainly has made good since the 1970s when he was working with several of the other carrier-makers in Gikomba. In December 1977, he took his machines with him and set up in Eastleigh, and then when the Gikomba Light Industries Society was formed in 1978 in order to get plots from the City Commission, he acquired one along with about another 140 people. He had stayed there for almost ten years, but the big change had come when he had got electricity in 1983 and also a loan from a Finance Company to allow him to buy his first two press machines, which themselves were locally produced by an Indian engineer. 'They made the difference between life and death in terms of production. This was the turning point.'

Initially he had applied his knowledge to making entire coffee machines (for sorting and grading coffee), but, doubtless because of the down-turn in the coffee market, he had had to diversify. The press machines then allowed him to take on a much more factory-like mode of production. In fact by 1989, he had some ten large, foot-operated press machines, and these were able enormously to raise productivity. However, he was anxious to move further and get three fully automated electrical machines with which he thought that he could break into the market for shovels.

Obviously by the time the press machines were accumulating in his small Gikomba workshop, it became necessary to move on to larger premises which he duly did in 1987. He was perhaps one of the first of the true Gikomba 'graduates', someone whose production had significantly outgrown the space available. He moved on therefore, but we may not say whether in Nairobi or elsewhere, since one of the conditions of talking to him and of visiting his factory was that there be no reference to his name or his location. Unlike Peter Kagotho, his operation was undeclared. There was no sign over his premises, no advertisement except by word of mouth (see figs 2.16 and 2.17 on p. 65). And so the boxes of drop-bolts, pad-bolts, tower bolts, and hinges that emerged from the premises were also unmarked.

The reasons for not wishing to be identified are again connected with the whole issue of jua kali status and definition. This particular entrepreneur would argue that he is threatened still by the upper millstone of the fully automated Indian factories, in the formal Industrial Areas of Kenya, and also from the nether millstone of the completely manual, or simple, hand-operated machinery of some of the jua kalis, making similar items without the expense of premises, electricity, packaging etc. As to when he would no longer call himself a jua kali, he considered that that would not happen until he was fully established in, say, Nairobi's Industrial Area. He still felt he had a long way to go.

TAXING JUA KALIS: THE CATCH 22 OF POSITIVE
DISCRIMINATION?

This particular example underlines the trade-off for policy between encouraging jua kalis to compete with foreign or local non-African industry on the one hand and the failure to get tax revenues from even the more successful jua kali enterprises on the other. It has become almost accepted that in the fragile world of encouraging real competition to foreign or non-African domination of business and industry in Kenya, there does need to be something of a kid glove policy. However, Kenya's small-scale industrial estates have been taken as failures because they have allegedly been featherbedded much too much, with the result that almost no one has graduated from their protected environment. They are said effectively to have failed to be nurseries for enterprise (World Bank, 1987).

If failure to collect tax from jua kalis is one of the ways that African enterprise is given a boost, that may prove a much blunter mechanism than what seems to have happened with the plot allocations for Gikomba or for Komo Rock. There it looks as if the process was not exactly transparent but the result appears to have been that a large number of people who were determined to be in business got an opportunity. Whereas with the informal tax-break for everyone who claims to be jua kali, it may mean that businesses get used to doing business in a way that can't really be compared with those they are competing against, and hence are not well prepared for any eventual competition on equal terms.

The issue of jua kali graduating to being taxpayers, however, is much more complex than this, and is ultimately inseparable from the question of probity in the public service more generally.

James Giathi: urban artisan/rural household

Another of our group from the early 1970s, James Giathi (see fig. 2.18), is also still in the same trade. Like Kairu, we have already mentioned that he had taken advantage of acquiring a plot in Gikomba, but had not been able fully to develop it, though he had managed to build on it. Satisfactory renting proved problematic, and led eventually to a court case which was won. He was then able to buy a much larger place in Komo Rock, which again he had not been able to exploit by the beginning of the 1990s. Giathi illustrates, however, a number of the characteristics that make quite a lot of the Nairobi artisans somewhat different from jua kali in other countries, particularly Latin America. This is that they have worked in Nairobi for the best part of 20 years, and yet they have continued to live in the rural areas. Even though Githiga is as much as 40 km from Gikomba, travelling every day to work is still preferable to the cost of living and renting in town.

Hence at marriage, it made more sense to put profits from the business into land in Githiga, so that his spouse could contribute directly to the family income through agriculture, than into parallel investments in the business. And so K.Sh.18,000 went towards one-quarter of an acre in 1976 for this purpose. And another K.Sh.60,000 to a stone house in Githiga. What is intriguing about Kenya is that for those who live in high-yielding agricultural land, there is a real tension and alternative between town income and rural income. On at least two occasions, Giathi actually came and operated his business from the rural areas, once in 1977–8, and once in 1981–3. And it seems not impossible that he could have continued to work there, just as some of the artisans discussed in Chapter 4 could come and work in town, but have elected to stay in the rural areas. In any country one of the successes of agricultural development must be that people can feel they can make an adequate living in a rural area, as opposed to feeling that they must take the whole family and live in town.

Fig. 2.18: James Giathi, on left (1972).

Githiga should not therefore be seen as a commuting suburb, merely offering a different and cheaper environment for the family home, but rather as an alternative work site for many of its urban jua kalis.

A GIKOMBA GRADUATE?

Giathi had in one sense graduated from Gikomba. He had sold up his permanent premises, but had not moved on to larger ones, and was in the late 1980s and early 1990s back sharing a plot on which there was no permanent structure, just a shade over the area where the many machines were housed. Giathi would appear to have moved backwards a step or two, since he was now sharing this quite large open site in California with his brother, Gacuiri. However, as the site had electricity, it was possible to do many or most of the things that Kairu did in his premises, and even a few more, as we shall see in a moment (see figs. 2.19 and 2.20, colour section).

The question around Giathi was perhaps how he would get the capital together to allow him to make a real start on the plot that he bought in Kariobangi for his larger-scale industry. He had put no less than K.Sh.130,000 into developing this two-storeyed building. And yet to the casual observer, his production at the moment might not seem very different from other groups which did not have the advantages of secure premises, but which just worked as a loose conglomerate on some open ground about half a mile from him over at Mlango Kubwa. There had been ups and downs in his business over these almost 20 years. He no longer had the old Peugeot pick-up he had had when he was obliged to look after his own and his brother's business when the latter was in jail. In one way he looked like he was an example of the very case of over-competition that his older brother had articulated so exactly, back in 1973. If this were true, it was a state of affairs that he and the others had helped to bring about, by training so many in the intervening 15 years in the very skills that once were the property of so very few:

> Now they don't get much profit. They operate now in a way that doesn't look like a business. You see, business has got some hard points to understand. For instance, some time, if you are in business and have a lot to sell, you don't let the buyer know; otherwise the price will go low. Now, however, these people order against each other. I have told them many times that they can make the goods if they like, as individuals, but only one man should go round to get the orders, so that they may all be selling at one price, instead of all going round trying to find out an order for themselves. The shops are muddled to find that they have got five men apparently ... they should do it as a society or co-operative and one man should make all the arrangements. (Gacuiri, quoted in *The African Artisan*, King, 1977: 121)

And yet Giathi did now have a two-storeyed building. He did have plans to make shovels, but for that he would need heavy duty press machines of the sort we talked of with our invisible jua kali entrepreneur above. It looked like he had reached something of a plateau, even though he is potentially in so much better a position than the majority of jua kalis. However, the kinds of surpluses that the metal products industry had generated in his best years (1986/7/8) when he had been producing jembes (the commonest agricultural implement for East Africa) seemed to have passed. In Giathi's view this fluctuation cannot be separated from what was happening to tea and coffee prices at the end of the 1980s and the early 1990s. When farmers are not paid properly, either because of corruption or because the world prices are falling, then there is a knock-on effect, and farmers don't buy new implements. If he was to get the money to make a transition from his present production to a higher level, it looked like he would need a loan rather than relying on the profits from his current work.

LOANS RELATIVELY UNKNOWN AMONGST ORDINARY JUA KALI

The world of loans was really a closed book to Giathi and to many jua kali despite the huge number of schemes that we have talked about in Chapter One. Or rather he only knew about the system for getting a loan from an Indian in one of the companies in the Industrial Area. This was apparently a piece of local knowledge in the jua kali world of Nairobi, since he had heard that about 800 had taken advantage of this rough-and-ready system. The advantage from his point of view was that you didn't need to have influence, nor go through a lot of complicated paperwork. You just gave in your title deed, and borrowed – in his case K.Sh.15,000 at a rate of 18 per cent for one year. And it was immediate, unlike what you heard about some of the other people who had tried to get a loan from the banks and various jua kali schemes.

RESPECT FOR AND HEAVY INVOLVEMENT WITH INDIAN BUSINESS

It might be thought that as the group who were immediately beneath the world of Indian business and industry in Kenya it would be the Indians rather than the larger international firms in the Industrial Area that would be the targets of jealousy, criticism, and unfair practice for artisans like Giathi. There is, after all, in the jua kali thinking quite a strong thread of anti-Indian sentiment, which is usually expressed in the examples of how a particular product, having been once made entirely by Indians, was now in the hands of the jua kali, while the Indian firm had been put out of business.

The opposite is the view by Giathi and others we have met. They regard the Indians as very important for their own businesses. For a number of reasons. The Indian wholesalers are prepared to take large orders, and like the loan business just mentioned, the money is on the table on the day mentioned. In Kairu's words: 'They don't procrastinate – the Indian traders, but they pay on the spot. If they say tomorrow, they mean tomorrow.' But Giathi would go further, and link the very success of his kind of jua kali to the Indians. They were the people who actually came to his plot and gave him orders. Indeed, on one occasion, an Indian had placed an order for 5,000 pieces @ K.Sh.12 each (K.Sh.60,000). But in general:

> Our business is related to Indians. If we miss them, we shall do nothing. Our big orders are from Indians, and frankly very little from Africans. The Indians know how to keep stock. They know about business more than we do. (Giathi, Oral interview, July 1992)

The line that is frequently heard, critical of the Indians, is that what can be bought in an Indian furniture or hardware store in the middle of Nairobi can be bought for a fraction of the price from the jua kali direct. The implication of this line (which is much more likely to be heard from individuals in MTTAT or ordinary consumers than from the jua kali themselves) is that Indians are somehow exploiting the jua kali. The view from jua kali such as Giathi is that whether it was 20 years ago with bicycle carriers or now with jembes, it is the fact that the Indian hardware stores or contractors are prepared to place a large order that has given them, the jua kali, significant amounts of money at a single time. They are very critical of some of the African hardwares, by contrast, for exploiting the jua kali by simply not paying on time, and keeping on telling them to come back tomorrow.

The early promise of Gacuiri Kagotho: 20 years on

In many ways the most dramatic of the 1970s machine-makers was Gacuiri

Fig. 2.21: Gacuiri, on right (1972).

Fig. 2.24: Gacuiri in his half-constructed engineering workshop in Githunguri, Kiambu District.

(see fig. 2.21). His enterprise had been the model for several of the other Githiga people. He had pioneered many of the developments and the contacts in Nairobi, and had effectively extended Mutang'ang'i's range of products to the city. At the time we left him in 1973–4, he had commandeered an informal site on the waste-land opposite some of the Indian workshops on Kombo Munyiri Road (*The African Artisan*, King, 1977: 112 and 127), but he had shown his readiness to drop Nairobi for the rural areas by moving back into Githiga when the City Council were trying to clear Burmah in 1972. And he started another business in Githunguri, a somewhat larger town, a few years later.

There were two major setbacks over the next ten years. The first, allegedly connected with *magendo* (stolen goods or trading in goods of doubtful provenance), put him in jail for two years. Some ten years later, he had a very bad road accident, and was out of commission for one-and-a-half-years. It would appear that being in jail in 1977–9 made it difficult for him to profit like the others from cheap plots in Gikomba that became available at that very time. On the other hand he appeared by 1989 to have control of a large site, which he shared with Giathi, his brother, in California, and he had also started a major building project for an engineering workshop in Githunguri.

The California site was often continuing without Gacuiri's personal presence. And there was plenty of evidence still of large runs of bolts, hinges, and other construction-related items being undertaken by the employees. The workshop was a good deal more formalized than back in Kombo Munyiri days, with power supplies, for grinding, electric welding, but still with the Heath-Robinson look of the various cutters, punchers and benders. No longer mounted on temporary wooden poles, but fixed to various steel frames.

What was different from the early days, and from several of the other 1970s jua kali who had been his associates, was that Gacuiri was still taking on new things. For instance, one of the contracts in 1989 was for a major piece of vehicle body building (see fig. 2.22, colour section). This involved a very different set of skills than a later contract where a maize mill was being put through its final tests (see fig. 2.23, colour section). But in 1989–90, possibly because of the major accident, there was not yet a direct or single approach. There was considerable evidence of diversification, with land purchase for the family, with the development of the Githunguri site, and with California. But it did not seem that Gacuiri was planning a breakthrough into higher technologies of the sort associated with our invisible jua kali entrepreneur.

One thing is of particular interest for rural–urban imbalances, and that is that Gacuiri, one of the more dynamic and profit-oriented of the 1970s jua kalis, was still in the 1990s one of those who could see that a good return could be made by having a proper engineering workshop in a small rural town, Githunguri (see fig. 2.24).

Njenga Mbereri: the challenge to innovation and change

The last two of the metalworkers met in 1970s are those who have moved, in some way, least far from what they were doing in that period. Andrew Gachangiu and Njenga Mbereri are not actually located in Gikomba. Gachangiu has his machines, still very temporary looking, in one corner of the Kamukunji jua kali site, and Njenga is just a few hundred metres away at Shauri Moyo and also has a small berth in Kamukunji. They do not appear to have made substantial progress in the 20 years. They are the only two that have some link to the new schemes for giving small plots (2.5m x 2.5m) to jua kalis.

Njenga would regard himself as having been in on the start of the machine-making project by jua kalis. His own account would have him, Gacuiri and Magotho making the first cutting machine as early as 1970 (though Mutang'ang'i had surely done so earlier). For Njenga the golden years were after this breakthrough, from 1972. Initially, he and Gacuiri, before they went their separate ways, had no less than 30 casual labourers working for them. The demand for these very cheap, jua kali bicycle carriers, foreguards and stands was huge, and they were the first people to try and meet it. Njenga had even opened a bank account in 1971 (though he had closed it a few years later). Then towards the end of this period, in 1977 and because of marriage, he had started to construct a house in his home village, Githiga, and had put as much as K.Sh.100,000 into it. This was of course a considerable diversion of potential business investment funds, but, as explained earlier it meant that the marriage could become also a source of revenue rather than a drain upon a single income.

SCHOOLING COSTS VERSUS BUSINESS INCOME

Njenga was not the only jua kali from the 1970s who at the beginning of the 1990s was starting to notice the very real trade-offs between business investment and school investment. As someone who had only had Standard VII himself (seven years of primary schooling) he was keen that his children should get the best chances. His first two were girls, and they were by now both of secondary school age. Both were in boarding secondary schools, for which the cost in the early 1990s was some K.Sh.6,000 to K.Sh.7,500 each per year. Then there were three boys almost finished primary schooling. He would soon have to cover at the same time no less than four secondary school fees (i.e. about K.Sh.25,000 per year) on an income, he estimated, of something like K.Sh.1,000 per week.

As the profits from his traditional business seemed to stagnate and fall, so his social expenditures were rising steeply. On the business side, he continued to make some machines for sale, and he did runs of agricultural implements (see fig. 2.25, colour section), but he clearly needed more machines himself – an electric welder and a drilling machine. He was beginning to wonder, however, if he could not do better just by getting the money together to build some accommodation to let, perhaps a block with 24 simple tiny rooms.

75

Andrew Gachangiu: a subsistence metalworker?

The last of the metalworkers, who we have linked quite closely with Njenga in terms of status and movement, is Gachangiu (see fig. 2.26). In *The African Artisan* (King, 1977), his journeys from employment to self-employment had been detailed (pp. 114–18). He had, like Nene after 1973, tried to concentrate on something other than carrier-making or machine-making, and had taken small labour subcontracts from a local contractor, and through him had since 1982 tried to specialize in making gutters and gutter brackets. At times actually he had gone back into employment with him. More commonly, he could be found carrying out a small contract for guttering or some similar building task such as water tanks, and he would use his access to workshops like Kairu's to allow him to complete some of the more complex parts of his various tasks.

Fig. 2.26: Andrew Gachangiu (1972).

He had not broken with the metalwork side of things, but kept his small number of machines on his plot in Kamukunji. Like other jua kali who were members of the Kamukunji Jua Kali Association, he had a small plot, and had no access to light or power. Nor was Gachangiu's plot under the shaded part of the site, but out in the open, as they had been a hundred or so metres away in the Burmah Market area in the early 1970s (see fig. 2.27, colour section). He clearly held on to his machines because of the irregularity of the building work. But he doubted that there could be much development of this metalworking side. Indeed his judgement on the blacksmith business was:

> There is no improvement in the blacksmith area over 20 years. In one week you can get enough for your daily bread, but no profit. (Gachangiu, July 1989, Oral interview)

Of all those we have revisited, he seemed the shortest of money. He now had five children, but it seemed that he had not been able to make the kinds of investments in agricultural land that would allow marriage not to make further major incursions into his small income. In early 1995, he was to be found in Bondo in Nyanza Province trying to make ends meet through a small contract.

Conclusions on machine-making revisited

One of the questions raised at the end of the relevant chapter on the machine-makers in *The African Artisan* was whether this small group constituted a freak, or would be one example of a moving frontier as more and more once foreign or formal sector products began to be made in the jua kali sector. On balance our judgement was that the successful making of bicycle carriers, stands and foreguards would by no means be the last example of a local product made by local machinery (King, 1977: 138). Twenty years on, this originally very small group of individuals whose access to tool making skills had been a single source in Githiga had each trained a significant number of others who could make similar products. We shall also see shortly that there is a rather large number of individuals who can put their hands not only to this particular generation of machines (hand-operated) but also to power tools.

Several of our group clearly also have this capacity, inasmuch as they can make maize-mills, zero-grazers, and wood lathes. Only one has gone full-time into machine-making, and derives his main income from machine manufacture. Arguably the most successful of the group has stopped making his own machines and has a production line made up of electrical machine tools that have been purchased.

In summary, they can be described broadly in the following terms:

Metal products manufacturer with power tools, and press machines (1)
Agricultural machinery manufacturer (1)
Jobbing metal products for building industry (3)
Plumbing sub-contractor (1)
Part-time sub-contractor and metal products maker (1)
Metal products and some hand operated machine-making (1)

But for all these eight people it is difficult to put a single category description on any of them except the first two and the plumber who have clearly all developed specialized production or trade expertise. All the others are really quite difficult to fit into any traditional industrial categorization, because they are mixing several kinds of work, depending on demand.

As to permanency of premises, there are again definitional difficulties. Only three work out of permanent, stone-built premises with electricity supplies, phones, offices etc. But that is somewhat misleading since another two, who might appear just to be working out of rather informal premises in California, in fact have major permanent business accommodation that is either complete or nearly complete. The three others are very different again. The plumber has no contact office, beyond a shared P.O. Box in Kiambu town, while Njenga and Gachangiu just have their small plots in the Kamukunji jua kali scheme.

In terms of labour employed, the differences are again deceptive. Clearly much larger numbers (over 30) are employed on the production line of our invisible metal products manufacturer than in the smaller shops, but the quality of the labour and its lack of security may not be very different. The preference amongst most owners across the informal sector is for casual (*kibarua*) labour. Predictably, there is more to be learned by the casual labour in Gacuiri, Giathi or Kairu's workshop than in working all day on a semi-automatic press machine.

Most of them are urban artisans with a very strong rural base. Again, we suspect that rather major differences exist here between those with permanently built rural homes, very adequate land and some cash-cropping facility, and those with much less, such as a timber house and a small plot. Such differencces are going progressively to make it hard to raise the educational level of their quite large families (most had five children already and had not completed their families).

None of them considered that he had graduated from the jua kali sector, but if they can all be defined as jua kali, then the term may not have much definitional usefulness.

However, perhaps one of the more interesting things to be asked about them now in the mid-1990s is how common are the level and range of expertise that they represent. In the early1970s they stood out as being really almost the only Africans in Kenya (bar one or two formal engineering firms that Africans had bought over from Europeans) to be in the business of very basic machine-making. Accordingly we turn back to Gikomba in the following chapter to see to what extent their neighbours have equalled or even surpassed what was so unusual in the 1970s in the area of machine development and innovation.

But before that, we shall need to visit Starehe, just a hundred yards down the road from the COTU building and some of the other peripheral Gikomba areas, to look at the second of the small enterprise categories that were examined in great depth in the 1970s – the tinsmiths who specialized in making tin-lamps or 'candles', as they are called in Kenya.

Revisiting the tin-lampmakers of Nairobi[3]

We had a number of questions to address to the tin-lampmakers, or candle-makers as they were sometimes called. (This latter term did not mean that they made candles in the normal sense of the word, but referred to the manufacture of the small, tin oil-lamp, from scrap metal and from scrap food and oil tins.) Would some of the same people still be in business? Would there have been diversification beyond candlemaking? Would anyone in the candlemaking trade have graduated from the wasteland or roadsides of the 1970s to set up in permanent premises? Would any of the children of the 1970s makers have continued in their fathers' footsteps

Figs. 2.28: Joseph Kamande, on right (1972).

Fig. 2.29: Joseph Kamande (1989).

Fig. 2.32 Kimotho (1972).

(there was only one female candlemaker discovered in the 1970s in Kenya)? And what about the most dynamic of those met in the 1970s – Jacob Njiru in Nairobi, and Joseph Kamande in Thika, the latter even at that time employing a swivel punch machine to take some of the manual labour out of the quite demanding series of processes needed to make all the different parts of the kerosene oil lamp – would they have moved on?

We were interested in the fate of this industry because we felt that it was typical of many other jua kali activities. It did not have the excitement and apparent potential of an industry that was wrestling with basic machine-making. It was just making a single product, and it was difficult to see how they could graduate from this degree of specialization.

It did not take long in July 1989 to discover the whereabouts of the main groups of candlemakers in Central Nairobi. There were two groups just a hundred or so yards past the COTU headquarters building in Gikomba. They were strictly speaking now in a section of Nairobi called Starehe (Peace), and they were both somewhat off the beaten track, in a small compound where charcoal was also kept. Their own premises were exceedingly temporary, just a rough structure of wood and plastic, open on three sides, but shaded from the sun. In point of fact it made a good deal of sense for it to be open to the air, since the fumes from the five or six braziers (jikos) would have been unpleasant in a completely enclosed space. The men (older and younger – there were no women) mostly still squatted on logs of wood or upturned, makeshift stools. In the larger of the two groups of some 20 candlemakers, Joseph Kamande (see figs 2.28 and 2.29), met last in Thika in 1974, was still playing an important role, but had been joined by his son who had reached as far as Form IV (see fig. 2.30, colour section). With him was Francis Njagi Nyagah who had

80

joined candlemaking around 1959, and had already done 13 years in the trade when we encountered him in 1972–3 (see fig. 2.31, colour section). They had been on this Starehe site since 1978.

One of the other main candlemakers of the 1970s had been Kimotho (see fig. 2.32). He was not far off, on the edge of a housing estate in Jerusalem. He too along with a small group of others was in a very similar temporary lean-to, and he too was assisted from time to time by one of his sons, who had left school at Standard VIII (see fig. 2.33, colour section). There were also one or two secondary school graduates there, including James Kang'ethe.

Njiru who had been one of the most active in the 1970s, with employees and exports outside the country, was now to be found about 2 km off in Mlango Kubwa, now very much working on his own, but again in extremely temporary accommodation. He seemed still to be mixing candlemaking with the making of rat-traps, but had added some part-time brewing also. He no longer had employees working full-time on candle-making, however.

Starehe had the largest of the various groups (and the total number of individual candlemakers in the five main Nairobi sites of Starehe, Kamu-kunji, Mlango Kubwa, Kimathi/Jerusalem and Kariobangi came to 86). But it was interesting to note that the composition was by no means made up of a whole group of older men continuing from the 1960s and 1970s. Of the total of 22 in one of the Starehe groups, no less than 17 had joined this particular candlemaking industry in the 1980s, and of them more than half had joined between 1986 and 1990. By contrast only two had joined the group in the 1970s and only three had continued from the 1960s. This is hardly therefore an industry which is gradually winding down, as younger men do step in to replace the older men.

A job that is not really attractive to Form IV graduates?

Although young people have recently come into the industry, it is not clear that there is an established profile of the younger workers having significantly higher educational qualifications than the older – which would be the case with the other growing industries in the Gikomba area. Indeed with the exception of the two sons of established candlemakers, there were almost no Form IVs in candlemaking at all. And in the case of Francis Kamande, the father regarded it as fairly 'disgraceful that his son, a Form IV boy should be doing this entirely unskilled job'. This may be somewhat unfair to the character of the job, for it certainly involves a very considerable amount of deftness and manual dexterity, although it is true that all of the cutting and measuring can be done against existing profiles. Indeed, the old Francis Njagi commented that compared to the 1960s and 1970s when he feels people despised and looked down on them, the work now has much more meaning to people. In addition, he feels that they are now much better off.

Nevertheless from the boy's perspective, it was strongly felt that this job had no future. We shall look in a moment at the scope for diversification in this industry, but the absence of Form IV boys (not to mention the complete absence of girls whether of primary or secondary level) may say something about its perceived status as a job in which there can be development. It is intriguing in this situation that in the revised 8.4.4. syllabus with its strong emphasis on practical skills for primary schools, there is encouragement for the children to be able to make things like candles. In reality, Kamande, the father, says the children come and buy the candles here and take them to school as if they had made them. 'Some even get them folded differently so as to make it look more as if they had done the job for themselves. It's just cheating. But there is a big trade from schoolchildren at a particular time of year!'

One reason why the job may be thought not to be appropriate for secondary school graduates is the differential between the cost of primary school and of the complete four years of secondary school (the latter comes to between K.Sh.25,000 and 30,000 for the full four years of boarding secondary school). When it is then calculated how difficult it is, as a single self-employed person, to get more than a certain amount per day, week, month or year out of the candle trade, it may well seem to the parents and the secondary school graduate not to have been a good 'return' on the money invested. This is not to say that parents do all have this kind of investment approach towards schooling – they clearly do not. But undoubtedly it is amongst those with lower incomes such as Kamande and Kimotho, both of whom had families of eight children in the early 1990s, that the burden of schooling is most acute. Indeed, Kamande admitted that he had a 'lot of luggage' on his back.

The limits of individual income from candlemaking

One of the reasons that secondary schooling, not to mention other expenses, does pose such a challenge for candlemakers is that it is so very clear what are the income elasticities (or rather inelasticities) in the trade. Working all day from 8 am until dusk will allow the production of just three score (candles are counted in scores [*koria*] of the individual tin-lamps, and that is provided there are already available the requisite materials, such as tins, solder, charcoal for the brazier etc. It would therefore be safer to say that an average would be 50 candles per day, and that would be less with the very old workers perhaps, and with those who were just learning the trade. With the price for a score being around K.Sh.45 in the early 1990s, the gross income for a day would be K.Sh.112, and for a week of six days (which is the norm in the informal sector) would be K.Sh.672. Monthly gross income would therefore be of the order of K.Sh.2689.

Against this, the individual candlemaker has to set the cost of solder (approx. K.Sh.100 per month), soldering flux (K.Sh.80 a month), charcoal (approx. K.Sh.50 a month), and the cost of the tins at 10 cents each (K.Sh.120 a month), plus the additional tins for the tops and other parts (say, K.Sh.70 a month). This would total K.Sh.420 a month. Normally, even in Nairobi candlemakers pay little or no rent (for instance the Starehe group pay about K.Sh.20 each a month). Even the candlemaker with a month or two in the trade can see that working at full speed, it should be possible to clear K.Sh.2000 a month. That this kind of figure is not far out is confirmed by a number of the candlemakers saying they would not even consider a job that did not offer them more than K.Sh.1500 (King & Abuodha, 1995).

This figure of, say, K.Sh.1500–2000 a month may seem very small, but just as its equivalent in the early 1970s (K.Sh.250–400) was much better than the so-called urban minimum wage, so in the early 1990s there were significant numbers of employees who had spent relatively long periods in the formal sector of the economy, and had some responsibility, and yet did not get more than K.Sh.2000 a month. Indeed, we have encountered some of these formal sector incomes in our analysis of other industries in Gikomba, and in our discussions about why the move was finally made to self-employment. It should be remembered also that income from candlemaking would normally be completely untaxed; whereas in some formal sector firms, there would be deductions of various sorts made on all regular employees.

The absence of employees in the candlemaking trade

The very transparency of what can be made, linked to the availability of both supplies and a continuing strong demand, is also one of the reasons why there are so few employees in this trade. Occasionally in the 1970s a candlemaker such as Jacob Njiru had four to six employees, but that was when he had some very large orders for exporting to Uganda and elsewhere. Nowadays, the local market is able to absorb as many candles as are made, and it appears to be difficult for one maker to dominate or monopolize the orders. In addition, there seems very little reluctance to allowing a former trainee to shift sideways and become an independent maker, even sharing the same fire and tools. However, since the shears, anvil, hammer and punch – the essential tools – do not come to much more than K.Sh.400–500, there is very little in the way of initial capital that could prevent entry either. The nearest the industry comes to employees now is the use of casual labourers from time to time when there is a big order, and when some basic cleaning, cutting or preparation work is required. Casual labourers do not make complete candles.

Technology unchanged since early 1970s

In one way this is the most remarkable difference from the machine-makers who were also studied in the early 1970s; there really has been no discernible change in the product or the technology for the manufacture of candles in 20 years. There have been small changes in respect of collecting the scraps of tin and the filings, and in the local manufacture of the solder by some who used to be candlemakers, but as to the main body of the candle, and its component parts, there has been no change. There has not been any counterpart to the movement which was very significant in the parallel trade of making jikos (charcoal burning braziers) where there was a whole series of fuel-economy jikos developed. A good deal of this latter innovation was sponsored by appropriate technology movements of various sorts and by external funding. But as far as is known, there has been no similar interest expressed in making this source of ordinary light, cheaper and more effective.

It might be mentioned in passing that this could well be a suitable candidate for some kind of appropriate technology attention. In poorer families, both in urban and rural areas, the little tin-lamps are often the sole source of light for children doing homework, or for parents cooking, and they are in many ways very inadequate especially for reading and writing tasks. Compared to what was almost a 'jiko-mania' of schemes for the improvement of the basic cooking brazier, it has been surprising that there was been such a neglect of what is still one of the main sources of low-cost light.

What innovation there has been has come from individuals linked to the trade. There has been some experimentation with a battery-cum-kerosene lamp, but this has not proved popular, and obviously the battery's life has even more severe limitations than kerosene. There has also been an attempt by a nephew of Kamande, a Standard VIII boy at the time, to link a small windmill to a motor and then to a candle; but this had not yet reached a stage where it was more than a prototype in the early 1990s.

The scope for diversification through associational activity

We have already looked at the different aspects of development associated with the rise of Jua Kali Associations, but here it may be worth noting that there is at least some expectation that these associations could assist the candlemakers to diversify. In addition, the objectives of the associations are seen to be ones that might assist the candlemakers in two of the things that they feel they need – some security of tenure, and some scope for acquiring small-scale loans.

Even though there is a healthy degree of cynicism about the possibility of candlemakers getting loans – after all, when had the government ever helped them? – several of the most senior candlemakers in their respective sites have had a role on the committee of their local jua kali association. This is true of Kimotho, who had emerged as the chairman of the Kimathi Ward Jua Kali Association, and also of Jacob Njiru who had become the secretary of a local group of some 35 members over in Mlango Kubwa. And Kamande had played a role in getting all the Starehe candlemakers to register on the official forms, and get their jua kali identity cards.

Jacob Njiru's view was that if it worked out, then they would get plots; the plots would give them title deeds, and on the basis of these, they could get loans of up to K.Sh.40,000. However, if that distant possibility came to pass, there would be no purpose in just building up more and more stock of candles (they rust anyway if kept); rather it would allow him to diversify.

There was some advantage in membership of these societies, even if very little had arrived from the state. According to one candlemaker, Kang'ethe, who was working on the same site as Kimotho, the status of being members had prevented the city council askaris from harassing them to the same extent as before. In earlier days, it was possible to wake up and find the bull-dozers outside your temporary accommodation. As to loans, he was ready to apply for one, and would not mind if there were interest attached, up to as high as 20 per cent. Alternatively, if the members of the jua kali association all contributed K.Sh.100 a month and then each month the total, of say, K.Sh.3000 was given to one member without interest, this would give the person concerned the chance to try a different development. Another advantage that he felt might come to pass through the development of associations and the possible increased security of tenure would be electricity. That would be very important in making diversification possible.

Ideas such as these about loans, development and diversification have begun to circulate more widely once associations have come into being, and they have also been helped by there being at least one candlemaker who had successfully applied for and received a loan. It was known in the community of candle people that this had actually happened, and that the person concerned was John Ngumba who was a tinsmith in Kamukunji in the early1990s. His outline history gives some indication of his own restless search to add to his existing skills and to diversify from the narrow base of candlemaking, his original trade.

After minimal schooling (just four years) Ngumba had joined Jacob Njiru in Nairobi, and had been trained and then employed for two years at K.Sh.5 a day. He had undertaken some casual labour as a stone cutter to raise the money for his tools, and then from 1972 started his own business on candles, and funnels in Race Course Road. Although he had not been interviewed at that time, he had started operating at the very time of our early interviews in Nairobi. He then moved to Thika and managed to get a slightly higher price than in Nairobi. He even managed to employ two people there in his business. Once again, in 1975, he moved, this time to Muranga. He was able to charge even more there, and he therefore stayed in the work until his trainees undercut him. Again on the move, he went back to Thika but met continuous harassment from the municipal council askaris.

Finally he moved down to Nairobi in 1982, and after the President had come to open the first jua kali sheds in Kamukunji he was lucky enough to have one of the plots that was laid out by the Kamukunji Jua Kali Association that was formed after the President's visit. He then was successful in applying for one of the first jua kali loans, through the Kenya Commercial Bank scheme. With the loan money of K.Sh.5,000 he was able to employ one person to work for him and carry out many of the kinds of production that can be found in Kamukunji, i.e. different types of *jiko*, sufurias (for cooking), water jugs and tin boxes. The loan also seems to have allowed him to get into the production of low energy jikos.

What is interesting is that the consequence of the loan would appear to have allowed him to diversify completely out of candlemaking, apart from employing someone to carry out some orders for candles. Indeed his future plans are to try and go into mass production of a small clip for sealing cardboard boxes rather than any direct outgrowth of candlemaking. The only link being that he would still, if successful, be working with the same type of metal sheets he had used as a tinsmith.

It is not possible to derive a great deal from this single case, but with a number of the other candlemakers with whom there were discussions on loans, it became clear that diversification in a trade like candlemaking has to involve either employment of someone to do the candlework, which is problematic for the reasons given above, or it has to involve coverage of a larger number of tinsmith and sheet metal items. In a way, this diversification is really a statement about the need to make the current tinsmith's trade somewhat more general like the range of the original East African Asian tinsmith's trade – of which it once was just a part.

Conclusions on candlemakers in the 1990s

This notion of the candlemaker's specialization being integrated or re-integrated is potentially important as one path for further diversification. Another one might be the pursuit of low-cost light alternatives to the candle, in a way that has been very successful with low energy jikos. But the clear constraint on either of these options for the present generation of tinsmiths is that the sheer economics of what has been established as their relatively good salary in informal sector terms is conditional on their spending the whole of six days a week working on the trade. This gives no possibility or scope for experimentation or development work, and especially so once the candlemaker has the additional requirement to find school fees. In a word, the candlemakers are simply too busy to think about changing their business. Only a loan of the merry-go-round type described by Kang'ethe, or of the type acquired by Ngumba can make possible this kind of re-direction or enlargement of the candlemaking trade.

In this respect, our candlemakers do stand as a kind of metaphor for many other jua kali workers; they are constrained by the work process itself and the relatively narrow skill base from any obvious route to diversification. The notion of graduating from being jua kali to factory style production that we were discussing with a few of the machine-makers, as they made their plans to move to the light industrial area at Komo Rock, does not really seem to arise. And yet, this particular jua kali constituency has been dealing with and producing one of the most crucial elements in many tens of thousands of poor homes for over 40 years since Kimotho and a handful of others started in 1950 – light for studying and light for cooking and other domestic tasks.

It may be coincidental but none of the candlemakers were aware of the myriad schemes for jua kali development that we were mentioning in Chapter 1. As far as we know, no NGO, local or foreign, is working on more appropriate technologies for effective low-cost light, and there have been almost no consequences yet for this community of the many different kinds of apparently very positive small loans associated with K-REP and other bodies. If there were such an interest, it is clear from this re-visitation of candlemaking that there exist highly skilled and productive artisans who could be used for product design and development.

* * *

In terms of our distinction between subsistence self-employment and entrepreneurial self-employment, the contrast between our two groups is in some way more clear cut now than in the early 1970s. At that time neither our candlemakers nor our metalworking machine-makers had premises, and one or two of the candlemakers were doing a very good trade, with their own employees and even foreign exports. Nowadays, there is a huge gulf between the income of the most successful of the metal-workers and the candlemakers. But it is important to note that there is very little differentiation of income within candlemaking whereas those at the bottom end of the metalworking group that we examined are certainly closer to the world of candlemaking than to their fellow metalworkers with plots in the light industrial area.

Having looked in quite some depth at the jua kali connections of the 1990s with the 1970s in respect of both our machine-makers and our tinsmiths, we turn now to examine their neighbours in Gikomba and its peripheries, and consider to what extent what was rather uncommon 20 years ago – a regular income from the informal sector – has become wide-spread now.

Notes

1. We retain the use of the term Indian though the term Asian is now commonplace. In Swahili the main term is still *Wahindi*.
2. During the fieldwork period of July–August 1989 the exchange rate was K.Sh.33 to one pound sterling; and the following summer, July–August 1990 it was K.Sh.40. This may be contrasted with the rate in December 1995 of K.Sh.85 to the pound sterling. (I am indebted to Zia Manji for supplying this data.)
3. As part of this research project, Charles Abuodha produced a paper after interviewing many of the candlemakers in the Nairobi area, under the title: 'Passive production in small scale enterprises: the case of low-cost light in Kenya' unpublished manuscript, 1990, Nairobi.

Three

Industrial Diversity
in Gikomba
in the early 1990s

Having looked at just a small number of artisans who had some initial connection with the Gikomba area in the 1970s, it may be useful to look at some of the others who are in permanent stone built workshops in the densely packed few streets that are the heartland of Gikomba as well as some of those who are less securely located under the shade of the President's scheme at Kamukunji. (It is interesting to note that this latter location is actually referred to colloquially in Kenya as 'Jua Kali', because it was the first site of jua kali that came to the attention of the President.) Our aim is not to take a random sample, but instead deliberately to pick out particular examples of different kinds of skills and expertise and examine the most critical dimensions of their formation and development. The emphasis here will be particularly on the range of what is being attempted technologically, and on some of the factors that come together in Gikomba to make this possible. However, after reviewing these more dynamic aspects of jua kali development in Gikomba, we shall then look quite closely at what is the more general picture of the informal sector in this part of town. It is important to pay some attention to this more ordinary aspect of the informal sector in Nairobi. It is certainly not the case that everyone in Gikomba and its peripheral concentrations of jua kali is busily making coffee grading machinery or designing a new machine. There are many jua kali who are involved in the production of just one or two basic items. In this sense, therefore, we continue our interest in the distinction between the subsistence and entrepreneurial jua kali that we have touched on earlier. But even with the more enterprising, there are still questions to be raised about their growth potential and technological confidence. However, we start with a search for whether the skills that set apart our machine-makers in the 1970s have become much more widespread.

Fig. 3.1: Karoki (left) and Njeroge, in their Gikomba workshop, with one of their electrically powered wood lathes. Note that both are wearing formal style work-coats.

The spread of machine-making in Gikomba, 1975–95

On the third of the Gikomba streets that runs off the busy road down from Pumwani Road, there is a bamboo-walled cafe on the corner doing a brisk trade in rather substantial Kikuyu foods. In the next door yard, there is a tiny office, normally closed, with a sign proclaiming it to be the Gikomba Jua Kali Association. From time to time, a secretary can be found, but almost nobody goes in – suggesting that it plays little part in the daily life of these very busy streets. In this same yard, there is an engineering workshop. Most of the area is still open to the sun, but there is a back portion covered over, where there is a small office and metal lathe working almost all the time. In the front section of the yard there are large separate sections of a coffee grading machine that appear to have been completed some time earlier.

Case studies of machine-making in the 1980s
This is the workshop of Peter Njeroge and Karoki Kihara from Kiambu District and Nyeri District respectively. They suggest an interesting progress towards their present work, at first sight rather different from the outlines we have offered with the 1970s metalworkers. Njeroge in particular offers an example of someone who had both formal educational exposure to vocational and technical training and had a very wide range of technical exposure to different formal sector firms. We noted above that one of the policy issues that is often raised when wondering about building jua kali technological capacities is whether the mix of employment and self-employment

Fig. 3.2: Njeroge with part of a whole coffee grading machine which the client had been unable to pay for.

Fig 3.3: Njeroge (right) and the very ancient metalworking lathe in Gikomba. Note the dress distinctions between owners and workers in the informal sector. And the temporary roof in the permanent building.

is valuable, and in particular whether exposure to relevant firms in the formal sector of the economy contributes to an important dimension of technological confidence. We noticed that really only one of our 1970s group of metalworkers had this kind of exposure to the formal sector.

In Njeroge's case, he not only excelled in art in primary school but went into the technical stream at the secondary level. In some countries this is equivalent to a second-rate secondary education, but in Kenya in the 1970s, some of the heaviest competition was to enter the small number of national secondary technical schools, since there was a scheme that encouraged modern sector firms to draw their first-year apprentices from these. This duly happened with Njeroge, who was taken from Machakos Technical Secondary to Bamburi Cement Works. One of the attractions of the apprentice scheme is precisely that it was often possible to get the firm to release the apprentice for further technological education, in Njeroge's case to Mombasa Polytechnic. However, the attractions of life were greater than the Polytechnic could offer; he dropped out and went back to Kiambu District.

The next set of experiences (from 1978 to 1983) was quite wide-ranging though in no case very lengthy. They may however have been important in providing exposure to many different engineering skills. As discussed in the last chapter, it will be noted that several of these work experiences are with relatively small firms, and several of them were Indian-owned. This was his real apprenticeship, not the one after school. He was first a welder/fitter with African Synthetic Fibres in Thika. After eight months he joined Hammers Engineering in Nairobi's Industrial Area, where he learnt turning and milling as well as welding and fitting. After just two months, on to a new firm Auto Auxiliaries, which made springs, dies, centre bolts etc. He learnt a good deal, including heat treatment and machining of bushes. He was learning a lot, but not yet thinking of starting his own job. The next move was to being foreman of Chuma (Iron) Engineers, an African-owned engineering workshop which was possibly bought over from an Indian. Its owner was a civil servant in the municipality. Here too there was experience with lathes, and in the making of bushes and centre bolts.

After two years, and despite the fact that his salary had risen from K.Sh.378 a month in 1978 to K.Sh.1300 in 1983 he left to go into business with his present partner, Karoki. The two of them came over to Gikomba with no machines except handshears, a hack saw and a vice. No more complicated machinery. However, like a number of people making the transition to self-employment, he had used a little time in his previous employment doing 'side-jobs'. And in an important instance he had constructed a woodworking lathe. It was extremely popular, and he was able to exchange a second one for a spot welding machine. We shall return to the significance of the woodworking machinery in a short while, but here was certainly an example of how the capacity to produce a key woodworking tool gave a considerable advantage to the very small group of those who were first able to make it.

Shortly, because of the demand, he was able to respond to orders from as far off as Kisii and Meru and Machakos. And now it was no longer the basic model, but a combined model of woodworking machine that did several different operations, and of course brought in more money (see fig. 3.1). From this, the workshop went on to make a bandsaw. The first of these he claims to have made in 1986, and it took quite some time because of the client's problems with money. Next there was an order for a machine that made chain links – incidentally a kind of machine that is very popular in Harare's main jua kali area, Durawall – but very few seem to be made in Nairobi. Next, and still connected with the wood industry, there was a special order for a roller bench, a log-cutting machine, for someone at Nyahururu and then a further order, somewhat different again, for one without rollers.

Finally, the move into coffee grading machines, which involved putting together into a single complex: a rotary feeder, a pulper, a pre-grader and a re-passer. Although there is no direct evidence of Njeroge or Karoki working there, it may be important to note that whole coffee machinery assemblies were being put together in an Indian business just at the end of Kombo Munyiri Road. Again, the possible importance, at a certain stage of technological development, of just seeing what was possible. Their first machine was made in 1985, but not enough money was forthcoming from the client to finish it. But with other orders, they had by 1989 completed three entire coffee grading assemblies, which at that period were selling for K.Sh.70,000 each. The sudden downturn in the coffee prices and the failure of the government to pay coffee farmers led inevitably to the stagnation of what might have proved a steady market. The coffee machine lying in the forecourt of their workshop constituted evidence of a client's inability to pay, once the government had first failed to pay for its purchases of coffee (see fig. 3.2).

In addition to machine-making, one of Njeroge and Karoki's main lines of work was threading pipes in plastic, metal and in aluminium, and making bushes. This was made possible by their having purchased, at at least second or third or fourth hand, a metalturning lathe (see fig. 3.3). It was exceedingly old, and had no longer any name on it. But they had been able to modify it, even removing the engine, and putting in different gearing, so that it could be used for threading pipes. This K.Sh.10,000 investment was exceedingly valuable, since it allowed a whole series of small job orders to continue when no machine-making was being undertaken. The other important thing about this lathe in 1989–90 was that it was one of just two in African hands in the whole of the Gikomba area. Many small jobs that would once have been taken to an Indian workshop would come their way.

For Njeroge a new lathe, e.g. a Congester from the UK at about K.Sh.400,000, would be his highest priority, but he knew that it could not be bought by instalments. Failing that a secondhand lathe for about K.Sh.80,000 would be very valuable, and, failing that, a pick-up.

The relevance of formal sector experience to the informal sector

Njeroge was dramatically different from all the jua kali metalworkers we have studied thus far. He not only had relatively high levels of formal (technical) education, admittedly not completed or fully taken advantage of, and also some five years of very diverse exposure to different formal sector engineering firms. The same was true of Karoki. He was in a true sense an Indian graduate or more specifically a graduate of the Sikh or, in Swahili, *Kalasinga* sector). He had much less education, but had had eight years, from 1955 with a Sikh firm building bodies for vehicles, then two months with another Singh. Then to a firm making posho mills. Finally in 1972 to one of the Sikh body-building firms (vehicle bodies, of course) which at that point was still operating in Gikomba. The move to self-employment came almost ten years later, when he moved to Kokota to try his hand at body-building and fabrication of window frames. A couple of years later he joined up with Njeroge. But in his case, he had no less than 26 years of formal sector experience before trying his hand at self-employment.

In looking at this great difference between five years of formal sector experience in the case of Njeroge and more than 25 in Karoki's case, some attention needs to be paid to the fact that in the fifties and sixties it was near to unthinkable that Africans could start in business on their own. There were no role models around, and no supporting structures for transporting or acquiring materials. Whereas in 1978, when Karoki was working for the Sikhs in Gikomba, he could presumably see that a lot of African businessmen were acquiring plots just near by. Technological confidence came along a good deal later than political confidence at Independence, but particularly during the mid-eighties, there was a sense of 'can-do' amongst many African artisans who might have been contented earlier with being long-term employees.

This means that there is no such thing as an optimum period of formal sector exposure. A great deal depends on the wider political and economic environment of the period when a person was in the formal sector. So it is not a question of Karoki needing 25 years perhaps because of his lower educational levels as compared to Njeroge. It is rather that the one had much of their formal sector experience at a time when few Africans would have queried the value of employment for life. However, by the early eighties the idea of a few hundred shillings a month in employment was beginning to look very unattractive compared with what might be gained outside.

Having mentioned Njeroge's manufacture of the wood lathe, bandsaw and roller bench, it may be useful to put this particular sub-set of machinery into the context of the furniture industry and its jua-kalification before examining some of the range of other machine-making skills in Gikomba.

The transformation of carpentry and joinery in Gikomba

Wood lathes and band saws

Starting at the bottom of the road down from Pumwani, just where it reaches the Nairobi River is the first of a whole jumble of little temporary wooden shelters in which there is everywhere the whir of electricity. They stretch along the river bank for two or three hundred metres and then upwards to the road again. In each of them there is a small collection of workers, and also several woodturning lathes, and here and there also a bandsaw. This is the heart of Gikomba's wood industry, and perhaps the largest concentration of woodworking machine tools in Kenya. At the height of activity here, before it was temporarily threatened by clearance in the run-up to the elections, there must have been well over a hundred jua kali wood industries here (see fig. 3.4).

Although we shall note shortly that there are furniture firms installed in some of the solid stone buildings of Gikomba, it is the dynamism of the large number of temporary structures, and the speed with which they have come to exist that is such a remarkable feature of Kenya's jua kali. There is little doubt that it has been the wood lathe and the very informal access to electrical power that have been the keys to the dynamism of the latest phase of the wood industry.

It is difficult to exaggerate the importance of this particular innovation in jua kali woodworking machinery. In many ways it would appear to have done as much for the quality and character of wood products in cities and towns of Kenya as the simple cutting machines did to metal products in the 1970s. Like many of these important changes and developments it is difficult to identify who was the individual who did make the critical move in machine-making. We have already mentioned that Peter Njeroge was able to make such a lathe just before he moved into self-employment in 1983. But it may be instructive to look a little at some of the other Africans who from as early as 1979–80 began to make these mechanized machine tools for the furniture industry.

One of these is clearly Ambetsa, from Western Kenya, or possibly Uganda.[1] He and his brother, Harrison, are now working in a very small workshop in Gikomba, without any of the scale of those we have described for Njeroge or Kairu. Both were graduates of the Indian furniture industry, since they had worked with Dodhia in the Industrial Area of Nairobi, before moving to Kombo Munyiri Road in 1973 to start on their own. There they concentrated on making cupboards and beds for some five years before the site was cleared by the City Council. It was on their return that the breakthrough took place. They went one day, in order to get some wood carved, to an Indian who used to make coffins. There, they said, they 'discovered the wood lathe' in a corner. They tried to make it in November 1979, and they succeeded.

This episode is worth unravelling a little further. If the two brothers had been working for an Indian furniture firm, there is no way they would not have already seen a woodturning lathe. It must be something else that they had seen at the coffin-maker. A visit to that particular Indian coffin-maker in July 1989 made things clearer. Right at the back of his workshop, behind all the coffins, and no longer used, stood an antique wood lathe.

Fig 3.4: Part of the densely packed area of electrically powered wood lathes in Gikomba in 1989. Much of this area was cleared in the troubles of 1990.

Fig 3.5: Bedan Macharia (right) in his riverside factory checking a wood lathe which can do all the turning jobs illustrated on the bed behind.

It was made from angled steel, just bolted and welded, and its mechanism was quite transparent. It could well have been an inspiration, by its very simplicity, for Ambetsa to work on. Whether it was the one that made it possible to capture the essence of the woodturning lathe cannot be determined with finality. But this potential link with an Indian coffin-maker is too good not to repeat.

Meanwhile the other Ambetsa (from Uganda), after working for a time with his father in Kampala as a carpenter, came to Kenya. He joined Allen Construction Company as a carpenter in 1978, and then moved to Gikomba in 1979 to do woodcarving. This Ambetsa claimed to have developed his first wood lathe that same year, and to have done so as a result of looking at a wood lathe he saw at Allen Construction Company.

Both of these initiatives were claimed to be in 1979 and Michael Ndoria, who is now mass-producing wooden rulers in his workshop or riverside, would also claim to have been the first person to make a wood lathe in the late 1970s. We had already noticed that Njeroge had made one before 1983. Then a year later, in 1984, Peter Githinji from Nyeri claims also to have made his first one. By that point he had been apprenticed in the in-formal sector in a garage, passed his trade test in car mechanics, but then gone into the Indian firm of Victoria Industries as a vehicle mechanic. Quite shortly he quit in order to pursue his own work, and for four years up to 1984 he made steel window frames with a welding machine he had bought.

It took him just three weeks to make his first wood lathe in 1984. Since then he has made some 20 each year, and he calculated that by 1989 he might have made 100. Githinji had done all this without a permanent workshop but had tended to operate out of Bedan Macharia's, another man who had started to make wood lathes in a big way. During that time he thought that the price had, predictably, dropped, from some K.Sh.10,000 initially to K.Sh.5,000 or less at the end of the 1980s.

Bedan Macharia came at machine-making from a very different route, in one way closer to Njeroge with his technical secondary school experience. In Macharia's case, he elected to join the National Youth Service after school and got two years with specialization in electrical engineering, as well as certification through trade tests at both ordinary and advanced electrical engineering. At graduation, there were no jobs, but he joined his brother selling timber in Gikomba in 1984. There he saw some of the earlier wood lathes, which were power-driven, and he decided to build his own (see fig. 3.5).

Whoever was the first to have made the basic wood turning lathe, it is evident that by 1984 when Macharia and Githinji decided to make theirs, there were plenty of examples available (see figs. 3.6 and 3.7). What is intriguing is that something which was simply not available to African furniture makers in the 1970s was suddenly essential by the mid-to-late 1980s. The differences made possible by woodturning in the legs and in all the rounded elements of furniture were so dramatic that few urban furniture makers could afford to be without this facility. And even in the rural areas they began to make their way.

One of the earliest and most innovative in the rural areas around Nairobi was Joseph Gitau Mwaura of Thogoto Village, near Kikuyu. When he too had finished formal vocational training in the Kiambu Institute of Science and Technology (KIST) in 1984, he found he had acquired some useful level of skills, since KIST was one of the institutes that believed in having a production unit, and also in the encouragement of self-employment (for which purpose it insisted on some management and book-keeping skills). When he left the institute, without any tools, it did not take long to discover that good quality handtools, e.g. a planer, were the same price as an electric motor. He decided to go into power tools, but designed them on wooden frames, whether these were circular saws, woodturning lathes, morticers, planers, or band saws. Between 1984 and 1989, he had acquired for his small rural workshop some eight to nine machine tools, all through improvizations with wood and electric power.

If these machines which he had constructed were compared with the price of imported machines he would have been looking at K.Sh.60,000 for a planer, K.Sh.18,000 for a band saw, and K.Sh.20,000 for a wood lathe. But, and this is the important point, it was not a question of whether he could get a loan to purchase such essential machine tools. If he had been granted a loan to get these, he would simply not have been able to pay off the loan, since the initial capital outlay would have been so much greater than the return that could have been expected from his local production.

A further development, he felt, which might be worth a loan, however, would be to get a good supply of high quality wood, varnish etc. in order to allow him to enter commercial production of all kinds of turned, wooden goods, from candlesticks, to sugar dishes, ash trays, lamp holders etc.

African 'graduates' of the Indian furniture industry

Here and there we have mentioned that a particular individual worked for the Indian furniture industry before setting up on their own. But still right in the centre of Gikomba is the rather un-Indian sounding furniture firm, McCrae's, which has been responsible for a large number of the successful African entrepreneurs around the area. As was said earlier Indian firms like these were not responsible in the sense of setting out to train Africans for self-employment. Rather, the level of the skills and expertise required for the Indian firm's work was eminently transferable elsewhere. We have also already mentioned that firms like these once had a majority of Indians working in them as employees. But by the early 1990s McCrae's had no less than 80 African employees, making it by far the largest of the furniture firms in the Gikomba area. The firm has a certain amount of very old machinery, but the emphasis is still a good deal on first rate hand work, chiselling out complex designs patterned on to the wood. There is some very modern machinery including a spindle moulder.

McCrae's Furniture, when it was bought over by Sukha Kalsi at

Figs. 3.6 and 3.7: Several wood lathes and band saws along the riverside in Gikomba. One being transported elsewhere.

Independence, would still have been amongst many other Indian, small-scale manufacturers. Thirty years later, in the early 1990s, like the Sikh temple nearby, McCrae's was also something of an island in a sea of African enterprise. To compete, McCrae's had to rely on the use of better, more seasoned woods, more modern designs, and finer finish, but with the access to power tools and designs, the much smaller stone workshops of African Gikomba were now able to turn out bedroom furniture that could also go into the showrooms of the main Nairobi furniture dealers. In some cases, in these rather small workshops, enormous double beds are being fashioned, with drinks cupboards, lighting systems and highly ornate head-boards; there are also what look like faultlessly oval dining tables with dark polished wood, and ornately carved legs and every kind of wall cupboard, chest of drawers, and drinks cupboard with mirrors glinting. Most of the work is carried out on an order basis for lack of room in the workshops. But the image of jua kali making rough-and-ready second rate goods for the poorer people in Kenya is clearly challenged by the extraordinary range of what is now available in the African wood industry of Gikomba.

The journey from employment through sub-contracting to self-employment
Symbiosis Furniture, run by Paul Njine Kfanya in Gikomba, is a very good example of informal Indian capacity building, followed by independence in self-employment. Njine had only four years of schooling before he had to leave because of his father's death just a year or two after Independence. He managed while making money from digging to attend a youth centre in Nyandarua, and get rough skills in carpentry and joinery. He was able to make crude folding chairs for just K.Sh.3 which can still be found in rural bars and houses. It was a far cry from the items he was selling in the early 1990s for K.Sh.15,000 each.

He came to Nairobi and after a short time 'tarmacing' (i.e. being unemployed, and just walking up and down, on the tarmac), he got into the Indian sector. First in 1972 he was with a Kalasinga (Sikh) in the building industry, then he was with another Kalasinga in Master Joiners doing fitted kitchens, doors and polishing. He was still, he remembers quite clearly, just thinking of employment, not self-employment. Finally he entered furniture firms, Technova for six months in 1974, Max Furniture in 1975, where he met his future partners, Githira and Wanjau, and then in 1977 he entered Eros Furniture, getting a salary of K.Sh.900.

> It was here that the subcontracting began. If you were prepared to make ten chairs on your own, you would get K.Sh.5,000 from the Indian owner. We also began to realize that when we were employed, we relaxed, but when we were working on our own, we worked very hard. It was at this point that we began to think: if we make x, we must save y. And in this way we soon had enough to buy our own timber.
>
> The next stage was going to another Indian, Troika, who was prepared to treat us completely as subcontractors. By this time we had got a small workshop in the suburb of Kawangware, but because we were making classic furniture,

there was no market there. We were being allowed to cut our wood in Eros, and then transport it to our workshop where we completed the work, but just using a bench and clamps. It was all possible through a special relationship with the Indians. And it was finally when another Indian, Sultan Glass Market, came and gave us a contract of K.Sh.15,000 that we realized we could be completely on our own. That was in 1981. We decided to go to town and look for a machine of our own. We got one from Kivunja for turning and cutting in January 1981. (Oral interview, 1989)

It can be seen in this outline account that some of the Indian furniture owners themselves helped to make it possible for their African employees to go it alone. Again, it must be stressed that this was no 'Jua Kali development project' on the Indian side; it was obviously just good business sense. There was no longer a point in paying people as employees if the same quality of work could be guaranteed without the responsibilities of employing large numbers of people, and having to deal with the social security and other social costs of employment in the formal sector. As a contractor, the Indian buyer need pay no attention to whatever conditions of work or pay were practised by the sub-contractor.

On the African side of this particular example, there had been something like a ten year 'apprenticeship' in various Indian firms, which had had the effect of transferring the skills of classic furniture design and manufacture. But at the point where a transition to self-employment was decided, it was not entirely coincidental that machines could now be purchased from the jua kali machine-makers. However, in 1981 when they started up in Gikomba itself, they still had to rely on an imported band saw (K.Sh.18,000) for the first band saws were not going to be made in the jua kali sector until 1986–7 (see fig. 3.8). Similarly, they had to rely on an imported planer costing K.Sh.18,000.

What is also worth underlining is that in 1981, there were apparently only a handful of African independent furniture makers in Gikomba (e.g. Kanini, Kiganda Furniture and Comfort), and there were none of the hundreds of furniture makers that were to be jostling each other for space along the riverside. So within the same decade, the remaining Indian firms lost some of their monopoly to the new African furniture people with their little workshops, and then quite suddenly these new Africans lost their monopoly to the much larger number of jua kalis who were ready and able to work without permanent premises. What we noticed in the position of some of the metalworkers with their permanent premises vis-à-vis those without is therefore paralleled with the furniture makers.

There may be an important issue embedded in the intensity and speed of this jua kali competition. In the case of the Indian small-scale sector, they were granted several decades of virtual security, during the 1940s, 1950s and 1960s to build up their businesses without the threat of competition. By contrast, the first generation of entrepreneurs like Njine had much less than a decade in which to establish themselves before there was massive competition unleashed by the next generation of jua kalis.

Fig. 3.8: Band saw of the type made by Ambetsa, and now very common in Gikomba.

Appropriately now Njine is planning to get higher grade machinery, in the form of a new lathe and a spindler. Also a vehicle. He has to get closer to the Indian sector in terms of standards, and he finds himself like them encouraging partial self-employment amongst his staff. Is he still a jua kali? Yes, he answers, like several others: 'We're still just in the middle. Perhaps when we reach the Industrial Area...'

The experience of Njine could be multiplied with other 'Indian graduates', including J.M. Kuria, now manager of Kihoto General Furniture, who had been with McCrae's from 1968 to 1973 and then with Uzuri for 10–11 years. He only made the move to self-employment as Uzuri wound up its business. Unlike those out on the riverside, he had taken out registration and a license. But like others he had started by paying just for a repair licence rather than for a manufacturing one ('You have to climb the tree from the bottom; you can't start at the top', he said in extenuation.). But by 1989 he was paying for a regular manufacturing licence, and he was also paying K.Sh.2000 to the City Commission. As to what characterized jua kali, he judged it was someone with good ideas but no money. Not just someone with brains (*akili*), but someone with experience to make something (*ujuzi*).

Conclusions on the 'jua-kalification' of the furniture trade

There seems little doubt that, in combination, the development of the key woodworking equipment between 1979 (wood-lathes) and mid-1980s (the band saw and roller bench) and the arrival of a number of highly experienced, Indian-trained, furniture craftsmen made possible a revolution in furniture in Kenya. This particular example of the Africanization of Indian enterprise was not like candlemaking (tin-lamp manufacture) where some Africans took a single item (the tin-lamp) out of what was originally the whole inventory of the tinsmith's trade, and made its production a highly specialized activity. With furniture, the evidence is that the African fundis took over a very wide range of the skills and products involved. They were consequently in a position to service a market for furniture that was very large, and which covered a spectrum from all but the most discerning corporate, government and private customers right down to the very modest clients who simply wanted a better quality of domestic furniture.

Kenya's second stage of import substitution: the 'jua-kalification' of products from the Industrial Areas

Returning to the range of machine-making in and around Gikomba, it may be useful to pick out some additional examples of types of what could be called second stage indigenization or localization. In the first stage, the particular product became a part of the formal Industrial Area in Mombasa or Nairobi through import substitution. Effectively, however, the whole process was kept quite separate and insulated in a purpose-built factory. But it was critical that exactly the same quality product, whether a soft drink or toothpaste, or a machine, be reproduced in Kenya. The most Kenyan part of the operation was on the employment side. But even the term import substitution was often not accurate. A number of key components continued to be imported, and those that were not were either made in the plant or sub-contracted to other firms in the Industrial Area. Not surprisingly, given the state of development of African enterprises in the seventies and even into the very early 1980s, there was very little from this first import substitution process that affected African business.

What we are calling second stage import substitution was when African small-scale enterprise carried out a further level of localization, during which the entire product was made in the jua kali sector rather than in the relatively protected environment of the Industrial Area.

Shifting the balance towards local manufacture

One of the more intriguing examples of this process comes from the second stage indigenization of machines for weighing and measuring. In the first stage, firms like Avery, Berkel and Kenya Scales made the same scales as the parent company, either as a branch plant or under licence. However, during the mid-1980s a number of the 'graduates' of these firms began to make the entire weighing scales, often in several different models. Luke Maangu was one of these scalemakers, who operated principally from Shauri Moyo near Burmah Market, but came over to Gikomba to get some finishing work done. Unlike many of those mentioned thus far who were Kikuyu, he was a Kisii brought up in South Nyanza. He was meant to join the priesthood, but after seminary, he joined Kenya Scales instead, which was actually a Scottish firm run by Cowie and an African sleeping partner. This firm had gone a good deal more local than Avery, and did quite a lot of the production of the separate components in Kenya.

This was probably quite a good thing for Maangu, because it exposed him to a greater degree to how items could be locally made. Kenya Scales sponsored him to the Kenya Polytechnic where he did higher accounts, but within the firm he managed to get his Grade 1 (the first stage) of the International Weights and Measures examination. He then left Kenya Scales and joined Avery for better prospects. In fact they stopped his sponsorship to the polytechnic, but he still managed to get his higher accounts and the second stage of his Weights and Measures examination. This was 1973. The last part of his exposure to the import substitution situation came in 1977 when he left Avery and joined one of the other major companies, Berkel. He stayed there till 1985. By this time, he had had close to 15 years working as an employee in the weighing scale manufacture and assembly plants.

In fact, it was while he was still at Berkel, he began, on the side, to try making counterscales. He made his first complete scales a year after leaving, in 1986. Initially there was considerable opposition from the existing importers, who alleged that his manufacture was substandard, and one of the firms, Avery, tried to take out a patents case against him. Looking back, Maangu would admit that his first models were not very high quality. But now they do get passed by the Kenya Bureau of Standards' weights and measures department.

At first, he had had to send out to a jua kali caster in Mombasa to make the castings for him, but when his prices went up he decided to make his own castings. Within a couple of months, using sand from Kenya Breweries and a mixture of molasses, he made moulds, and by 1987 was making all the castings for himself (see fig. 3.9). For this and all the other stages of shaping and finishing he employed 12 people of whom three were fundis (see fig. 3.10). The most demanding element was cutting the knives for the balances, and making the weights. For this he had eventually to get an old lathe machine (for about K.Sh.50,000) but he still had to go to Gikomba, to one of the two other lathe machine owners for finishing.

Originally he was only able to make about four of the basic model a month, but by 1989 it was nearer to 30. At that time the Avery model was selling at around K.Sh.5,000, and his version at between K.Sh.3,500 and 3,200. What is particularly interesting in terms of his status as a jua kali machine maker is that all his machines have to get the official stamp of the Kenya Bureau of Standards if they are to be used in Kenya. So here is an example of an entirely jua kali operation which gets the official mark of approval by the formal sector authority.

But how would Maangu himself judge his jua kali status? At the moment, because his casting and machining go on in the open air in a small yard at the back of the Burmah Market, he does not feel that he could get a manufacturing licence. He is still doing things in a 'jua kali way' but, he says, 'we are on the way to an industrial mode'. He is aware that there are very few genuinely African-run buinsesses of any complexity in Kenya; he thought there might be as few as 20. His feeling was that 'to be a real firm, you needed to have tried raising your own finances, and have got your own money. You also needed to have your business at heart, and not be pursuing it as a second string or a hobby.' His own plans were to transfer to the new light industrial area at Komo Rock, where in fact he already had secured a plot in a building.

Maangu is aware of the need to cover the range of weighing machines up to the 250 kg model, and ideally he will need to move on from weights to machines that have a self-indicating read-out, and for this he would need a proper lathe and a drill machine. But he is not anxious to get involved in large loans. Far too many people's businesses he has seen flop once they got involved in large loans. 'The loan seems to kill off most business potential', he avers.

This is far from being a new monopolistic market he has entered. But there were in Nairobi alone in 1989 some five of these second generation weighing machine-makers. One was an Indian, but the others were all Africans, most of whom were Avery 'graduates'. It might be that their

Figs. 3.9 and 3.10:
Moulding parts of the weigh
scales in Maangu's workshop
in Shauri Moyo, near
Gikomba, Nairobi. Finishing
some of the parts of the
weigh scale on one of the
very few lathes in the area.
Note here, too, the use of
factory coats by the staff.

Fig. 3.11: A completed pair of weigh scales, of the type now made by several jua kali manufacturers in Nairobi.

Fig. 3.12: Fedha James' workshop in one of the Gikomba streets. Note the mass of powerlines going off to various workshops.

experience would not be dissimilar to Maangu's. But certainly, Otiende, one of the five who was sharing a workshop in Gikomba, had a remarkably parallel history, with his relatively high levels of formal technical training, and over ten years of exposure to experience in Avery prior to using his retirement money to go into competition with his previous employer. Like Maangu, he had had to depend on one of the only two lathe owners in Gikomba to get some of the finer parts of the work completed (see fig. 3.11).

It would be interesting – though beyond the scope of this present account – to do some mapping and monitoring of what we are calling this second stage import substitution, in which the product moves out of the one or two initial importing firms in the Industrial Area, and becomes something that is the repertory of several small-scale or micro-enterprises. We have, for example, noted the attempts by machine-makers to develop a method of making nails, which has not worked out thus far. But there are probably a large number of others that have. Sometimes the particular item is very small, like a button for use in sofa-making; sometimes very large like a coffee grading assembly, and sometimes in between, like exhaust systems for cars. They would also include the welding machines that Samson Odote began to experiment with while still working with W. Hope, before finally moving to Gikomba and making his own welding machines. But our impression is that the ones we have mentioned constitute just the tip of the iceberg, and that their number is certainly growing quite rapidly. And not in the small-scale industrial estates, but in the ordinary workshops of Gikomba, Komo Rock, and elsewhere.

Further cases of Gikomba's new engineers

We need perhaps to look at a few more of the people whose growing technological confidence has helped to make this second stage import substitution possible. Again, we shall restrict ourselves to Gikomba.

A first brief sketch covers Ferdinand Mwambulu (otherwise known as Fedha James), just a workshop or two down from Paul Kairu. As a Taita, he got his secondary education down at the Coast, and then in 1972 entered City Engineering Works, where they made dustbins and did galvanizing, using very old machines. He left after two years and entered another firm, Lunga Lunga, which made blockmaking machines and even presses. After a further two years, he left and started doing his own welding in Kibera, a suburb of Nairobi. Most unusually, he was able to purchase an old metalworking lathe at K.Sh.65,000. This was in 1982. He concentrated on machine-making and jobbing work from then on.

At one point he had made woodworking lathes, but as prices dropped with the competition from K.Sh.7,000 or more to about K.Sh.3,000, he left this and made *posho* (maize) mills, blockmaking machines, and band saws. He has also made potato chip-making machines. Like Peter Kagotho, he has not sought to be invisible, but has his sign up over his shop (see fig. 3.12) and he has taken courses at the Eastern and Southern African

Trade Promotion and Training Centre, and also attended a seminar for the metal and allied trades organized by the Kenya Association of Manufacturers. As one of the only people with a lathe in the whole of Gikomba, and with semi-automatic press machines, he finds he is not short of jobbing work, apart from his own orders. He has given a foothold in his workshop to the weigh scale maker, Otiende, we have just discussed.

Where Mwambulu came out of exposure to formal sector engineering, our next example, Stephen Ndolo Kivindio, from Machakos, had relatively little formal sector experience. He had had some training in a so-called Technical Institute in Nairobi which had a notoriously poor reputation, and after that began to get training with the informal metal workshop his father ran on the side while working for the Kenya Railways. With this background, he entered the Indian firm, Arrow Motors, as a mechanic, getting K.Sh.900 in 1985, but like many young people at that time, he found this a poor reward. He left and went back to his father's, and it was from there that he saw one day what was being done in Gikomba. 'I saw a wood lathe, and said to myself: "Why can't I make that machine?" '

In order to get access to the knowledge, he got taken on at Bedan Macharia's, just along the river bank, and made a wood lathe as well as a band saw. This would be in 1986 and 1987. 'There were no secrets. Everything was out in the open.' He became known quite shortly as one of the most expert band saw makers, and he was able also to comment on the pros and cons of the local versus the imported machines. It was, interestingly enough, not just the cost factor that militated against some of the foreign machines. For example the imported aluminium ones were about K.Sh.18,000 and the cast iron model was nearer K.Sh.28,000. The problem was that it was exceedingly difficult to adjust or repair the cheaper aluminium models by the use of arc welding.

In terms of technological capacity, it is also interesting that Kivindio does not work from a precise design when making his band saws. It is almost as if he sees what he is making in his 'mind's eye'. And it is the same with several of the other machines he has attempted. He sees an existing machine, understands how it works, and is then confident about making it himself. This is, for example, the case with a spray paint machine he has made for his father's workshop. New this would have cost about K.Sh.48,000, but he was able to make one for a few thousand.

His own longer-term plans were to be the first person to have this machine-making capacity out in his home town of Tala in Machakos District. This again is an important consideration; that like the Indian fundis some 50 or 60 years earlier, the modern jua kali fundis do see it possible to make a good living in the rural areas. This has to be a positive feature of jua kali development.

Before leaving the machine-makers of Gikomba, we should just mention Kanyale Coffee Machinery, at the other end of the street that we started at, at the beginning of this chapter. Here, a group of three entrepreneurs have been running one of the most diverse machine-making operations

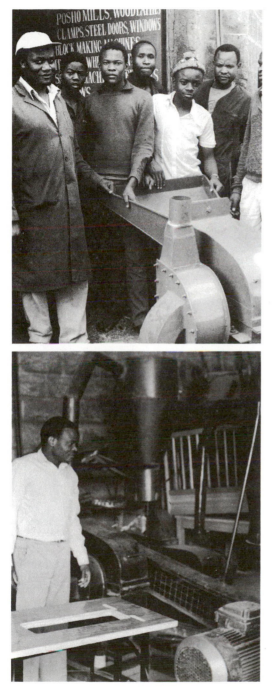

Figs. 3.13 and 3.14: One of the owners of Kanyale Coffee Machinery (top left) with one of the products, a maize mill, and several of the workers. Another of the owners with an entire maize mill assembly.

Fig. 3.15: Mohammed Asgar, one of the remaining Indian workshop owners in Gikomba, with an ancient power punch and a metal sheers, of the type now common in African metalworking.

Fig. 3.16: Bedan Macharia in 1989, outside his workshop on the riverside, Gikomba, at an early stage of experimenting with a metalworking lathe.

for several years. Again, it is interesting to note that the prior experience of one of them, Fanuel Otieno, covers a significant range of formal sector operations: from carriage repair and maintenance on Kenya Railways (in 1966), to exposure to electrical components through African Electronics (from 1967); then on to a more general spectrum of appliances with Car and General, and from that to coffee machinery fabrication for some seven years. Finally to working for an African on coffee machinery in Kombo Munyiri Road, before moving with two others to set up their own premises to fulfil their first orders in Gikomba in 1982–3. No less than 15 years of formal sector experience were behind him before the move to self-employment took place.

With this exposure, the group (Fanuel Otieno, Remjus Onyango and Charles Muga) were able to do full assemblies of coffee machinery, from 1984 develop maize mills, and then a wider range of commissioned work, including zero-grazers (see figs. 3.13 and 3.14). Their total equipment was valued by them at around K.Sh.146,000 in 1989–90. However, by November 1994, it could be noted that this very promising-looking firm had broken up. The premises were being used by a different firm, and only one member of the original trio remained in Gikomba, in a tiny office, with no space for machinery. The precise reasons for the break-up are not yet known, but it may well be that the three partners were not able to continue to collaborate, as Marris and Somerset (1971) had noted was so commonplace in Kenyan business failures.

Industrial diversity in Gikomba: Indian and African

We probably should not leave Gikomba without paying a fleeting visit to some of the Indian workshops that still remain. The reason for mentioning them in this section is not only to reinforce the notion we have mentioned several times about their role as sources of skills and knowledge for the jua kali sector. It is also important to note that in the case of several of the Indians, their own lives reflected a move from being employees to being self-employed. For instance, one of the most jua kali-like of those still in Gikomba is Mohamed Asgar Mughal. His father had come over to Kenya and during the war had got experience with the firm of Haartz and Bell in the Industrial Area in blacksmithing and moulding. His father had then set up on his own, and had made his own first little machine, a hand-operated swivel punch machine, in 1952.

Mohamed Asgar saw this as a rather similar experience to what he perceived the jua kali going through now. The difference however was that at that time, just after the Second World War, there was a great deal of relatively inexpensive secondhand machinery around (see fig. 3.15). And it was also possible then to import secondhand machine tools. More recently, in the Independence period, it had become impossible to import secondhand machine tools, one reason on the government side apparently being that it could lead to a loss of foreign exchange through over-invoicing. With the benefit of many years in the business, Mohamed Asgar doubted that in some cases the local demand could justify the very high cost of new machine tools. Which was the very point made by the machine-maker we mentioned earlier who used combinations of wood and metal in Thogoto for his machine tools. And if that was the case in 1989–90, how much more so would it be in 1994–5 after the further devaluations of the Kenya shilling had made the cost of imported machinery even more prohibitive.

A similar case would be made by the manager of Lotus Engineering Works, Harjinder Singh Bilkhu. Contrary to the view that the Indian engineering firms started with generations of tradition behind them, he felt it worth emphasizing that his father had started just after Independence with a drill and a lathe. The difference, however, between now and then, he confirmed, is that it was very easy to get secondhand machines then. Many of his current machines are 'extremely old workhorses'. As far as machinery development is concerned, it was only in the 1970s that he began to go in for heavy duty band saws, and roller benches for the saw-milling industry. And it was only in the 1980s that he had begun production of the power presses that two or three of the African jua kali had profited greatly from buying.

But if someone were to take on or try to reproduce the kind of production machinery he now had, they would need about one million shillings' worth of equipment, in 1989–90 prices; they would have to acquire milling, shaping and press machines, as well as regular metalworking lathes. He knew that in the UK for instance it was possible to get excellent second-hand machines for just a few hundred pounds. Even with the cost of shipping them, these would be invaluable. Indeed, he knew that they were being exported to other countries, such as Pakistan.

The cost of high quality machinery for such engineering operations as crankshaft regrinding is one of the things that is protecting some of the other Indian fundis that are still operating in Gikomba (and who have not moved out to the formal Industrial Area). This would certainly include Sehmi Engineering in Kombo Munyiri Road. Again there seems to have operated in this case the exposure to mechanical engineering in the army during the Second World War (from some accounts the East African corps of mechanical engineers had a large number of Sikhs from India). But at the same time what we may call this formal sector employment (in the army) was reinforced by the strong cultural and community sense that precision engineering was something that Sikhs gravitated towards. This itself was much aided by customers in Kenya preferring to see their job done by 'Kalasingas' than by others.

Down on the riverside, a few hundred yards from Sehmi, in the much smaller African workshop of Bedan Macharia, there would be substantial agreement with the views of Mohamed Asgar on the prohibitively high cost of new machine tools. He had become acutely aware that he needed a metalworking lathe, in order to repair bearings and other jobs. But in despair at being able to acquire one that he could afford through a loan, he had decided to fabricate one himself back in 1989–90 (see fig. 3.16). It is not known if the obvious technical problems to doing this without major castings had been overcome in the last few years, but certainly in some ways this aspiration to develop a metalworking lathe, as the jua kalis had done for woodworking so effectively, can stand as a metaphor for Gikomba and its very powerful 'can-do' attitude to technological development. The idea that an artisan should try and make a metalworking lathe, a welding machine, a spray paint machine or a nail-making machine is no longer absurd or unthinkable.

In fact it is worth reporting that since the bulk of the interviewing for this research was completed, there has appeared also on this riverside road a further workshop which would appear to have achieved just such an objective, and to have built a local metalworking lathe, and to have established in addition a rather diverse engineering workshop using a range of different machine tools. Developments by this innovator will be well worth researching.

We have looked up and down two or three of the small streets of Gikomba and come across many examples of this type of initiative and innovation. But what of the more general picture of Gikomba? How is it viewed by government, and in particular by the responsible 'Jua Kali Ministry'? And what about the profile of those Gikomba artisans who actually joined the Gikomba Jua Kali Society? They are a minority, but they may shed some further light on industrial diversification in central Nairobi.

An official angle on Gikomba

Jua kali activity in Gikomba today is no longer just a collection of small groups of entrepreneurs perching on waste-ground, outside the scope of permanent buildings, as it was in the early1970s. But it could scarcely be described as the jewel in the Jua Kali Ministry's crown, since there is no major initiative taken by the Ministry to develop jua kali. True, in the late 1980s and early 1990s, we have noted in Chapter One, the then Minister, Professor Ongeri, had visited Gikomba on a number of occasions, often with foreign visitors, in order to demonstrate something of the dynamism of the jua kali sector. And a number of the entrepreneurs have demonstrated their products and machine tools in the Nairobi Show and in other agricultural shows. We saw also in Chapter One that to a limited extent Gikomba and the nearby Kamukunji had been used as sites of special jua kali interest by the Ministry. Jua Kali groups from other parts of the country had been encouraged to come to Gikomba and Kamukunji in order to study their technology and consider the implications for their own industries in the rural areas.

It is very doubtful if Gikomba sees itself as a particularly favoured site for any specific government or NGO jua kali project. In fact, it could be said that Gikomba represents instead a typical example of jua kali development quite independent of government. It is a monument to local enterprise without intervention, without policy and without assistance. And from that viewpoint it is important to understand more fully the range and expertise of those who operate there.

A Ministry profile of Gikomba via the Gikomba Jua Kali Society

One way of capturing a more comprehensive picture of Gikomba within the emerging industrial society of Nairobi would be to look at the character of those who have chosen formally to register with the Ministry as members of the Gikomba Jua Kali Society.

The most obvious first point to be made about the names in the Ministry's register under Gikomba Jua Kali Society in 1989–90 was that they amounted to 64, whereas in the small office of the Society in Gikomba itself it was said at the same period that there were 170. By contrast with both these numbers, it is certain that the overall numbers of jua kali working in the Gikomba area are very much greater than either figure. This anomaly may perhaps be explained by their being some selectivity operating in the provision of the Ministry registration forms to different kinds of jua kali, which would allow the issue of Jua Kali Identification Cards. Whenever there is something of this sort available, there is a tendency for the economies of scarcity to operate, with the result that a form intended to be provided widely gets restricted in its circulation. But whatever the reasons, the number of just 64 gives the impression of their being a relatively small group in Gikomba. Even though the following analysis is based on a small proportion of the Gikomba total – just those who have registered – it may still be worthwhile examining the profile of this particular segment of the jua kali who have managed to get themselves officially registered.

Table 3.1 *Profile of trades in Ministry files for Gikomba Jua Kali Society*

Tailoring/dressmaking	25
Welding/metalwork	13
Manufacturing/engineering	10
Carpentry/joinery	12
TV/Radio	1
Basketmaker	1
Photoframing	1
Missing data	1
Total	64

The most obvious point about Table 3.1 is the apparent predominance of dressmaking and tailoring in Gikomba. Of course it is entirely possible that individuals who are tailors or dressmakers and who are located in some of the market stalls nearby Gikomba have somehow managed to register as Society members, but in terms of Gikomba's central area, there are really few if any tailoring or dressmaking shops in evidence. This is confirmed by figures from Dorothy McCormick's census of the garment industry in 1989 which points to just one garment firm in Gikomba proper but almost 30 operating in Quarry Road Market nearby (McCormick: personal communication, October 1994). On the ground, as opposed to on paper, Gikomba is a sea of carpentry, joinery and metal fabrication enterprises. There are, we have said, large numbers of people engaged at the entrance to Gikomba in the selling of secondhand clothes and of cereals and beans of every variety. And there are, near where our candle-makers in Starehe are settled, a number of tailoring and clothes manu-facturing enterprises, located in one or two of the oldest 'African' housing in Nairobi. But in the ordinary course of events, the clothes and food sellers would not qualify for jua kali status as they are in the retail trade rather than production, and the tailoring and clothing enterprises are not sufficient to give an impression, in walking round the heart of Gikomba, that this is a dressmaking and tailoring area. This official picture of Gikomba seems, therefore, very much at odds with the reality, and must raise some concern about the mechanisms for ensuring that those who register for a particular society are in some way representative.

One of the other problems with the profile in the Ministry files is that it has no very satisfactory way of categorizing those who are working with metal. This is not the fault of the jua kali artisans, but rather of the Ministry questionnaire which did not really ask them for sufficient detail on the business: (only for '*Nature of Business e.g. Wood work, textile, mechanic etc.*'). But there are also good reasons in the jobs themselves for finding it difficult clearly to categorize these activities. As we have seen in our case studies of people like Kairu, individuals tend to combine jobbing work with other development work. But by breaking up the completed Ministry questionnaires into those who had mentioned welding and metalwork as their trade and those who had mentioned machinery and engineering, we reached a rough distinction between 13 of the former and ten of the latter. Even so, the total came to less than the dressmaking and tailoring group.

Other anomalies that make the Ministry data much less valuable is that a single firm with three managers sharing the same equipment can be counted as three different enterprises. For example, Kanyale Coffee Machinery which we discussed briefly a little earlier has all three of its managers down as separate Gikomba Jua Kali Society members, each mentioning that they had equipment worth K.Sh.150,000 (Remjus Onyango, Charles Muga and Fanuel Otieno). It could of course be the case that several of the dressmaking and tailoring names are in a similar position; several of them could be in the same enterprise.

The profile, therefore, that can be gathered from these 64 members of the Gikomba Jua Kali Society seems to be insufficiently representative of the range of industry represented there. It can be seen that Table 3.1 really only has four trade categories of any size mentioned. It misses out many other categories that can be found in the area, including a large number of craftsmen who are working on wooden carvings, and others who are manufacturing items such as paint, welding machines, wood lathes.

Gikomba businesses: largely unlicensed and unregistered

With these dangers of double-counting and undercounting, the files on Gikomba in the Ministry look to be of limited value. Nevertheless they may be able to point to some directions for further research and possible action. For example, the bulk of the Gikomba members state quite openly on their forms that their business is neither registered nor licensed. This raises an issue that sooner or later will have to be confronted by both local and national government: to what extent does the jua kali 'sector' deserve a special status? If Gikomba had been one of the very basic jua kali areas of the city or of the smaller towns, where, as we shall note with Kamukunji, the capital and equipment may not be much more than K.Sh.1,000-1,500 per capita, then it might be acceptable not to try and ensure that businesses were registered and had a trading licence. But Gikomba is certainly one of the most developed jua kali areas in the whole of Kenya, and in many cases the capital stock of individual entrepreneurs is between K.Sh.60,000 and 100,000 (or sometimes much more).

Differentiating Gikomba from other jua kali areas of Nairobi

One possibly valuable contribution of the painfully collected and recorded Ministry data is that it might eventually assist in developing more sensitive policies towards the jua kali in different trades, and at different income levels. We have suggested at various points that behind a particular trade category, e.g. carpentry, or metalwork, there can be an enormous range of facilities. And the same may well be true of jua kali membership in a particular part of the city. Here in Gikomba, although we have implied that there are some people who have managed to get membership who are strictly speaking outside Gikomba proper, there is a certain pattern amongst the 64 members of the Gikomba Jua Kali Society.

Even if we bear in mind the danger of some double-counting, it is plain

Table 3.2 *Capital stock amongst the Gikomba Jua Kali Society members*

K.Sh.	
200,000 +	5
150,000 +	5
100,000 +	5
50,000 +	23
20,000 +	13
less than 20,000	8
Hires equipment or other	4
Total (including 1 missing value)	64

that a significant number of the registered Gikomba Jua Kali Society members have some considerable equipment and machinery behind them, let alone the value of their premises which is not included in these figures. Amongst those claiming to have more than K.Sh.200,000, for instance, there was Ferdinand Mwambulu, who we met a little earlier, as one of the only people in Gikomba with a metal lathe and press machines. He estimated the value of his machinery at K.Sh.500,000. And J.M. Kuria of Kihoto Furniture estimated his machinery (for which we have independent confirmation) at over K.Sh.400,000. It can be seen that the largest grouping are those with over K.Sh.50,000 worth of equipment.

The reason for underlining this point is that half a kilometre away – in the jua kali sheds of the Kamukunji Jua Kali Society – there is a very different picture of capital stock. Many of the individuals may call themselves metalworkers like their counterparts in Gikomba, but a glance at the capital stock values would indicate that the majority of them have as little capital equipment as our tinsmiths in Starehe. The following is not an analysis of all the files for Kamukunji, but the others not categorized were not significantly different.

It can be seen at a glance that two-thirds of the Kamukunji sample had less than K.Sh.2,500 of equipment, and of this group the majority had less than K.Sh.1,000. This should not be surprising when it is remembered that many of the Kamukunji artisans are tinsmiths, sheet metalworkers, and people who are forming griddles, and other heavy duty kitchen ware by manual operations with simple hammers and anvils. But these data do point up the very great danger of talking about, say, metalworkers as if they were a single category. Here in the very centre of Nairobi there are at least two very different levels of jua kali enterprise being undertaken.

Table 3.3. *Capital equipment size in Kamukunji Jua Kali Society*

K.Sh.	
5,000 +	5
2,500 +	10
1,000 +	19
Less than 1,000	25
Not applicable/missing data	9
Total	68

Differentiating Gikomba by its numbers of trainees and employees
Another indication of a different character of jua kali operation in these two sites would be the size of the trainee and employee workforce. The Ministry questionnaire had asked the owners for the numbers of 'trainees' and of 'qualified artisans' working in the business. We need not pay too

much attention to the notion of 'qualified' since the great bulk of those working in micro-enterprise would be informally qualified by experience but would probably not have trade tests or other formal trade qualifications. Nevertheless, it is interesting that the great majority of the 64 micro-enterprise owners in Gikomba did have either trainees or artisans or both. In the case of trainees, 49 individual enterprise owners had a total of 212 trainees; while in respect of trained employees, 55 of these enterprise owners claimed to have a total of 217 artisans. Thus we can see that there are 429 trainees or employees managed by this small group of entrepreneurs. Even if we subtract ten or 20 from this total for those situations where joint owners such as Kanyale Coffee Machinery are reporting on their trainees and artisans more than once, we are probably still talking about nearly 400 workers and trainees depending on some 50 individuals. This ratio of some eight dependents to one manager or owner is rather different from some images of the informal sector as consisting of tiny firms with just a man and a boy helper or a woman and a girl.

There was no independent confirmation of these figures from the government questionnaires, since they were basically self-reported, but for the individuals known to the present author (e.g. Kairu, Mwambulu and Kanyale) the figures of trainees and workers coincide with our own research findings.

Contrasting Kamukunji with Gikomba in terms of employment creation

We have already mentioned that as an example of differentiation in the informal economy the Kamukunji jua kali present a very different face to those we have looked at in some depth in Gikomba. It should not perhaps be surprising in a situation where two-thirds of the Kamukunji sample had capital stock of less than K.Sh.2,500 that they should turn out to be much closer to the image of one man-and-a-helper that we have just referred to. The figures for our sample of 68 jua kali firms in Kamukunji indicate that just a little less than half (26) of the owners had no trainees at all, and these 26 had a total of just 45 employees.

Altogether the sample of 68 individuals in Kamukunji produce a total of just 107 trainees and workers compared with a total of approximately four times that number for almost the same sample (64) in Gikomba. It is clear, therefore, that there is something very different about these two sites of jua kali activity. This would come as no surprise to anyone visiting the two sites, for one consists solely of little groups working in the open or under the government sheds, in ones and two, but with not a single temporary or permanent building, while Gikomba has a whole grid of small streets with single and double storey factories and workshops.

Comparing Kamukunji and Gikomba: lack of materials vs lack of machines

A last dimension on which it may be significant to contrast two contiguous but fundamentally different jua kali sites is on their development aspirations. Again, not a great deal can be attached to what individual jua kali owners say in answer to requests or questions such as *Suggest ways by which you think these problems* (just outlined) *could be lessened.* or *What do you need to improve your business?* However, it may be worth noting that one of the most frequent responses amongst the jua kali of Gikomba was concerned with machinery. Thus typical responses included:

> more machines; lack of lathe machines and shapers; machinery of all kinds; lack of good equipment; capital for machines.

Whereas in Kamukunji, where the main activity was metalworking and tinsmithing, the most frequent demand or comment was of the following type:

> getting cheap materials; lack of materials; markets.

Only one or two of the Kamukunji owners talked of the need for machinery. In part, of course, this can be accounted for by the fact that the site has no electricity, no real provision for security, nor even any permanent individual premises. But for whatever reason, this does amount to a major contrast between these two jua kali areas. This is not to suggest, in terms of our distinction between entrepreneurial and subsistence self-employment, that Gikomba fits the first and Kamukunji the second. Naturally, there are a number of successful entrepreneurs including innovative machine-makers in Kamukunji and there are others who are just surviving in Gikomba. But the overall contrast between two adjacent jua kali areas is instructive.

Conclusions on industrial diversification and development in Gikomba

We have said enough in this chapter to answer several of the questions with which we set out. It is quite clear that our machine-makers of the early 1970s, who we revisited in the last chapter, are by no means on their own in the mid-1990s. Rather, there is within this small area of Gikomba alone a very considerable diversity of basic fabrication talent. We have described this in terms of technological confidence – a sense of how to tackle a technical problem, in terms of design, materials and market. The results of this confidence, this technological capacity, are plain to see. They consist of products which have been import-substituted in a very different sense from how that term was used in the 1960s and 1970s. Now, as compared to then, there is no doubt that the manufacture of scales has been localized within Nairobi, to take just one example. The same would be true of all the basic woodworking machinery we have discussed. The capacity to design and develop discrete machines and basic production lines such as are used in the grading of coffee is now also in place.

We have also hinted at the fact that the close proximity of different metalworking and woodworking businesses has been important in the building of this micro-industrial society in Gikomba. The continuing presence of a small number of high-quality Indian engineering workshops, as well as furniture factories such as McCrae's, the availability of even just a handful of metalworking lathes in African workshops, the relative ease of access to electricity – however informally that may be arranged from those with permanent premises to those with temporary jua kali workshops – all these have deepened the technological capacity of Gikomba over against closely contiguous areas such as Kamukunji.

It is more difficult to reach a judgement about the implications for policy and for replication of what has come together in the very informal chemistry of Gikomba. Clearly one very crucial component was that a particular mayor in Nairobi in the mid-to-late 1970s was prepared to allocate plots very cheaply to those who had formed the Gikomba Light Industrial Society. In other words, the very thing – access to land – that had encouraged so many of the jua kali associations to get registered that we noted in the first chapter did actually take place in Gikomba. It may well not have been done fairly or openly, but access to those plots by that particular group of young men who were desperate to develop their roadside businesses was critical in the Gikomba formula.

Even if the land was acquired relatively cheaply, there was no further help. No premises, no access to electricity or water, no package of assistance with small industry development. Gikomba's history certainly bears no relationship to that of small-scale industrial estates in Kenya. The motto in Gikomba has been self-help, even if that has meant waiting ten years to be able to afford to build.

Beyond this, there is a readiness to face new challenges in Gikomba. Conversations with entrepreneurs suggest that they are frequently seeking to undertake what they have not tried before. Sometimes the odds seems to be stacked against the individual, as for example, when someone tries to design a nail-making machine or a metalworking lathe. But with the most talented, there is often a degree of success. It is important, however, to be clear about the basis of this technological competence. It is not a confidence that is generally founded upon an extended mechanical engineering education in a college (though we have noted a very small number of our sample have had some formal technical and technician education), but rather upon the capacity to design, to copy and to improvise. Most of the Gikomba 'engineers' are not engineers at all in any formal sense. Most have few if any formal qualifications. Their experience is their key qualification, and in the case of many, this experience has been grounded principally on many years of employment in the formal industrial sector of the economy.

In one way, this exposure to formal sector standards and procedures over a considerable period has acted as a substitute or an alternative to extended formal education and institutional training. The majority of those we have been analysing in Gikomba have had, at most, four years of secondary education, and more commonly have just seven or eight years of primary education. Often their expertise was built up over ten or

15 years of formal employment. But now that they are independent owners with employees of their own, it is by no means as clear that their young trainees will wait as many years to build up their own technological capacity as those they are learning from. In such a situation of impatience to become independent, it may become more necessary for this hands-on technical capacity, learnt on the job, to be linked to formal mechanical engineering education. There is otherwise the danger that only a partial understanding of the trade or the skill is acquired, and that there arises either specialization in just one small area, as was noticed in the candle-making trade in the previous chapter or that the skills are not secured in the wider context of the product, its materials, market etc.

A good deal will depend on how rapidly some of these new found capacities are transferred to younger generations of entrepreneurs. Much of what can be seen in Gikomba suggests that this process is happening very fast. This makes it a highly competitive theatre of enterprise. But it does raise a question mark about the engineering frontier. The handful of Indian engineers left in the area, and the many others to be found elsewhere in Nairobi, are probably no longer dependent on just learning on the job in their family businesses. Almost certainly the younger generation of Indian engineering managers, such as those appearing in the businesses in the Industrial Area will have joined their on-the-job expertise to some engineering college or polytechnic degree. And it may well be that to make the transition from the basic fabrication of machines such as we have seen to higher order machine tools, some greater understanding of the technology of these processes and of materials science is required, as well as an exposure to electronic systems.

At the moment, however, the jury is still out on the question of movement towards this next technological frontier. Gikomba's African artisans have certainly moved very fast indeed between 1972 and 1995, and there is every reason to expect continuation of their new style import substitution. It will be important to examine to what extent education and training in schools, training institutions and in colleges seem likely to reinforce some of the trends we have analysed here. This formal educational support to technological confidence may well prove much more critical in crossing the next technical frontiers than it has been in assisting jua kali get to where they have reached today.

Before we turn to education and training, we need to look at whether the rural areas illustrate similar trends in jua kali development, and for this purpose we return to the rural area some 40 km to the north of Nairobi where also we visited artisans some 20 years ago.

Note

1. Ambetsa Mukkwanga claimed to have come from Western Kenya, and was a Luhya. Another Ambetsa, in a separate interview, claimed to have come from Uganda.

Four

Revisiting Rural Kenya's
Jua Kali

Defining jua kali in the rural areas is a challenge. Historically in a previously White Man's Country like Kenya, it might seem easier. And certainly on the road to Githiga from the district town of Kiambu, in Central Province, passing mile after mile of coffee plantations and, as we get higher, fields of tea, all of which used to be in the Settled (i.e. White) Areas, it is tempting to contrast the formal sector of the large farm, whether colonial or contemporary, with the small plots and the little villages in what were called the Reserves. By this criterion, the labour lines and the workers on the large farms would be in the formal sector and the little villages such as Githiga, outside the former Settled Area, could be thought of as informal. Even today labour on the plantation sector, whether producing tea, cotton, coffee or sugar, is regarded as formal sector and counted in the government statistics as such. Thus the figure for formal sector employment in agriculture in the rural areas is still largely made up of wage labour associated with these plantation crops and large farms. However, the distinction between formal and informal employment is increasingly difficult to maintain, since there are large numbers of casual workers who are not enumerated as formal sector employees and yet they are picking the tea, coffee, pyrethrum and other cash crops in the so-called formal sector. Such casual workers can often live in villages such as Githiga which are just on the edge of what was once the Settled Area.

But as the car swings off the Kiambu road through the estates and down to the river and up again to the ridge on which Githiga is laid out, other contrasts are presented with the jua kali we have been describing in places like Kamukunji and Gikomba in Nairobi. Here, as we pull up in Githiga, at the 'stage' where the line of *matatu* taxis waits to fill up with passengers for all the nearby towns, there is an immediate sense of most of Githiga being constructed of sturdy stone buildings. On the three sides

Figs. 4.1 and 4.2: The village green in Githiga, with shops and workshops on three sides. And one of the other streets, off the square. Note the abundance of pickups and lorries.

of the village green, all the buildings are of stone, and they are all occupied for trade or commerce (see fig. 4.1). The same is true for the other broader and bustling streets behind each side of the central square (see fig. 4.2). Most are built of stone, though there is the occasional kiosk of wood, and most have a small fenced in yard behind. Almost all the trades that we shall be referring to in a moment are being run out of these permanent premises. Jua Kali Githiga is, therefore, not really Hot Sun work as it still is in many urban areas. It is mostly covered. There are just a handful of vegetable traders who keep their wares in front of them on the ground. And once or twice a week this group is hugely added to by the market men and women displaying their wares all over the village green. But that is an institutionalized form of trade on the ground, quite different from the hawkers with their goods spread out on the pavements of Gikomba and Pumwani and their eyes on the look-out for the city askaris.

It must be borne in mind that the trade names we shall come to later on – the metalworkers, knitting-machine operators, photographers, dry-cleaners and paint-makers, and almost all the tailors and dressmakers operate out of formal premises. And there must be a demand for such premises for it can be seen that several of the most recent building projects in the village are to construct little rows of trading stores, with their big padlocks on their mild steel doorways.

One of the paradoxes of the differentiation of jua kali activities in urban and rural Kenya is that in some of the big concentrations of jua kali in Nairobi, metalwork is being done without any access to electricity, e.g. in Kamukunji, whereas in Githiga the metalworkers can get access to power if they can pay the price. As we begin, first, to look at who aspires to be a jua kali in Githiga, and then later look at some of the earliest fundis in the village, we shall be continually thinking about what defines a jua kali artisan. Is there anyone practising trade or commerce, full or part-time, who could not consider themselves to be jua kali?

Change and development of rural jua kali, 1972–92

I returned to Githiga in 1989, 1990 and 1992, almost 20 years after I had originally started to do field work in the little Kiambu village, some 40 km north of Nairobi. It had been chosen in the first place since it had turned out to be the home of several of the young men who were found to be experimenting on wasteland in Nairobi in the use of their hand-made, manually-operated machines for the manufacture of metal products. Most of these young men who appeared in the chapter on 'indigenous machine-making' in *The African Artisan* (King, 1977) had acquired their skills in Githiga at the hands of an innovative entrepreneur named Mutang'ang'i.

But having lit on Mutang'ang'i as the source of a network of skills that spread out from this particular village into Nairobi and further afield, occasion was also taken to examine the wider technical context of this village (King, 1977: chapter 6). A picture was thus captured of one ordinary village in the Central Province of Kenya between the years 1972 and 1974. Its primary school leavers were examined over a period of ten years before this, and they were traced into different kinds of skilled and unskilled jobs in the village and further afield. In addition several of the main groups of skilled people, in the building trades, in transport and vehicle mechanics and in metalwork were examined in considerable detail, to illustrate the dynamics of skill acquisition and transfer, as well as the interaction between the rural and urban clusters of such skilled people. One of the recurring themes in this early account of 'the technical form of a Kenya village' was the impossibility of describing rural or urban skill as a self-contained category. It had also been amply demonstrated in the analysis of a significant number of this particular village's skilled people over a 30 or 40-year period up to 1974 that it was also not possible to divide the skilled community neatly into what were then called formal and informal sectors.

In many cases, the key skilled people in the village had acquired their skills originally from 'Kenya Asian' (or Indian) enterprises or from European firms, farms or government concerns. This should not have been surprising since these were then the major sources of the new skills that had entered Kenya in the previous 30 or 40 years. But a pattern had already begun to establish itself whereby these originally formal sector skills were being passed on from African to African by what looked like an emerging local apprenticeship system.

A number of major questions were left up in the air at the end of this first examination of Githiga in the early 1970s:

- Would this small village, built during the Emergency in the mid-1950s as an alternative, protected village to the attractions of the Mau Mau, be able to attract more of its skilled young people to return and ply their trades in the village?
- Would the 18 or so trades that we were able to detect in the early 1970s expand in the next decade or more? At that time one or two of these, such as window-frame maker and knitting-machine operator, were represented by just one person, newly arrived.
- Would these pioneers be able to thrive, or would there be insufficient demand in a small village to sustain them?
- In 1974 there had been a Presidential initiative to make primary school free for the first four years, and there had been other reform proposals in the pipeline that suggested there would be a major attempt to orient the basic cycle of education towards self-employment. Almost two decades later, would the village school system itself be more identified with a contribution to skill development than it had been (apart from the general skills of language and maths) in the period since Independence in 1963?
- And what about the trades that were already in the village in the early 1970s? Would they have continued with the same lines of business, or

would they have graduated to new technologies? Would there be any evidence of greater technological confidence amongst the community of skilled people?

• Would the one or two people identified with machine-making in the early 1970s have been joined by others?

These and many other questions were in mind in revisiting the area. In so doing, it was of course understood that if there was much discernible change at the local level, it would not be the result of isolated rural initiatives, in one village, rural town or district, but rather the outcome of policies and developments that might have originated far from the rural areas. In Kenya's case, one of the most salient of these national policy papers to have focused on the rural dimension was *Economic Management for Renewed Growth* (1986).

In one of the key chapters of this Sessional Paper ('Rural–Urban Balance'), the four sub-sections were: growth centres and infrastructure; financing and managing urban development; the informal sector; and energy requirements. The growth centre concept laid out the plan for 200 Rural Trade and Production Centres (RTPCs) between 1986 and 2000. It is interesting to note that the notion was not restricted to trade but quite specifically mentioned production. It is not at this point known if Githiga was to be identified as an RTPC, but it is instructive to note that the investment package aimed to make good some of the missing infrastructural elements. It could as easily have applied to Githiga as to many of the other hundreds of small trading centres around the country:

> This package should be restricted to essentials only and typically would include some combination of rural roads, water, power, post office, telephones, youth polytechnics, markets, and other facilities directly related to agriculture or small-scale manufacturing and trading enterprises. (Kenya, 1986: 46)

Equally, as has already been noted in Chapter 1 on the Policy Environment, this was the government Sessional Paper that had given more attention to the potential of the informal sector than any since the International Labour Office (ILO) had identified Kenya with the new found concept of the informal sector in its Employment Mission, *Employment, Incomes and Equality in Kenya* (ILO, 1972). Apart from the more general attention given in this Sessional Paper to the incapacity of Kenya's modern, urban industrial sector even to begin to provide sufficient jobs for Kenya's aspiring entrants to the labour market, there was good deal of comment that saw the informal sector as a crucial component in Kenyan villages and small towns:

> Unquestionably, the majority of future non-farm job opportunities will be in the informal sector – in small-scale manufacturing, marketing, repairs and other service activities – located mostly in market centres and moderate-sized towns throughout Kenya ... the self-employed and small-scale enterprises represent the major part of business activity in market towns and smaller urban

centres. They fulfil key functions in support of agriculture and other local production by marketing inputs such as fertilizer, making and selling small tools, providing local inhabitants with a wide range of inexpensive basic consumer goods and services for everyday life. Small local firms can be especially efficient at producing bulky or heavy items such as building materials, especially brick and tile, and furniture, thus saving on transport costs. (Kenya, 1986: 54–5)

A whole series of proposals was associated with this recognition of the importance of the informal sector, and, as we have seen, many were drawn together in 1992 and taken a good deal further – at least at the level of policy recommendation – in the *Sessional Paper No. 2. of 1992 on Small Enterprise and Jua Kali Development in Kenya*. Very few of these proposals for support to informal and micro-enterprise have yet had any discernible impact on the village of Githiga. The only thing that did have some implication for Githiga was a recommendation originally made by President Moi in late 1985. This was a direct encouragement to artisans to consider forming themselves into groups in order that 'they could more easily be helped by Government' (*Kenya Times*, 1985). From that point on for several years, as we saw in Chapter 1, all round the country, groups of artisans began to organize themselves, hoping that through registration and recognition, there would be preferential access to shelter, sites, loans and marketing.

This process was not able to proceed very rapidly until a special unit had been established for Jua Kali Development within the reshaped Ministry of Technical Training and Applied Technology (MTTAT). It was from this Ministry that a letter was sent out in 1988 to all District Commissioners, instructing them to use the local channels of chiefs and public meetings to encourage the development of groups. And it was to this section that embryonic jua kali associations had to apply, in order to get the application forms which their individual members would complete in order to acquire recognition.

Githiga's jua kali artisans begin to organize

Githiga, despite being close to Nairobi, was by no means early in thinking about forming an association. However, they had held a first meeting in mid-1988. The initiative appears to have come from officialdom in the form of the Assistant Chief. But whatever the source of the suggestion, a meeting was duly held on 10 July 1988 formally to develop a Githiga Group. It is interesting to note that, according to the minutes of that event, 20 people were present, of which five became office-bearers and a further six, committee members. Apart from the elections, only two other items were minuted as decisions of the new committee. They decided that the appropriate name for their organization should be the Githiga Jua Kali Group, and that it should be registered with the Department of Social Services in neighbouring Kiambu.

It would seem that the process of registration of what might prove a very large number of new societies across Kenya did lead to some competition amongst Ministries (such as Cooperative Development, Culture and

Social Services, and MTTAT). Some groups were clearly encouraged to call themselves cooperative societies or groups in order to link in with traditions of cooperatives or of registering self-help (*harambee*) groups, while MTTAT was suggesting that they call themselves Associations and register with the Register of Societies through the Attorney General's Office. While none of this may seem very significant to the artisans in Githiga, it does perhaps point to the fact that the jua kali were for a time conceived by officialdom and politicians to be a whole new class of clients for ministries and MPs to relate to.

Behind the initial decision of the Githiga artisans to call themselves a group may have been the idea of registering as a *harambee* group with the Ministry of Culture and Social Services. It is not clear whether anything very much happened in this first year after the initial meeting, but one of the next pieces of correspondence appears to have been written on the very day, 8 August 1989, I returned to the village after an absence of almost 20 years. This was a letter to the Ministry of Technical Training and Applied Technology asking to be registered as the 'Githiga Jua-Kali Co-operative Society', as part of the 'national jua-kali co-operative movement'. It is not known how MTTAT replied, given their own preference for associations not to become cooperative societies or *harambee* groups. But in any event within a couple of months there was, finally, an opportunity for eligible artisans to register with the new society.

It is interesting, in this connection, to note that the only other item minuted a year earlier had been concerned with the question of membership, and in particular the issue of women or children being members when their husbands were already members. The Committee 'passed that nobody is allowed to be a member of the Group together with his or her children or wife'. The wording is not exactly clear, but it probably points to a desire not to have several individuals in the same family becoming members of an organization that might just mean getting access to land, loans, special favours etc.

In any organization that may qualify for access to scarce resources, there is probably no such thing as equitable arrangements in deciding on membership. This particular minute certainly looks as if it would discriminate against a woman jua kali, however independent her business might be from that of her husband. Still, before reaching such a judgement, it may be worth looking at what perspective on village skill can be deduced from an examination of jua kali membership in Githiga.

Githiga: a preliminary attempt at jua kali membership

The first illustration that is available of those who wanted to take up jua kali membership is in a listing of 54 names that was attached to the original application for the Jua Kali Group. In the government thinking at this time about how to define jua kali membership, the emphasis was very certainly on productive artisan skills, in contrast with hawking, vending and service skills. It was stated, in an interview in the Ministry (MTTAT), that the emphasis on production would more easily allow for training and upgrading, and for the eventual development of new products. That would be much more difficult with hawkers. The Ministry, in fact, was coming round to a definition of the jua kali and related areas that fell into three categories: 1) jua kali proper, consisting of the productive trades and the vocational services sector, such as vehicle repair; 2) there would be the small traders' group which, in fact, already had its own professional association, the Kenya Small Traders' Society (KSTS); and finally, 3) there was the group of hawkers and vendors, who were really a less formal version of the more established small traders who had fixed or permanent premises (Mutiso, oral interview, July 1989).

With this perspective on who the Ministry was encouraging to come forward as jua kali, what does the initial set of names put forward by the Githiga Committee members look like? The first point about it is that 52 of the 54 names are male. We shall notice shortly that when it came to individuals completing the government's application forms for jua kali recognition, some further women did apply, but it is interesting that in the first conception of the committee, jua kali did not include, for example, any of the well known women tailors or seamstresses in the village.

Of greater interest in this preliminary listing, however, is the significant number of names sent to the Ministry of those who were in terms of their job very far from the core idea of productive artisan skills. The list included at least the following rather unlikely candidates for jua kali status:

2 full-time farmers	the son of a shop owner
2 drivers, 1 for Kenya Breweries, 1 in Githiga	an owner of a tea shop
a photographer	a shop assistant
a court clerk in Kiambu	a bar owner
an ex-chief	an owner of a general store
2 transporters	a local teacher
	a butcher

In other words of those who could be readily identified, 16 were at first sight rather inappropriate candidates for jua kali status. But, as has been mentioned already, there are strong pressures in economies of scarcity for individuals to seek to be included whenever there sounds like an opportunity to get an advantage. When in fact, in response to the Githiga request, the Ministry had sent application forms for individual membership, most of these initially dubious candidates appear to have fallen away. We turn accordingly to the list that can be constructed from the responses to the Ministry forms. These are held in the offices of the Ministry (MTTAT) in Nairobi.

The Ministry's profile of Githiga's jua kali

Githiga's registered jua kali artisans

It should not perhaps be surprising that there is some uncertainty about the number of jua kali artisans from Githiga that have been fully registered with the Ministry. It was a massive task that the Ministry had taken on – to register tens of thousands of artisans across the whole country, filing their application forms, banking their K.Sh.20 registration fees, and entering the registration numbers painstakingly in files and ledgers, prior to sending out batches of completed jua kali identification cards to the associations concerned. In the case of Githiga, in August 1990, there appeared to be some 72 names in the MTTAT ledgers, but only 59 appropriately completed forms. But this could well be explained by the sheer scale and complexity of an operation that was being done entirely manually with just two or three staff. A small batch could have been unavailable because of being processed.

Even though the figures are not completely reliable, it is still worth asking the question: what could the Ministry deduce about the shape and profile of a jua kali community in a trade centre or a village like Githiga from the data that they have themselves collected? Before looking in much more detail, later on in this chapter, at the individual artisans who have been interviewed in our own sample, is it possible to give what could be considered a Ministry snapshot of the registered jua kali group in this village? We should point out that, as far as is known, the Ministry has not in fact had the time to make this kind of assessment of a village association by drawing on its own data. But with some quite small-scale support to data processing, there could be some valuable insights derived from the thousands of forms that came into the Ministry from all over the country in the years following the Presidential announcement.

Obviously the quality of any such analysis would depend a good deal on the information the Ministry sought to acquire in the application forms that were issued for artisans interested in acquiring jua kali status. The four pages of the questionnaire, in fact, covered a good deal: a section on personal particulars, including previous jobs, education and qualifications; and the basic details about the business (its nature, when started, whether licensed, and registered; a section about economic activities, including the means originally employed to raise funds to start, and the actual amount of initial investment; then a section on profitability which included an estimate of money spent on materials, as well as data on numbers of qualified artisans and trainees working for the owner, and what they are paid. A fourth section was on management, which included questions also on what equipment was in use and what it cost. Then a final section dealt rather extensively with needs. This asked rather coyly if the owner thought the income from their activities was satisfactory, what were the major problems they faced, their suggestions for dealing with the problems and improving their business, and lastly a sub-section asking how long they could afford to be away from their business on training courses and seminars. The overall impact of the questionnaire would be to suggest that there were a number of good things in store for well-organized jua kali associations. Indeed it is some confirmation of the expectations attached merely to filling the registration form that no less than nine of the forms came from individuals who were not jua kali at all but who wanted to start a business and become registered jua kali. These individuals have not, of course, been counted in the following analysis.

It is also interesting to note, given the original male bias noted in the Githiga minutes of the Jua Kali Group, that the form is strongly entitled in a way that would encourage women jua kali to register:

A Survey of Jua Kali Artisans
This Form is to be filled by Women and Men Jua Kali Artisans.
(Note: This form is free and nobody should sell it.)

The Ministry's quantitative data on Githiga's registered jua kali artisans
The 59 completed forms in the Ministry of Technical Training and Applied Technology from the village of Githiga provide an intriguing angle on this community that is the target of our research. Indicative perhaps of the major influence cast over the community by the metalworking, foundry and blacksmithing skills of Mutang'ang'i are the quite large number of individuals who described their business as metalworking. Generally it is clear from the detail given that these are not tinsmiths, making the assortment of metal boxes and other goods found in many market centres. Instead, this group of individual artisans give themselves a range of different titles: blacksmiths, foundry workers, welders, metal engineers, and in a couple of cases an even more elaborate occupation: 'mechanical engineering, welding and general fabricator', for one; and, for another, 'metalworker of processing machines'.

Table 4.1. *Githiga Jua Kali Association applicants by trade*

Metalwork/smith etc.	17
Tailor/dressmaker	4
Retreads	1
Curios	2
Maizemilling	1
Cycle repair	1
Shoemaker	2
Catering/hotel	5
Clothes-seller	1
Hawker	1
Carpentry	4
Timberyard	1
Plumbing	2
Watch-repair	2
Electrician	1
Motor mechanic	8
Kiosk	4
Charcoal	1
Missing data	1
Total	59

An additional reason for the large number of metalworkers applying for registration may well have been the fact that most of the Committee of the Jua Kali Group in the village were from the metalworking trades. But whatever the reason, the metal trades were certainly well represented amongst those who first registered for jua kali status.

This rather important group of metalworkers were not all older individuals either. Half of the 17 (nine) were over 30, but half (eight) were under 30. Again this probably is a comment on the longstanding possibility in the village of acquiring skills directly from Mutang'ang'i or some of the others he had trained in earlier decades. (Mutang'ang'i had been operating his metal business since approximately 1960.) Some of these previous trainees were operating on their own account in the village. But, equally, young people interested in the metal industry could have got their skills from many other well known Githiga people who had their factories or workshops in Nairobi.

The other Githiga applicants in this Ministry sample are also revealing, as much for how the term jua kali is being defined at the level of the village association, as for what is the actual profile of village skill. Apart from the metalworking, blacksmithing, welding and fabrication sector, there are really only two other groups of any size, at least as far as the Ministry's profile through these forms is concerned. One is motor vehicle mechanics, and the other is catering/hotel and kiosk services (if these categories are combined). There are smaller numbers of carpenters and also tailors, but after these two trades the numbers for the rest appear to be very small.

We shall suggest in a moment that this profile is not particularly representative of the village skill environment; nor is it very close to the ideal of what the Ministry was prioritizing as jua kali skills. Even if the earlier list which had contained several non jua kali aspirants for jua kali status and registration had been improved upon through the completion of the formal questionnaires, there were still nine applications on the official forms that were in the catering, food kiosk and hotel trades. These would not qualify in any strict Ministry definition of 'vocationalized' skills oriented to production. Nor of course would the charcoal-seller, the solitary hawker, the seller of ready-made clothes, or the seller of retread tyres.

Female jua kali applicants

One of the difficulties about a very strict definition of jua kali, emphasizing the 'vocationalized trades', is that, despite the heading of the questionnaire, they tend to reinforce the bias against women qualifying. Amongst the 59 applicants for registration, no less than 13 were women, but most of them fell into the categories of tailoring, hotel and kiosk workers. And women were also represented in several other trades which would really not fall within this Ministry notion of core jua kali skills, e.g. the charcoal-seller and the clothes-seller. However, the Ministry simply did not have the capacity to sort out applicants very systematically, and probably these women were granted jua kali identification cards.

Revisiting Rural Kenya's Jua Kali

Change and development in Githiga's micro-enterprises, 1970–90

Bearing in mind that this sample is a rather incomplete snapshot of Githiga skills in 1989–90, it may still be worth asking what it suggests about change in the character and composition of micro-enterprises in a village situation such as Githiga, over a 20-year period. And here perhaps one of the most obvious questions to ask about these almost 60 applicants for jua kali status is how many of them were already in business in the early 1970s when we last studied the area. Would the jua kali in Githiga who were captured in a Ministry sample at the end of the 1980s turn out to be just the older and more established artisans such as Mutang'ang'i who had played such a key role in the process of training others, some 15 or 25 years earlier?

Age of businesses amongst jua kali applicants in Githiga

As far as the age of the various businesses is concerned, the data available are quite intriguing. One expectation of a situation where economies of scarcity operate is, we have suggested, that power and influence may well determine access. It had been thought likely, therefore, that if there were limited opportunities to register for jua kali, it would tend to go to those who had been established in business for quite some time. Very new businesses might be asked to wait their turn. The opposite would appear to have been the case. The application forms were only available for Githiga in early 1990, and yet the largest number of businesses had apparently just recently started (21), and of these, 12 had started in 1989 itself. And we have already noted that nine mainly young people acquired forms who had no business at all, but just wanted to start one. By contrast, the village's most distinguished businessman, Mutang'ang'i', did not even appear amongst these 59 first applicants for jua kali status (perhaps because he had not bothered to apply, or he had not been given the forms to complete).

Table 4.2. *Numbers of jua kali businesses starting in Githiga by year*

1990	3
1987–89	21
1984–86	15
1981–83	5
1978–80	4
1975–77	4
1972–74	3
1969–71	2
missing	2
Total	59

Overall, the recency of business start-ups is very marked amongst the set of applicants for jua kali status. No less than two-thirds of all these businesses had started up in the seven years between 1984 and 1990. And

133

as far as the numbers whose businesses dated from the early 1970s are concerned, it can be seen that there were only five.

Of course, this table says nothing about the age and possible seniority of those starting businesses in the late 1980s. It could still be proportionately the older generations who were getting into business at this period. An outline of the age profile of the group is, again, suggestive of the opposite conclusion:

Table 4.3. *Age profile of Githiga jua kali applicants*

60+	3
55–59	1
50–54	3
45–49	10
40–44	5
35–39	11
30–34	7
25–29	12
20–24	6
20–	1
missing	1
Total	60

The village community of those calling themselves jua kali (and taking the opportunity to apply for registration) certainly entered business very recently, but a third of them (18) were under 30 years old; another third (18) were in their thirties, and the remainder (22), a little over a third, were in their forties, fifties or sixties. It still remained to be seen if it was the younger people who were starting their businesses in the late 1980s, or whether the group of relatively new starts also consisted of older people

Table 4.4. *Age of Githiga jua kali starting businesses in 1984-6 and 1987-90*

Age	start-ups 1984–6	start-ups 1987–90
60+	2	
55–9	1	
50–4		1
45–9	2	4
40–4	2	4
35–9	2	2
30–4	2	1
25–9	2	9
20–4	2	3
Totals	15	24

(who might have been employed earlier) deciding to start up perhaps after many years of being employees (like some of those we met in Gikomba in the last chapter). It would certainly seem from Table 4.4 that for the late 1980s, and especially for the years 1987–90, there are significant numbers of both young and old deciding to start their own ventures.

For instance, in this most recent period, nine of the business people starting off were 40 or over, another three were in their thirties, but half of this group of entrepreneurs (12) were in their twenties.

Education levels of Githiga entrepreneurs

As far as education is concerned, the expected picture would again be that the younger the entrepreneur the higher the level of education. Thus it might be expected that the bulk of the (secondary) Form IV (F4) and Form VI (F6) leavers would be in the under thirties age group, while those with only the (primary) Standard VII (S7) or Standard VIII (S8) would be much more likely to be in the older groups. The results from this data set are somewhat more intriguing, as can be seen from Table 4.5.

Table 4.5. *Education of Githiga jua kali applicants by age*

Age	F6	F4	F2/1	S7/8	S3/4	Adult Literacy	Missing	totals
60+					3			3
55–9						1		1
50–4					1	1	1	3
45–9		1		3	1	2	2	9
40–4		2		2			2	6
35–9	1	4	2	4				11
30–4		3		2			2	8
25–9	1	4	3	4			1	13
20–4		4	1					5
Totals	2	18	7	15	5	4	8	59

More than half (11) of those with F4 or F6 are actually to be found amongst the over thirties group, and there is still a small group of the under thirties who have not more than S7 education. What is clear from the table is that those with just a few years of education (S3/4), or merely adult literacy skills, are all in the over 45 year old group.

What may help to explain this initially puzzling situation where most of the secondary school (F4/F6) group are over 30 years old is that this is a part of Kenya which has had its own, originally *harambee*, secondary school since the mid-1960s. We noted in *The African Artisan* that the first group of F4s left Githiga Secondary School in 1969. So quite apart from the opportunities to go to the many other government secondary schools nationwide, there has been a day secondary school in the village for more than 20 years. Those who left in the early 1970s at 18 years old would be almost 40 by the end of the 1980s.

The issue that needs more explanation is the presence of a number of young business aspirants with just primary education in a society which has had the possibility of secondary education for years. Here the reason is probably to do with the absence of money for fees in the case of poorer families, mixed with the feeling by some parents and pupils that to pay a good deal of money for a secondary education that will still not offer the certainty of a job is a difficult investment decision. In the words of one father, John Nene, who we met in Chapter 2 and whose son was at the transition point between primary and secondary in 1989: 'If he fails to get into a government secondary or a good *harambee*, it is better for him to be a driver than struggling in a poor school and then getting nothing.'

Trade licences and business registrations in Githiga

It is often said that the urban micro-enterprise sector manages to avoid registration and licensing in a way that is not possible for rural entrepreneurs who are much better known to the community and to local officialdom. This difference is not borne out, at least by the small numbers of Githiga jua kali admitting to having registered their business or having obtained a trade licence. Of the group of 59 jua kali, only two blacksmiths admitted to having registered their business, and in respect of trade licences, only 12 of the total appear to have obtained them. This is in fact a somewhat higher proportion than we found in the urban area of Gikomba, and much higher than in Kamukunji where not a single one of those who sent in their forms to the Ministry admitted to having either registered their business or applied for a trade licence.

Again, as in Nairobi, this does raise the question of whether central and local government can afford not to secure some local tax revenue from the very large numbers of artisans working out of regular premises.

Initial capital, expenditure on materials, cost of equipment

Although this kind of questionnaire data is notoriously unreliable when it comes to figures for income, expenditure and profits, there may nevertheless be some indication of patterns in what is admitted to. No less than 30 of the 51 who answered the question about their initial investment indicated that they had between K.Sh.1,000 and 5,000. Though this was obviously more in real terms when they actually started than when they completed the application forms or now, it still suggests that individuals have been entering businesses with very little behind them. Only a handful (7) admitted to starting up with K.Sh.20,000 or more (and of these, six said it was just K.Sh.20,000).

On weekly expenditure for materials, it is the same story. Thirty-four out of the 44 who answered this inquiry admitted that their weekly expenditure on materials was between K.Sh.1,000 and 5,000. And this time only three admitted to spending K.Sh.10,000 or more on weekly materials.

The cost of their equipment was another indicator of their relatively small scale. But here the figures need to be treated with particular caution since, as will be clear later in this chapter, a great deal of the equipment used in village workshops is actually made by the artisans themselves. Apart from those not answering or stating that they were hiring or had not any equipment (12), there are really just three groups. About a third of the remainder possessed equipment of less value than K.Sh.2,000; a little over a third held equipment of between K.Sh.3,000 and 10,000; and another third had machines worth between K.Sh.20,000 and 250,000. But of this group only three were over K.Sh.50,000. Again we shall seek in our more qualitative analysis to make more sense of these rather bald indicators of scale. But if we recall the pattern in Gikomba where the majority of those registering as jua kali had equipment worth over K.Sh.50,000, we can see that this particular sample of the Githiga jua kali has a very different level of capital stock. On the other hand, the Githiga sample was actually better endowed than the artisans in Kamukunji, the bulk of whom had less than K.Sh.1,000 of initial capital stock.

Trainees and employees: employment generation by Githiga jua kali

In some ways this is the most interesting dimension of all of those mentioned in their application forms to the Ministry (see Table 4.6). The artisans were asked to indicate how many trainees they had and how many 'qualified artisans'. Only 33 of the 59 admitted to having trainees, and a little fewer (30) to having employees. In most cases those who had trainees were also those with employed artisans, since there were no less than 21 owners who had neither trainees nor employees (or at least did not admit to having any).

Table 4.6. *Numbers of trainees and employees (artisans) by numbers of owners (Githiga jua kali sample)*

No. of trainees in enterprises	No. of owners with this no. of trainees	Total no. of trainees	No. of artisans in enterprise	No. of owners with this no. of artisans	Total no. of artisans
1	6	6	1	11	11
2	11	22	2	16	32
3	5	15	3	0	0
4	4	16	4	0	0
5	4	20	5	0	0
6	1	6	6	0	0
7	1	7	7	0	0
10	1	10	9	3	27
Totals	33	102	Totals	30	70

What is of interest in this small sample is just how many trainees there are: 102 (an average of three per master or mistress, though there is considerable dispersal around this mean). As to employees, there are less, at 70 for 30 owners (an average of just over two). But in total, trainees and employees make up the rather extraordinary figure of 172 people working in micro-enterprises for just over 30 owners. Again a more qualitative analysis would need to look more closely at, for example, the three metalworking owners who all claimed to have nine artisans, in order to ensure that there was no double counting. But we have here a pattern that is not so dissimilar to what we found in Nairobi's Gikomba, where we encountered some eight dependents for one micro-enterprise owner.

There was an opportunity given in the Ministry forms to comment on ways in which jua kali problems could be lessened or their businesses improved. Not many jua kali applicants took the chance to express their views, but amongst two of the more substantial contributions were two men (plumbers) who both commented on the potential for developing quality local goods. (They would appear to have collaborated on their answers!):

> Our local activities are being imported and we are able to make these on our own. We, Kenyans, would like to cooperate ourselves (jua kali artisans) to make more types of activities to ensure that our government will no longer import such activities. (plumber, 1990)

> We in Kenya we have to be proud and assist jua kali because there are some activities we are making locally very useful which tomorrow are more better than the imported ones; so let us build a strong Kenya. (plumber, 1990)

An alternative survey of Githiga's Jua Kali

In conjunction with looking at what profile the Ministry might have been able to draw if it examined its own jua kali file on Githiga, we also carried out a kind of establishment survey of who owned the various shops, stores, kiosks in Githiga, what they specialized in, and who they employed as workers or trainees. We also inquired about their date of setting up the business. This small survey was not intended to cover the many individuals who would only conduct their businesses on market day in the village, nor the many farmers (male and female) who would carry on some occasional commercial activity from their homes. If these latter two categories had been included, the numbers would have been very great indeed. As it was, however, this mini-survey, done with the help of secondary school pupils who knew their village well, turned up some 150 enterprises, but noted that over ten of these were not currently in operation.

Compared with the first table in this chapter on the applicants for jua kali status, this listing (in Table 4.7) not only shows some major differences within the same categories, but it also adds a significant number of

Table 4.7. *Comparison of Jua Kali Society trades with village survey trades (Jua Kali Society applicants in brackets)*

Trade type	Nos.		Trade type	Nos.	
Metalwork/smith	3	(17)	Hawker	0	(1)
Tailoring	13	(4)	Carpentry	1	(1)
Retreads	0	(1)	Timberyard	0	(1)
Curios	0	(2)	Plumbing	0	(2)
Maizemilling	1	(1)	Watch repair	3	(2)
Cycle repair	3	(1)	Electrician	2	(1)
Shoemaker	7	(2)	Motor mechanic	3	(8)
Catering/hotel	9	(5)	Kiosk	0	(4)
Clothes seller	6	(1)	Charcoal	4	(1)
Second-hand clothes	5		Dry-cleaners	4	
Knitting shop	3		Retail store	25	
Music store	1		Hardware	4	
Butchery	9		Paint shop	1	
Shoeseller	3		Grocer	3	
Hair saloon	7		Bar/restaurant	8	
Post Office/shop	1		Insurance	1	
Photo shop	1		Clinics	4	
Wholesaler	1		Agrochemicals	1	
Darts/social	1		Milk store	1	
Totals	74	(34)	Totals	65	(21)

categories that were not represented at all in the earlier table of applicants to the Ministry. One of the reasons for this difference is that the earlier table was made up very much of personal applicants. We have also suggested that a set of application forms is a very unreliable way of securing a comprehensive coverage, since (quite apart from the merely logistical problems of having enough duplicated forms available) there may well be tendencies to restrict the distribution of forms if it is thought there could be advantages to being registered. The Ministry forms tended to assume that the applicants would be the owners of the businesses they described, since distinguishing 'owner jua kalis' from 'worker jua kalis' had been one of the intentions of the Ministry in designing the questionnaire, but there is evidence from our analysis of Gikomba that sometimes three different people from the same enterprise had applied for jua kali status. This might have happened also with the Githiga sample, and hence increased the number of metalworkers. The establishment survey, by contrast, had gone systematically from door to door asking for the names of the store and the owner.

This is still not quite sufficient to explain some of the very large differences between the two tables and their listings of occupations. But already for one small village in Central Kenya, we are faced with a serious statistical set of inconsistencies. In the case of the Ministry, were it to interrogate its own data on jua kalis in Githiga, it would find a different figure in the ledgers of individual names (72) than the actual number of original forms (59). But if this is compared with a careful survey of business owners in the central grid of the little village itself, the Ministry has captured less than half of what an enterprise-to-enterprise or shop-to-shop survey would reveal (139). If these kinds of inconsistencies were to be paralleled in other towns and villages, then the Ministry's estimates of jua kali size could prove massively misleading.

These discrepancies are worth discussing a little further. Tailoring, for instance, had only four applicants represented in the Ministry forms, but there were 13 establishments identified in the enterprise-by-enterprise survey that were clearly tailoring shops, and there were several others that combined tailoring with selling of clothes. Metalwork, smithing, foundry work was by far the largest jua kali category in the Ministry forms (with 17 individual names going forward), and yet the enterprise survey only picked up three such industries. The category, motor vehicle mechanics, was quite large in the earlier sample (eight), but only three operations were identified in the later exercise. It is also striking that there could be just four kiosk operators identified in the early listing but no less than 25 individual establishments are found to be trading as general or retail stores a little later on. And if restaurants-cum-bars are joined with hotels and catering in the more recent survey, there are no less than 17 as compared with just five earlier.

One of the most intriguing explanations of these differences, not just in these categories but in a large number of the others, is that the enterprise survey was done in July 1992; whereas most of the Jua Kali forms were filled out and sent to the Ministry during March or April of 1990. There was therefore a little over two years between the two surveys. Now, in many villages in OECD countries, or indeed in other parts of Africa, differences in the number of businesses, especially in a village, would not be expected to change very dramatically in the space of 26 months. It

Table 4.8. *Start-up year of businesses in Githiga enterprise survey*

1990–92	52
1987–89	40
1984–86	29
1981–83	6
1978–80	10
1975–77	0
1972–74	1
1969–71	0
Before 1969	1
Total	139

would appear however that in Githiga that the time difference in the two surveys was perhaps the single greatest reason for the change in the figures (see Table 4.8).

It can be seen from Table 4.8 that 121 of the 139 operations claimed to have started within the previous eight years, but by far the largest group (52) had started in the two-and-half years up to August 1992. Given that the earlier survey was done at the beginning of 1990, it can be seen that almost all of the 52 new business starts had taken place in the period since the Jua Kali questionnaires were issued and completed. Even allowing for some reporting error, this is a very substantial amount of new activity in a very short time, and it must provide some of the explanation for the discrepancy.

The diversity of the village business profile

But what is intriguing in the more recent survey, and which has been confirmed by field visits to the village also in 1992, is that it is not just the quantity of new starts that is impressive; it is also the diversity of the businesses that have been coming into the village in the early 1990s. The table of trade types points to a number of developments that presumably illustrate the rise in rural demand for goods and services. These were the very things that the Sessional Paper of 1986 had been looking for when it talked of small non-farm enterprises 'providing local inhabitants with a wide range of inexpensive basic consumer goods and services for everyday life' (Kenya, 1986: 54–5). In this category would come, certainly, the basic support services to business and general life, such as the Post Office, the insurance business, the several different clinics, and the frequent communication by *matatu* to all the neighbouring towns. Then more specifically on consumer goods and personal services would come the carpentry, plumbing, electrical, and the paint selling (and paint making), the maize-milling, dry-cleaning, shoemaking (and repair), hairdressing and several of the other personal services (e.g. music, photographs, and leisure) which would allow residents to do locally what would in earlier years have meant a bus journey to Kiambu Town or to Nairobi. Even though there was not yet any bank in Githiga, the sheer number of tailors, clothes sellers, butchers and retail shops speaks to a substantial rise in local surplus from agriculture.

Also, as hoped for in the 1986 Sessional Paper, the arrival of electricity had made it possible much more easily to make in the village the large number of basic metal products that could be used in the improvement of local houses. This is not to suggest that the many metal workshops were depending on village demand. This was certainly not the case, as we shall see in a moment. But it did mean that retailers could get their stock of bolts, padlocks and many other metal goods required for housebuilding and agriculture directly from village producers, and without going to town. And individuals could order such items as iron gates or metal grills from one of the many local smiths without having to order and transport them from town.

Labour and trainees in village businesses

Only 89 of the 139 businesses in the enterprise survey of the village admitted to having workers or trainees. In total, these 89 said they had 215 people working for them (50 trainees and 165 workers). This was a rather different picture than was received from the approximately 30 owners amongst those who had applied to the Ministry as jua kali applicants; they had admitted to having a total of 172 people working for them (102 trainees and 70 workers). This difference in the owner-worker : trainee ratio of about 2 : 1 workers and/or trainees to one owner in the larger survey versus almost 6 : 1 in the smaller survey can partly be explained by the fact that, through the element of self-selection, the smaller sample of Ministry applicants did, with some exceptions, probably focus on some of the larger enterprises, and especially included the metalworking industries which appear to have had much larger numbers of workers and trainees.

Thus although the enterprise survey had picked up significantly fewer metalworking industries than the Ministry forms had picked up individual metalworkers, those firms they had identified had large labour forces, by village, or indeed town, standards. One (Gathea's) had five trainees and six workers, another (Kariuki's) had seven workers and five trainees, and the third (Kahindi's) had four workers and two trainees. In other words, three enterprises had a total of 29 workers or trainees altogether. It must be remembered in talking about labour force that this is a very loose concept. It most certainly should not be thought of as suggesting that these three enterprises, or many of the others, have anything remotely like a fixed number of employees or apprentices.

When an owner has a contract for so many hundred metal items to be delivered to a wholesaler in town, then workers will be re-hired, trainees that were not around will suddenly re-appear. What had been a dead-looking yard will spring to life. When there is no contract, it may be easy to overlook the fact that there is even an industry present in that little backyard at all. The same is even more true of those micro-enterprises that really operate on a labour contract basis. Thus there are plumbers and masons in and around Githiga, a few of whom had applied for jua kali registration. But it should not be surprising that their 'businesses' were not noticed by the enterprise survey. Usually there is no office and no sign advertising a mason or a plumber's presence, nor even a workshop. Such trades are normally operated just through networks of contacts. In a village situation, the plumber most certainly would not have a whole series of bathroom or kitchen fixtures in stock. He could not afford to keep such stock. In fact, in the ordinary labour contract, all such items would be bought directly by the individual giving the plumber a contract, and the plumber would then only negotiate a 'labour contract' just to do the job. And when he got such a contract he would know who would be available as a mate or as a trainee.

As invisible as the plumbers, painters and masons, as far as business premises are concerned, are the quite substantial number of people, usually young men, who can be hired for the digging of pit latrines, bore holes or septic tanks. In 1993 for example it was possible easily to identify some ten young men in Githiga who were ready to turn to this type of labour on a regular basis (Nene, personal communication, 1993).

Specialization and diversity in village enterprises

Another difficulty with producing a really accurate profile of a village from an enterprise perspective is that it is not always possible to allocate an individual to a single, particular trade type, and thus be able to say that there are so many welders or cycle repairers, or tailors in the area. Quite a number of individuals deliberately have more than one trade or activity that they are able to practise, again depending on what is demanded. It is, in this connection, interesting to note how many of the businesses in the enterprise survey admitted to carrying out multiple activities. A few examples will illustrate this tendency:

Welding, bicycle repair and clothes repair
Dry-cleaning and clothes dyeing
Battery charge and cycle repair
Shoe repair and agrochemicals
Retail shop and shoe seller
Household utensils and tailoring
Bar and butchery (very common)

Apart from these, there is the much larger number of people, as has been mentioned already, who are basically dedicated to farming but who also do a small amount of many different non-farm activities. One aspect of the scale of this can be seen in the number of men and women who appear on the regular market days on the village green.

Conclusions on jua kali data available from two samples

This first view of the village, from the angle of these two listings, takes us some way to answering the questions with which this chapter began. To the question about whether the village would be able to attract more skilled young people to operate from it, the answer would seem to be yes. We have noted that a very significant number of the new businesses in the village were associated with young people, and it is also interesting that more than half of those who used the Ministry jua kali forms to say that they wanted to start a business, but had not already done so, were also young. Seven of the nine such applicants were 32 years or under.

As far as the question about trade diversification is concerned, there certainly seemed to be new operations that had moved into the village during the 1980s and early 1990s, and which were not present when this village was surveyed in 1972–4 (King, 1977: 171). Paintmaking and maize-milling would be two of these. But a lot of the new activities amongst those listed in Table 4.7 are really more in the service sector than in production. These would include music store, Post Office, dry-cleaning, secondhand clothes, insurance, agrochemicals and curios. Also where there had only been one or two operators in the early and mid-1970s, there were now many more. This was particularly marked with tailors and metalworkers.

Another factor that was intended to have some impact on skills and attitudes (whether in the village or the town) was the local school which like all others in Kenya had been exposed to the dictates of the new, much more vocationalized curriculum from the mid-1980s. We shall return to its possible impact in Chapter Five.

But perhaps the most significant question, however, was what had happened to the trades already in the village in the 1970s and which had been joined by others in the same trade category. What evidence was there of technological development? In *The African Artisan* (King, 1977), for instance, a good deal of attention was paid to the question of whether the emergent informal sector industries would continue to spread horizontally, with more people making basically the same products in more places, or whether there would be any evidence of vertical integration in terms of products and skills, which would result in there being substantial product development. Would the technological confidence that had allowed Africans to take over several of the originally Indian skills in East Africa get stuck at a rather low level of technical capacity?

It was hoped that by looking in more detail at the character of one of the very trades that had been examined in the early 1970s, some insights might be gained into some of the possible trajectories of skill and product development. It was also thought useful to examine one of the trades where women were more in evidence.

A more qualitative analysis of Githiga's metalworking skills

First, a word on the feel of this sector in the village economy. Unlike what is sometimes said of the informal sector, most of the village workshops are literally 'backyard industries'. They operate both in the shop itself and they spill out into the yard. Nor are they in temporary sites, just waiting to be moved on by officious police. The buildings, whether of stone or of wood, are on regular plots, set properly on the side of the few streets in the village. The only exception to this order is Mutang'ang'i's yard which is quite extensive (see below).

The actual number of working establishments seems to alter from time to time, as has been suggested in the very different numbers of enterprises and individuals reported by the two different samples or surveys. We have suggested that this may have a good deal to do with the presence and absence of orders. The result is that sometimes a shop and its abutting backyard are quite deserted with just a series of hand-operated punching, cutting and bending machines standing idle. At other times, this row of machines, tightly squeezed into the small shop premises, are being worked at full speed, and there may be as many as six to twelve young men (or recent school leavers) working on them.

We shall turn now to see if through a more detailed analysis of entrepreneurship in metal work we can answer some of the questions about its past and future direction.

Four different metalwork businesses in Githiga

Compared to the larger group of men who we noted were as many as 17, according to the Ministry's applicants for jua kali status, we had selected just four individuals for more intensive interviews. It is worth noting that at the time none of the four would appear to have registered with the Ministry. Two of these were metalworkers from the 1970s, Mutang'ang'i and Donald Gitau Kagotho; they were both from the same, traditional blacksmith family. The older of the two, Mutang'ang'i, had featured very prominently in *The African Artisan* (King, 1977) as the source of skills for many of the younger skilled metalworkers. Apart from what was learnt at his father's hands, a good deal of what might be termed the application of smithing to modern technology appears to have been picked up through a six-year attachment to a white settler farm in the 1940s, and through an informal apprenticeship there to the Italian foreman who was responsible for the maintenance of (and doubtless essential improvization with) all farm machinery. This was the only structured access to skill that he experienced, and conceptually it needs to be classified as originating from the formal sector of the economy. Once Mutang'ang'i was back in the 'reserves' as they were termed in the colonial period, the younger people who learnt from him were gaining a version of the technologies that had been available on the settler estate, without the electricity and also, perhaps, without some of the wider technical knowledge that an Italian tradesman would have acquired in Europe. (Mutang'ang'i had only four years of schooling in a Kikuyu Independent school.)

One of the issues that we shall note in a number of very different settings is the vexed question of skill transfer. Is the model we are working with one in which a person acquires skills through his employment in the so-called modern sector of the economy, and then seeks to utilize these within the constraints of his or her own enterprise in the informal sector? That enterprise is not so fully capitalized as the one that was the source of the skills and technologies, and so inevitably only a narrower version of the original range of skills can be deployed. It is these skills which are in turn taught to the trainees who come to assist. And with their trainees again, it may well be a narrower version still of the skills that were available at the source.

In the case of the younger relative, Gitau, (with four years of secondary education, not just four years of primary) he appears to have had no direct employment in any formal sector firm at all, but to have acquired most of his skills, from the late 1970s, in the jua kali sector in Nairobi, in the company of several of the other Githiga people who had decided to operate there rather than in the village. (Some of these we have already encountered in Gikomba.) His father had spent most of his working life on a settler coffee estate and had become expert at the construction of entire coffee grading systems which the farm had sold to other farmers. In the process, some basic machinery had been acquired, and it was this that his son inherited when he moved back to Githiga, and installed himself in premises right in the set of shops and workshops that go round three sides of the village square.

The third metalwork man, Gathea, had a very different skill development experience. This, too, illustrates that there is no single highway to micro-enterprise in Kenya. He had a year in the original African trade school at Kabete, but had to drop out for lack of fees. So he can scarcely be looked at as an example of an institutionally trained micro-entrepreneur. He also had a year-and-a-half in a vehicle body-building firm, but for most of his working life he had been a driver for the Ministry of Education. Until he retired in 1983, he was used to driving ministers and permanent secretaries, but it increasingly made him feel that it was degrading to be commanded by younger men, who were there, in the backseat, just by reason of their longer education. He accordingly began to do what was commonplace amongst a whole series of different people who had worked for years in the formal sector – he began to make plans to start on his own, by accumulating capital. He started out on his own in 1984.

The fourth metal businessman, Thuita, was somewhat different again. He also had long-term employment in the formal economy from the time of Kenya's Independence in 1964, but unlike Gathea it was in a series of firms that did offer some anticipation of the technical and mechanical skills that he would eventually use some 20 years later. These included working in Indian firms, in long-distance transport, and in farm machinery. He too became increasingly sure that he should begin to prepare for his own business, and from as early as the mid-1970s was 'straddling', in the sense of looking for jobs that would allow him also to develop his own business. This seems to be a particular strategy with many people who finally make the move to setting up their own business. They set it up gradually, first buying some tools or a bench so they can work at the weekends and evenings, then taking a bigger contract or two, then perhaps looking for a formal sector job that allows them more leeway. They finally move into their own business full-time. But the date that researchers (including ourselves) are always asking for – the single start date of the business – is really rather artificial. For the person has in fact been becoming self-employed over a period of years. Self-employment is a long-term process rather than a one-off event.

The relationship between employment and self-employment
This characteristic, shared by three of these metalworkers, of moving from

being an employee to being self-employed needs some careful consideration by those who are concerned with developing a healthy business sector.
First, it may suggest, in looking at the rural areas, that one of the most
effective preparations for self-employment is employment. We pointed to
this also in our analysis of Gikomba. But the experience of employment
should be viewed in two different senses. In some cases, e.g. Mutang'ang'i
and Thuita, the period of employment provided an exposure to the very
skills and technologies, some of which they would take and develop in their
own businesses. In the case of Gathea, the experience of being a driver
was not important for anticipating the character of the future business.
Rather, the employment experience intensified the view that there were
likely to be more financially rewarding activities elsewhere. Some of the
jobs in the formal economy, moreover, have probably failed to maintain
their attractiveness 30 years into the Independence period, as compared
with such a job taken in the year of Independence. For some people, as
they begin the process of diversifying into self-employment, such jobs
probably act more like insurance policies than the major source of income.
They may offer access to health provision, retirement benefits, holidays –
though these benefits are not generous, and they cover only a small
proportion of those counted as being in the so-called formal sector. They
also offer some security, and the relative certainty of being paid a small
sum monthly as opposed to perhaps much larger sums on an irregular
basis. And like a club, they also offer contacts. The latter was clearly
important in the case of Gathea, as his passengers were frequently high-
level civil servants or ministers.

The acquisition of technological confidence

The process of building technical capacity is very different from just turning
out more students who have taken science subjects at school. Those who
have been examining the origins of the discipline of technology (as
contrasted with science) talk about the importance of the acquisition of
figuring, designing and problem-solving skills – of the need to find a
solution to a challenge (Layton, 1994). It is something of this spirit that
can be seen in the approach of some of these metalworkers as they seek
both to acquire and refine technologies.

At its most basic, it can be detected in the strategies followed by Gathea
to acquire the capacity to build his own machines for metalworking.
According to his own account, he purchased one of the basic, hand-
operated, cutting, punching and bending machines, took it to pieces and
then started to manufacture them himself. He did the same with some of
the jua kali products. He would purchase them, open them up, draw them
to the specific sizes, and then re-assemble them. These capacities to 'see
behind' a process, understand how it works, and improvise with available
materials to reproduce it are all central to technological ability.

In Gathea's case in the same year that he decided to go full-time into
his own business he had made three punch machines, two cutters and two

Fig. 4.3: One of the many Githiga metalworking shops, with a battery of hand-operated shearing and punching machines, for use in making building components, e.g. hinges, bolts etc.

Fig. 4.4: A group of rural jua kali metalworkers, with a zero-grazer and a bellows. Note the use of a factory coat by one.

Fig. 4.5: Mutang'ang'i (1972).

bending machines. What had been a very special capacity back in the early 1970s, known to only a handful of metalworkers such as Mutang'ang'i, could be picked up in a few months by an ex-driver with a flair, and could be put to work. It is probably also the case that getting into machine-making in Githiga where so many people had operated them in different small village industries, and many had made them would be much easier than setting out to do this in some other part of the country (see fig. 4.3). In other words what may be seen in a very small way in a single village in Kenya is the beginnings of an area of specialization. It may be qualitatively different from the flexible specialization identified in whole districts of Europe, India, or the Far East. But it may still be seen as a very basic example of this process whereby a technical community is built that can, metaphorically speaking, take in each other's laundry. Metalworking becomes over the years something that all Githiga young people – or rather all young men – get to know about, simply because they all experience it in some way, as casual labourers, helpers, trainees, producers etc.

Amongst the many who had over 30 years become expert in metalworking in this little village, there were, by 1993, groups who usually worked in Nairobi, but commuted to Githiga at night, and others who stayed in the village (see fig. 4.4). But it can be anticipated that across this group there would be a shared expertise on the sources of raw materials, on outlets, and, as important as anything, on the use of neighbours' machines for carrying out specialist operations. This does not imply that any such advice or assistance would necessarily be given free. But the question of payment is less important than the growth of a culture of specialization. And such a culture would include, of course, the availability of a ready supply of young men, both school-leavers and those still at school, who could be used as part-time workers. Unlike labour in other parts of the country, this group would tend to know how to adjust machines as they went out of line or needed alterations.

Mutang'ang'i's technological development, 1973-93

Mutang'ang'i was such an important source and affirmation of this technical capacity that it is worth looking a little more closely at whether he managed to continue to develop over the 20 years after we first met him in the early 1970s (see fig. 4.5), and whether his technology at the end of these two decades was really any different from the beginning. And if so, what had contributed to that difference.

In the years preceding the summer of 1974 when we last saw him at the end of our first period of research in Kenya, he was able to make (with his exclusively hand-operated machines for punching, cutting, and bending) bicycle carriers, and foreguards, and large runs of aluminium serving spoons. He had also developed the ability to make fence-post nails from scrap wire. In 1974 itself he had successfully developed the capacity to make a fodder-dicing machine that used a fly wheel, and this required much less labour than the very simple machine pictured in *The African Artisan* (1977: 131).

By the mid-1970s, Mutang'ang'i had reached a point where he was very anxious to get access to power tools. Yet this issue of access to hand tools versus power tools is often a major obstacle to aspiring jua kali. In fact, this transition from manual to power tools is one that still exercises the several bodies that are interested in assisting with the development of technology in the jua kali sector. As we shall note in the next chapter, some are by no means convinced that there is something natural about such a shift, and seem to be anxious to avoid too rapid an adoption of power tools.

Be that as it may, by 1977, Mutang'ang'i was very actively looking for a loan specifically to allow him access to power tools. In due course he was successful in acquiring one of some K.Sh.130,000 from the Industrial and Commercial Development Corporation (ICDC). He used it to get electrical grinders, drilling machines and power presses. And these in turn allowed him to make further machines. including electrically powered machine tools. His access to power tools coincided with the electrification of the village itself and several of the surrounding areas. So within the space of just a few years he had moved from a relatively simple hand-cutter of maize stalks to the much more complex flywheel model (based originally on a type that is very common in village India) and then to the attachment of an electric motor to this latest model.

The name given – whether by Mutang'ang'i or his relative, Peter Kagotho who we met in Gikomba – to this electrical model was 'zero-grazer'. The name, we noted in Chapter 2, underlined the link between the technology and local veterinary environment where people had begun to acquire 'grade cows' in order to increase milk production, but because of the shortage of land, the cows were largely kept in tiny paddocks, and fodder was brought to them rather than the other way round.

By the early 1990s, this electrical model was being made by both men, in Githiga and in Nairobi, and was selling for some K.Sh.20,000. It was a very good example of the agriculture-related capital goods that the 1986 Sessional Paper had been looking for. It fitted the differences in Kenya's environment, since it could be worked by hand or by power. It was also a technology that was naturally protected from cheap imports by the fact that it was not made commercially in most traditional exporting countries. And appropriately, it made use of secondhand electric motors, which themselves could be easily repaired or renewed.

The further electrification of Mutang'ang'i's yard came in 1984. With the clearance of the first loan, a second loan of K.Sh.500,000 was negotiated, this time with the Development Finance Company of Kenya (DFCK). It was for further power presses and other machinery. His purpose now was to make shovels, and on the basis of a very large order from Tanzania, he was able to negotiate a third loan of some K.Sh.600,000 for materials. Not enough is known about the arrangement of the order and its profitability, but the sheer scale of the operation and the loan money involved had meant that from 1984 he had been required to take on an accountant to keep an eye on his finances.

The role of Kenyan Indians as wholesalers (and sources) of jua kali technology

It may well have been that the large export order to Tanzania was due to the Kenyan Indian firm in Thika that Mutang'ang'i relied on for many of his orders. This firm also seems to have been ready to supply him with raw materials. As we noted in earlier chapters, this dependence on Kenyan Indians has been historically very important for the jua kali sector, even though much of the rhetoric surrounding jua kali represents the Indian manufacturing sector as one of the prime obstacles to jua kali development. The reality as we showed in Gikomba is perhaps a little different. The Indian wholesalers and retailers in Nairobi and other towns were some of the first merchants to recognize that the products from the informal sector in the early 1970s could undercut imported items or local factory-made products. It was, for example, Indians in the early 1970s who had placed the first orders with the first generation of Githiga metalworkers to try their luck in Nairobi in making such items as bicycle carriers and foreguards (King, 1977: 111).

Many African jua kali entrepreneurs talk of the importance of the Indian wholesalers' network as being extensive enough to place quite large orders, and sufficiently businesslike to pay on the nail, rather than keep them waiting for settlement. We have also seen, particularly in the chapter on Gikomba, that a substantial number of the African entrepreneurs are in a real sense 'Indian graduates'. They acquired all their technology and expertise from the Indian furniture, vehicle body-building, and metal fabrication firms. The difference between this type of technology transfer and that of the several agency and non-governmental initiatives to support technology-for-the-jua-kali-sector is that the Indian firms were simply operating as regular businesses, and not seeking to 'develop' African technologies. It may well be, however, that this kind of informal, business-based technology development is much more sustainable and therefore more successful in the long term than special short courses for technology upgrading of the sort that were discussed in Chapter 1 and will be looked at further in Chapter 5 on Education and Training.[1]

Mutang'ang'i's yard in 1993

From being a small compound with a few machines strapped on to poles, and with two labourers in 1974, his business had developed significantly in the subsequent two decades. By the early 1990s it took in a large area and, as can be seen from the accompanying photograph, it still had the look of a factory that was very different from a regular small-scale enterprise (see fig. 4.6, colour section). For one thing, although most of the machinery was under cover, and in this minimal sense was not under the direct hot sun (jua kali), it had not been transformed into an industry that was run in a stone building with permanent premises like many of those we have noted in Gikomba. Much of the machinery was really under corrugated iron sheeting rather than secured on concrete floors in solid buildings. One reason for this may be lack of the kind of security risk in a small village that there would be in a densely packed industrial suburb, such as Gikomba. But whatever the reason, the result is that Mutang'ang'i's machinery, technology, and current production and orders are pretty easily on view. They are not hidden away behind a nameless facade of an industrial building, as is the case with a few of the jua kali entrepreneurs in Nairobi.

Nor had electrification meant the end of the old hand-made machine tools. Indeed in the early 1990s, there were no less than 60 of the manually operated machines, and between eight and ten electrically powered machines (see fig. 4.7). It was very much a mixed technology mode that was being used. On the one hand the modern power machines had themselves been adapted, and on the other, there were manually operated machines that had had power added to them, such as the zero-grazers. But there were also machines such as his huge rotating drum for burnishing small metal components that were home-made and electrically powered (see fig. 4.8).

Compared to the two workers of the early 1970s, there had been 22 to 24 during the late 1980s. But as has been said above, on any day or week, the complement would depend a good deal on the work load and orders. On one of my visits an order had been received for some 10,000

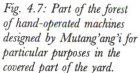

Fig. 4.7: Part of the forest
of hand-operated machines
designed by Mutang'ang'i for
particular purposes in the
covered part of the yard.

Fig. 4.8: A drum designed to
smoothe the edges of the
products, such as the hinges
in the wheelbarrow, prior to
painting.

steel 'knives' for use in weighing machines. On other occasions, there was some of the regular production of items for the building trade being carried out, such as T-hinges, washers etc.

Jua kali success and the jua kali dilemma in metalwork

Some of the technological learning that Mutang'ang'i had developed over more than 30 years, others such as Gathea, the retired ministry driver, were determined to acquire at high speed. This telescoping of what was necessarily a slow learning process with some of the original skill sources does seem to have gone particularly rapidly with Gathea. We left him in 1984 when he had already made seven manually operated machines in his first year. Within another year he had bought a grinder and a drilling machine. In 1986 with the help of a loan or a grant from one of his Ministry contacts, he had a welding machine. With these he was able to diversify production into fodder-cutters, wheelbarrows, spades and slashers.

He continued buying machines (a second welding machine and a heavy-duty drilling machine), and with these he made more bending, cutting and punching machines for himself and for sale. In 1989 he purchased two grinders. It was also when he began deliberately to try and further diversify production. In two areas: first he sought to develop capacity in making lorry springs which required understanding of foundry and smithing skills; secondly, he began to devote time and energy to a nail-making machine. This was something that several of the other Githiga smiths had also tried at various times, either in Nairobi or in the village.

By 1989, he had already made three attempts at nail-making. The last of these was a success in terms of product, but the process was just too slow to come anywhere near mass production. He had come to the conclusion, therefore, that he would need to acquire nail manufacturing machinery which was currently monopolized by the Kenyan Indians. But despite trying to use his contacts in the Ministry to assist, he had made no progress, and so was coming back to the idea that he would need to try and make machinery himself. To this end he was seeking to acquire photographs and blueprints, and making contact with other jua kalis who had more electrical knowledge to assist in making the machinery. Here, therefore, is a very good example of an entrepreneur who has rapidly acquired the basic technological know-how to reproduce the kinds of products which a number of Githiga metalworkers had first made. But he remained sceptical of the profits in some of these, and feels he is able to illustrate just how small a profit margin if anything there is in some of the jua kali products. As a consequence he has been seeking to go beyond the regular products, into an area – nail-making – where he would be competing with just a few larger firms.

In a way this is the jua kali dilemma. On the goods that can be made within the admittedly moving frontier of jua kali technology, there is often fierce competition. That competition, as we saw in Gikomba in the wood lathe business, is so intense that what was virtually a monopoly one year can become the common property of many small-scale manufacturers a few months or a year later. Such is the speed with which young trainees wish to become independent, and such is the difficulty of protecting a new design against the technological capacity of others. But in the new areas of production where it might be attractive to move, there is often a very different kind of competition – in getting access to much more modern machinery or to regular supplies of cheap raw material. For some basic products, it would seem that developing the machinery locally, using some of the accessible technology, is a feasible proposition. But for other products which are already being mass-produced in Europe or East Asia by highly specialized continuous process machinery, it would seem that there is a real entry barrier to local manufacture. As we also noted in Gikomba, the machine tools needed for certain kinds of local manufacture would be so expensive that it would not make financial sense to take out a loan to import them. It would simply be too costly to service the loan.

Where the Githiga metalworkers and their counterparts in town have been successful is in producing large quantities of very basic metal components for the building trade. The demand for housing has been rising dramatically, but more significant has been the demand for higher quality dwellings, with windows, secure rooms, and all the appurtenances of locks, hinges, bolts, stays, guttering, and plumbing. These product markets have offered niches where local manufacture, even if not to the standard of imported equivalents, has proved quite adequate for safety and consumer requirements.

Tailors and dressmakers:
another dimension of Githiga's jua kali

Thus far we have focused on the metalworking side of Githiga, for it is a very important characteristic of this small village. However, it would be appropriate to refer to one of the other trade groups, and since there are no women involved in metalwork, it is worth taking the trade of tailoring since that certainly is accessible to both sexes. It is also the second largest of the occupations in the village, according to the enterprise survey.

The other similarity with metalwork is that there are a good number of associated clothing-related activities. In Githiga, for example, apart from the tailors, both male and female, there were in 1992, no less than five dry-cleaners, five secondhand clothing sellers, three knitting machine owners, and at least one person concentrating on selling ready-made clothes. All in all, therefore, the clothing sector is quite significant. Nor should the number of tailoring establishments on the village streets count as the tailoring total. Altogether these might come to about 13 or 14, if the numbers from the enterprise survey and those from the Jua Kali applicants are merged. But tailors in the village estimate that there would be at least that number again operating from their homes.

Figs. 4.9 and 4.10: Two of the brand new tailoring shops in Githiga, built in stone with metal doors.

It is intriguing to see that the rather large number of tailoring establishments goes along with there being no less than five secondhand clothes sellers. It is often said, with a good deal of evidence, that the latter directly undermine the custom for tailors, but none of the tailors interviewed in depth hinted at this challenge at all. Indeed, it was conspicuously some of the new tailoring firm such as Njuno's and Sunshine Outfitters that were operating out of brand new premises (see figs. 4.9 and 4.10). This could suggest an optimism about the tailoring profession.

In one way, tailoring seems to stand at a very different end of the spectrum from the metal industries. For one thing it seems quite commonplace for would-be tailors or dressmakers to attend a college for a few months. There are many varieties of these, both those connected to particular machines, such as the Singer school in Nairobi, and other private colleges. This is not to say that many would-be tailors do not actually train on the job; this too is common, with trainees paying some K.Sh.350 a month in training fees, or some K.Sh.1,800–2,000 for a complete training.

The other difference is that unlike candlemaking or tinsmithing where the initial capital may be as little as a few hundred shillings, and unlike Kamukunji where we noted that almost half of the entrepreneurs started out with less than K.Sh.1,000 (and often a good deal less), the absolute minimum equipment needed to enter tailoring is the price of a sewing machine, and some money for materials. The machine can differ a good deal in price, but it seems that it is not uncommon in the case of a daughter or a wife, for a father, a husband or a mother to make this available as a gift or as a loan, as some examples from Githiga make plain:

Her mother loaned her money to buy her first machine, which cost about K.Sh.18,000.

Her father bought her her first sewing machine in 1988.

Her father bought her a butterfly machine for K.Sh.2,200.

She saved between late 1987 and early 1988. The cost of the machine she was saving for was K.Sh.6,300. She first found a deposit of K.Sh.2,200, and acquired the machine.

This may not be the same with men who are entering the trade. But Josephat Kirumba, who runs Njuno's along with his wife, bought his first three machines at K.Sh.8,000, K.Sh.15,000, and K.Sh.6,000 respectively. Some of the other examples we have from Githiga are principally from some of the older tailors, and they appear to have rented first and then bought, while some of the younger men seem to have raised money through other jobs and bought their machines outright. One of these older men, Muhoro, casts light on the way things have changed since the 1950s. He actually rented his first machine at K.Sh.50 a month in 1957 from a European, A.J. Stephen, who had a shop for tailoring in Kiambu town nearby. Another Githiga man, Kinyanjui, also rented first at K.Sh.60 a month, and at the same time started saving to buy his own machine. He bought his first machine, a secondhand Singer, for K.Sh.1,800 in 1978.

As to whether tailors are really jua kali, the women on the whole do not seem to consider themselves jua kali. One in particular said that she does not think she is a jua kali and would not like to join the association. She believes that jua kali are simply metalworkers. On the other hand, Susan Wanjiru said she would quite like to join the Society. From the group of 59 Githiga artisans who did actually fill out the forms for jua kali status, there were in fact four women tailors. Amongst male tailors who were interviewed there was also disagreement about joining, with a few thinking it might help them to get plots, and others thinking it would lead to more competition amongst themselves.

As far as products are concerned, it seems clear that increasingly the tailoring and dressmaking shops are catering to a more selective and discerning audience. Though there are still some standard items like school uniforms, the Githiga tailors have to show that they are up with the times, with pattern and design books available from which their clients can select a particular line of fashion. The more successful tailors are ready to diversify, combining some ready-made with repair and making of their own.

On the question of income, several admit to getting around K.Sh.4,500 to K.Sh.5000, while one man estimates that he gets as much as K.Sh.9,500 net. Doubtless for the many tailors and dressmakers without premises, working from their homes, part-time, incomes are very much lower and more irregular, but if these estimates are correct, even K.Sh.4,000 to K.Sh.5,000 sounds a good deal better than the K.Sh.2,000 our candle-makers were getting in Starehe.

Conclusions on revisiting rural jua kali

The conclusions from these reviews of the range of skills being deployed in this particular rural area are, we have said, encouraging. They point to a sharp rise in the range of services, products and industries available locally in the village over a 20-year period. The indications were that the increasing interest in entering business was not something that had happened many years ago; a lot of evidence would suggest that there is a continuing movement into self-employment. There could well be more services such as a bank in due course, since that would in addition to the recently established little Post Office, allow for more rapid communication and for some savings activities to be undertaken in the village itself rather than through the nearest larger town, Kiambu, some 20 minutes away (see fig. 4.11).

Apart from electricity, there is one service that has probably been very important to the encouragement of rural enterprise and that has been

Figs 4.11: The Post Office arrived in Githiga in 1990.

Fig. 4.12: Githiga, a small village, is linked by excellent rural roads within Kiambu. Note the lorries, and the line of matatus at the end of the road, waiting to fill up.

rural roads. Githiga is well connected to all the other smaller and larger villages nearby, and it is well linked to the district headquarters of Kiambu, and beyond that to Nairobi. But it is not the roads alone that allow Mutang'ang'i and others to connect with wholesalers in Thika, Nairobi and elsewhere, or several people to commute for their work in Nairobi. It is the availability of lorries for transporting materials, and the presence of large numbers of relatively low cost, competitive matatus, carrying people in stages between Githiga and Kiambu, and then others between Kiambu and Nairobi (see fig. 4.12). Obviously these services and infrastructural supports are assisted by the relatively dense population levels in these agricultural areas. There are, by contrast, many parts of the country where rural produce cannot reach the market very readily, and there are whole countries in the rest of Africa where the sheer absence of sufficient road networks and vehicles would make the very idea of commuting an impossibility.

Although Githiga is only some 40 km away from Nairobi, it could be 400 km away as far as there being much impact of what in NGO and agency circles in Nairobi seem like a multitude of jua kali projects and programmes are concerned. It is very doubtful that there is any single NGO project or initiative aimed at jua kali development in or around the village, and hence for this small part of Kenya the multiplicity of jua kali support plans, many of them externally conceived and funded, has had little or no direct relevance. This is not surprising. There are many much more needy parts of the country where NGOs can perhaps be of some assistance in encouraging income-generating projects or providing for micro-enterprise credit.

But the availability of roads, electricity, banking, transport or appropriate schemes for credit may all be of value in creating a supportive environment for the exercise of small-scale enterprise. None of them may be sufficient on its own or in combination with others unless there is a predisposition also to enter the world of trade and industry, and unless there exist systems for orienting and socializing young people into the culture of work. We shall be looking in the next chapter at the formal education system's contribution to the knowledge and skill base necessary for successful self-employment. But in doing so, we must be aware that the attitudes to work and to achievement are probably not principally fashioned by school nor by the provision of services. They are very powerfully affected by the ethic of the family and of the surrounding society.

In this sense, we need to be aware that we are talking of a small village, which although on the edge of the settled areas was predominantly a Kikuyu-speaking community. Doubtless it shared with other parts of what the colonial government called Kikuyuland some of the very features that Marris and Somerset captured so perceptively when they sought to analyse the traditions of business in Mahiga Location, less than an hour's journey north of Githiga, and still very much part of the Kikuyu heartland:

160

But whatever the individual circumstances which characterized the origins of these men, the most important factor was the entrepreneurial values of society as a whole, which gave scope to ability and enterprise. These values derived from the nature of Mahiga economy. Throughout the nineteenth century, it was still a frontier economy where an ambitious young man could hack his way into the forest and ... look back over his shoulder with pride at the land he had cleared. Inherited land rights mattered less than the industry with which it was cultivated ... Prosperity was therefore an individual achievement, won by hard work and good husbandry, and this was reflected in the distribution of status....Nor were these qualities seen as a natural endowment. If a man achieved little, he was scorned for his idleness without considering what his abilities fitted him to do. Wealth, ability and hard work emerged in a single conception of worth. Children were encouraged to compete for status while they were still young. (Marris and Somerset, 1971: 41)

These words were written almost 25 years ago, just before the concept of the informal sector became internationally known by the ILO Mission's visit to Kenya, and its discovery of this huge range of activity that lay outside the so-called modern sector of the economy. The term jua kali did not get used for a long time thereafter. But it is intriguing that in many ways the core values of jua kali (hard work, ingenuity, self-reliance, individualism) are the very items that Marris and Somerset pick out for the Kikuyu. The formal encouragement of a jua kali approach to work, by a non-Kikuyu president like Moi, may produce different resonances in different parts of the country.

And doubtless the same is true of the formal school system which has increasingly been called to adjust children's values to the realities and challenges of self-employment. This may well be a message that is heard by young people differently in different parts of the country. We turn, however, to examine the role of education and training in the creation of self-employment in the next chapter.

Note

1. The Asian industrial community is not monolithic, but a notable exception to this lack of targeted jua kali training projects would be the initiatives of the Asian Foundation, which, amongst other things, set up a Hawkers' Market in Nairobi in 1991.

Five

〳〳〳

Education & Training
for Self-employment
in Kenya

In the 20 years between the ILO Employment Mission to Kenya in 1971 and the publication of the *Sessional Paper No. 2 of 1992 on Small Enterprise and Jua Kali Development in Kenya* (Kenya, 1992a), an enormous amount has been written about education and training in Kenya. Our purpose in this chapter is not of course to review this general output, but to analyse the extent to which the education and training systems have changed in ways that may have some direct impact on options for self-employment and micro-enterprise. Kenya has often led the rest of Africa in educational innovation, in educational self-reliance, and in access to higher and higher levels of education. But arguably in respect of seeking to orient its system to new kinds of self-employment and vocationalization, it has also done more than most others. Even within this narrower perspective on education and training there has been a considerable outpouring of literature on Kenya over the years. For instance, in *Jua Kali Literature: An Annotated bibliography* (K-REP, 1993a), there are no less than 81 items that fall under the heading 'Education, training and entrepreneurship'.

As we look at some of the major dimensions of this attempt to make education and training both anticipate and reflect the policies on small-scale enterprise and jua kali development, we shall refer where appropriate to the experience of the jua kali we have been visiting and revisiting.

Schooling and self-employment

Vocationalization of basic education for self-employment in Kenya
There are several ways in which governments in the last decade and more have tried to alter schooling and training so as to affect employment. Some of these could be captured by the term vocationalization, and in these

initiatives, the curriculum whether in primary, secondary school or tertiary education has been altered in order to give it a greater orientation to work. The varieties of vocationalization are large, but they have tended, as the term itself might imply, to be most obvious in situations such as Commonwealth Africa, where there was not a distinct vocational school system of any magnitude. In such countries, where there might only have been a handful of trade or technical schools, there has been considerable interest in developing a more vocational orientation. In this respect these Commonwealth countries have not had very different experiences from the UK. Here too there had been no strong tradition of separate vocational and technical schools such as are commonplace in parts of Western and Eastern Europe, and yet in the 1980s there was a large-scale attempt to give a more technical orientation to the regular schools through the Technical and Vocational Education Initiative (TVEI).

There was a parallel in Kenya. Influenced originally by the UK, it also had no separate tradition of vocational and technical education but just a very small number of trade and technical schools. Only a handful of our *jua kali*, such as Peter Njeroge and Peter Kagotho had gone to these in Machakos and Kabete respectively. To these schools there were added in the 1960s and 1970s, with World Bank and Swedish funding, some schools that were termed 'Industrial Arts' or 'diversified' in the sense that they had workshops for wood, metal and electricity, as well as facilities for home economics and agriculture. Because these schools were high cost and dependent on donor-financing, they never reached large numbers of children (Lauglo, 1985). Nevertheless, these two types continued until the large-scale curricular and structural reform of the mid-1980s.

Running alongside this relatively small, donor-financed version of technical and diversified education, there has long been a local strain of policy in Kenya which has felt that in both the basic cycle and the secondary school system as a whole there should be a substantial practical emphasis. This goes back to the recommendations of the National Committee on Educational Objectives and Policies in 1976, and the Sessional Paper on the same topic in 1978, which had suggested that a whole range of new subjects should be found in the basic cycle, including business education, home economics, Swahili and traditional arts and crafts. Nor were these to be electives, but rather they should be part of the nationally examined core subjects. Similar recommendations were made for the secondary cycle (Kenya, 1978).

What was unusual about these recommendations was that they were linked very explicitly to new employment and technology policies that went back to the recommendations of the ILO Mission at the beginning of the 1970s, and argued for legislative and administrative measures that would abolish harassment and encourage growth in the informal sector (King, 1990c). In fact, it was exactly eight years later in December 1984 that the government moved decisively to put into place a new structure and content of education in what was called the 8-4-4 System of Education.

This with its eight years of basic, four of secondary school and four of university finally put into place in 1985 a curriculum that it was hoped would 'impart the kind of attitude more in tune with the development of the rural areas where 80 per cent of our people live' (Kenya, 1984a: 39). The new *Syllabuses for Kenya Primary Schools* (1984) made it quite clear that the curriculum was concerned with skills, knowledge, expertise and personal qualities for a growing modern economy. But it added this important emphasis: 'The country requires trained manpower, both self-employed and in paid employment' (Kenya, 1984b: ix).

The notion that schools should prepare young people both for employment and for self-employment, and that both sectors offered opportunities for modern incomes and wealth creation is one of the distinguishing features of the Kenyan education reform (King 1990b). By contrast in Tanzania with its 'Education for Self-reliance', it had been difficult not to conclude that there were modern sector jobs, protected by the selective entrance to secondary school and then for the great majority there was terminal primary education followed by work in the rural areas (King, 1984; Buchert, 1994). The 8-4-4 Reform produced a whole series of basic education syllabuses including Home Science, Art and Craft, Science, Agriculture, and Business Education where there was a strong emphasis on the awareness of income opportunities and of the notion that self-employment could mean making as much money as being in a salaried job. These syllabuses were in due course translated into textbooks and there was suddenly a whole range of new information about young people and micro-enterprises being offered through the regular school system.

Some of the flavour of this may be worth offering. For example, in one of the new subjects, Business Education, here is some typical exhortation being offered through a textbook to Standard VI (i.e. 12-year-olds):

> All that one needs is to be organized either as an individual or as a group and start a business. You do not need to stay idle in your father's home simply because you have no job in which you are paid regularly. You should actively keep yourself busy by engaging yourself in one of these activities. In other words, when you finish school, the question should not be: WHO WILL EMPLOY ME BUT HOW WILL I EMPLOY MYSELF? In many cases, you will find that self-employment is more paying than being employed by another person. There are many self-employed people in the rural areas who are very successful. (Gatama, 1986: 66; emphasis in the original)

This particular text goes on to argue that there are many more job openings in the rural areas than in town. And, as if the syllabus committees had known that it had often been said that small businessmen did not seem to know about or to keep accounts, the Standard VI texts give full information about keeping records and different types of personal records and personal budgets (Gatama, 1986; Waithaka, 1987).

But it is not only Business Education that is concerned with the business of being self-employed. Similar encouragement runs through the Home Science texts, Agriculture, Art Education and Craft Education, as well as

Primary Science. Here, for example, is an excerpt from one of the best written and most innovative of the Primary Science texts (Standard VIII):

> Soon you will be leaving primary school. You will have to decide what to do. There are many possibilities:
>
> 1. Self-employment
>
> This means you work for yourself. For example, you could start a small business such as making tools, rearing chickens, trading or growing vegetables...
>
> 2. Finding out about Self-employment
>
> To be self-employed, you need to have courage and skill. You need to work hard. However, many people enjoy working for themselves, being their own boss. Many of the following people are self-employed: mechanics, builders, watch-menders, taxi-drivers, tailors, fish-sellers, plumbers, traders, craftsmen, electricians, shoe repairers, potters. Find out what small businesses are needed in your area... (Berluti, 1985)

One of the problems about inserting a great deal of what might be termed 'developmental knowledge' in the primary school curriculum is that, even with the advantages of a progressive examination system (for which Kenya has been justifiably proud), it is difficult to know what happens to all this potentially valuable information (King, 1989b; Eisemon, 1989). There was already within a year or two of its being implemented, a good deal of critical comment on the impact of all these new subjects with their demands for practical experimentation and space in the crowded timetable. Indeed, the Presidential Working Party on Education and Manpower Training for the Next Decade and Beyond (which led to the *Sessional Paper No. 6 of 1988 on Education and Manpower Training* [Kenya, 1988c]) had looked carefully at the evidence of how the new system was bedding down. But it certainly did not retreat from the decision to ensure a measure of vocational education for all, both in primary and secondary education. In fact, as a result of the reforms, the proportion of time allocated to broadly vocational subjects in the upper primary schools was no less than 34 per cent, and that has continued to be the case until the present (1995).

The original intent of the reform had been that the practical subjects actually be examined both for their academic and their practical content. This suggested that pupils would actually be examined for their ability to make such things as simple tinsmith items, a blouse or a shirt, and much else. Because of the disparity in tools and equipment and workshop space, it has always proved problematic to carry out national examination of the practical side of these practical subjects. An interesting illustration of the problems of the practical examinations is that the tinsmiths whom we met in an earlier chapter reported that there was always an increased seasonal demand for their simple little tin-lamps from pupils wishing to provide evidence of their practical skills!

In Githiga Primary School in particular, four years after the reform had been implemented, it is perhaps typical of the difficulty of doing in school, for all children, what is commonplace in the self-employment setting for some, that teachers should be appreciative of the reforms but critical about their practical challenges:

> Many practical things are not practised because of the cost or the lack of the materials. Thus in Standard VII, they are meant to make pajamas, but many children cannot afford the material, and they are kept off school for that reason. Accordingly we only teach them the stitches. The smaller items are easier; and so with the tea-cloth which is only 1/4 metre of cloth, they can do that in school.

> There is the same problem with the woodwork. No timber. They are supposed to make some basic items. But because we have few tools, and no timber, we just show them the joints.

> In Standard VIII for Home Science, we are at the moment trying to collect enough flour to make cakes, but it is difficult.

> In Agriculture in fact quite a lot of the families do not have land – even in Githiga. So they cannot try things out practically; and the school has no room for practical activities.

> Business Education – they do enjoy it in the classroom. And now they do have some ideas about business that they did not have before. But unless they can put it into practice, they wont be able to understand the things that are suggested.

> Finally, though primary school is now eight years and not seven, the children nowadays, as compared with the 1960s and 1970s, are not big enough to do jua kali practically. (Discussion with teachers, 2 August 1989, Githiga)

In 1995, it is now a full ten years since the implementation of the 8-4-4. But it is worth underlining the fact that this is a very short period for effective educational reform. For example, children who started in Standard I in 1985 would still not have finished their secondary education. And there would so far only be three cohorts who would have left primary school (eight years) after experiencing the whole of the new curriculum. Researchers, therefore, have only just been beginning to ask what has been the impact on these new generations of primary school leavers of one-third of their time being allocated (in upper primary school) to more vocational subjects. Equally, attention has been paid to the impact of the science curriculum. Understandably, assessment has been difficult. For instance one Kenyan researcher discovered that the new primary school curriculum accounted – at least on paper – for 21 out of the 22 skills that were judged essential for welding artisans in jua kali workshops. But it was very difficult to be sure how many of these skills had actually been communicated in the very resource-poor settings of the basic cycle of education, such as we have referred to in Githiga (Digolo, 1990: 41–2).

Another researcher (Obura, 1993a) has investigated whether the new form of 8-4-4 education has been a 'help or a hindrance' to small and intermediate sized enterprises in Kenya. Her preliminary conclusions are that despite the lack of facilities, properly trained teachers and insufficient time allocations, there have certainly been some beneficial outcomes for the school leavers and the community from the reform. These would include:

A more positive attitude on the part of learners towards practical skills.

Increased recognition by many primary learners of the relationship between primary technical subject learning and employment in the informal sector.

Involvement of the wider community in technology learning at school, for example, in the agricultural activities.

The lessening of gender differentiated curriculum through compulsory core, nontraditional curriculum for everyone (including technical and Home Science subjects). (Obura, 1993a: 21–2)

The debate about the cognitive and attitudinal consequences for later work of the particular curriculum in primary and secondary schooling is going to continue for a long time. But it is at any rate worth noting that the Kenya Government has not been apparently influenced by the World Bank's very forceful argumentation against the vocationalization or 'diversification' of primary or secondary education. The Bank has commented that 'These "diversified" programmes are no more effective than academic secondary education in enabling graduates to enter wage or self-employment' (World Bank 1991: 9), and it has made a similar case for primary education. Indeed the Bank's general position, re-inforced by the latest draft of its *Priorities and Strategies for Education* (World Bank, 1995b), continues to be that because the social returns to specialized vocational education are much lower than those to general secondary education, vocational and technical education is best delayed as long as possible, ideally to the workplace, and is best preceded by general education (World Bank, 1995b). Admittedly, on this particular occasion it is talking about specialized vocational education, but it has in so many other places talked against the vocationalization of primary and secondary education that it is worth making the point that Kenya provides one of the most dramatic illustrations of following a reform process directly opposite to the tenor of Bank recommendations.

The fact is, as the Bank has itself admitted, that there hardly exist rigorous evaluations of such programmes (for the vocationalization of primary education); and yet the Bank argues very strongly against them. What research the Bank itself has supported in this arena is not strictly relevant to what the Kenya Government has done in the 8-4-4 system. Thus in Tanzania and Colombia, the Bank analysed the diversified versus the general secondary schools, and reached a judgement that the former were not cost effective (Psacharopoulos & Loxley, 1985). This research has been challenged for its relevance to Tanzania let alone to Kenya (King, 1987). In addition the Kenya government could legitimately argue that what they themselves have tried to put into place through the 8-4-4 system is not a high-cost, specialized vocational education system such as has been commonplace in Eastern Europe, but rather *a form of low-cost vocational orientation for all*. It could be emphasized, therefore, that Kenya's version of the vocational really treats it as an element of general education which every pupil should be exposed to. In addition in Kenya, because of the shortage of materials, tools, equipment and workshops, a good deal of the vocationalized curriculum – whether in primary or secondary school – is actually academic and theoretical, just as science education is frequently theoretical in developing countries.

While it may be legitimate to challenge the Kenya experiment on grounds of overcrowding the curriculum, and for expecting too much of children and their families in the practical areas, as Githiga teachers suggested above, it certainly cannot be dismissed as yet another version of the diversified school which the Bank believes it has judged and found wanting. Nor can much credence be given to attempts to correlate different kinds of primary school subjects with 'economic development' as has been tried by Benavot (1992). For although the latter research has suggested that science education has a positive and prevocational a negative correlation with economic growth, the same research has also had to admit that maths and language do not turn up positively in these correlations while aesthetic education does!

What probably has to be said is that a good deal of the research that links primary schooling to all kinds of positive developmental outcomes remains mystifying to many members of the policy community, and indeed to many researchers. The most heralded of these research results (many of them are associated with the World Bank) would claim that there are direct impacts of even four years of primary schooling on agricultural productivity, and there are equally renowned impacts on the reduction of female fertility (World Bank, 1988). And as far as the link between the informal sector and basic education is concerned, the Bank feels that basic education is probably one of the best ways to improve the productivity of the sector. Not of course basic education with a bias towards pre-vocational studies, but just plain basic education with a traditional emphasis on numeracy and literacy. Indeed in a Bank-financed study of apprenticeship in West Africa, one of the most important factors for improving productivity in the informal sector is said to be basic education:

> *Increased access to basic education.* This is critical in assisting wider entry to the microenterprise economy, particularly to the 'more attractive' activities and therefore to a more equitable widening of access to microenterprise opportunities. Completion of primary education has become a necessary, though not a sufficient, condition of apprenticeship. (Birks, S. *et al.*, 1992: 99)

Current research by the Bank which connects primary education to the jua kali development process ends up arguing that general primary education is highly beneficial to the informal sector, but not, paradoxically, those forms of primary education that seek explicitly to make the content of the primary school curriculum more relevant to self-employment (Riedmiller, 1994).

The Kenyan form of vocational secondary and post-secondary education

Unlike the Kenya of the 1970s where it was possible, as we have said, to identify at the secondary level a small number of technical secondary schools and also a slightly larger number of the diversified (industrial arts) schools, the 8-4-4 system heralded the end of both these as secondary level institutions. In their place, it was recommended that in the first two years all secondary schools offer Agriculture and one subject from either Home Science, Industrial Education, or Business Education. And in their last two years, they should still offer Agriculture as well as one other subject from Business Education, Home Science, Industrial Education or Religion or the Arts. In other words, two of the 13 subjects taken in junior secondary were explicitly vocational, and up to two of the nine subjects taken in the second two years of secondary schooling could be vocational (Kenya, 1984a). The 8-4-4 reform could therefore be seen as unifying the secondary education system, so that there were no longer just a small number of schools thought of as technical or industrial. Instead, all secondary schools now offer a modicum of what should probably be termed pre-vocational education, in the sense that these subjects are seen to be an important component of an all-round general education.

By contrast the more specialized institutions – the 19 technical secondary schools – have now become post-secondary, and have been renamed technical training institutes (TTIs). In this post-secondary role, they are now much closer to the 20 Institutes of Technology (ITs) which continue in the 1990s to have special connections with particular districts, reflecting their original self-help (*harambee*) beginnings.

The distinction between the element of some vocational orientation for all (and especially to Agriculture) in the general secondary school and the removal of the more specialized and intensive vocational preparation to institutions outside the formal school system is probably appropriate. The aims and objectives of the secondary school system are now more coherent, and it is likely that the clientele now entering the TTIs or the ITs are doing so much more because of their explicitly vocational or technical mission. In earlier days, as was shown in *The African Artisan* (King, 1977), it had always been unclear to potential employers whether entrants to the national technical secondary schools were more attracted by their being secondary schools than by their technical content.

Jua kali attitudes to school reforms for self-employment

It would be interesting to know more about jua kali artisans' attitudes to all these changes in schools, and especially when a great deal of the purpose of the reforms has been to make pupils more aware of opportunities in self-employment What is intriguing about those artisans for whom we do have data is that their attitudes towards schools are more concerned with school type (government versus *harambee* versus private) than they are with the content of the curriculum. This should perhaps not be surprising. School reforms in all countries take a very long time to reach small scale employers' attention, and Kenya is likely to be no exception.

What we can, however, note in some jua kali attitudes to schooling is a very shrewd investment approach. Schools, and especially secondary schools in Kenya, cost a good deal of money, and the good quality government schools are normally much less costly than the lower quality *harambee* schools, or *harambee* streams. Jua kali such as John Nene, we noted, were prepared to support their children if they managed in the competitive examinations to reach a government school, but they were not going to throw a great deal of hard-won money after a low-quality education, and then find that the children were no better off in employment terms; they would be better to learn a trade with their father rightaway, he had thought. In other words, jua kali like Nene are not even aware of what is meant to be the self-employment orientation of all schools, but are still operating on the basic contrast between government and *harambee*. The same was true of several of our other jua kali, including both the candlemakers, with their relatively modest incomes, and metalworkers. They were seeking to ensure that they covered the government school fees of their children, even if this was putting them under very severe pressure. And again the issue seemed to be good government school, and preferably boarding, as opposed to cheaper *harambee* day schools.

Effectively this means that jua kali with children of their own of school age seem little different from many other Kenyans in classifying schools according to their traditional capacity to provide better opportunities for a modern sector job. There is some evidence, however, from the next generation of jua kali who have just emerged from the exposure to 8-4-4 that they certainly appreciate some of what has been learnt, for example, about the pros and cons of starting a business.

Self-employment through vocational training institutes (VTIs)

It is important to make the point that not all vocational training institutions in Kenya are post-secondary. A very important layer of vocational training institute remains the youth polytechnics (YPs) which have traditionally drawn most of their trainees directly from primary schools, though many young people now enter them from secondary schools. In the early 1990s, there were no fewer than 573 YPs with an enrollment of some 40,000 students. Which means that they constitute by far the largest portion of post-school training in the country, and it is worth noting that they represent a much larger post-school training opportunity than is available in many other African countries.

170

Historically, the YPs emerged from the youth unemployment scare of the late 1960s, and they have continued to the present to have a very strong practical orientation towards skills for rural and urban employment or self-employment. Indeed it would be important, despite the YPs' emphasis now on formal certification, not to underestimate their long-standing contribution to making young people think about working independently in skilled occupations. However, along with all the post-secondary institutes they have increasingly been targeted by policies during the mid to late 1980s that expected technical and vocational training to be as much concerned with entrepreneurship skills as with technical skill content.

This particular strain of thinking was one that emerged from several of the key commissions and sessional papers in the 1980s. It was *Sessional Paper No. 1 of 1986: on Economic Management for Renewed Growth* which identified an inescapably central role for the informal sector, but linked to that policy objective a new mandate for many of the other sectors in the country. In the case of technical and vocational training, it was suggested that this would now 'play a crucial role in developing artisans, managers and entrepreneurs for the informal sector in both rural and urban areas' (Kenya, 1986: 57).

The same idea of inserting entrepreneurship skills on to technical content was picked up by the *Report of the Presidential Working Party on Education and Manpower Training for the Next Decade and Beyond*. By the time this reported in 1988, and had produced a sessional paper on Education and Manpower Training, it was clear that skills training for micro-enterprise was something considered very desirable for all trainees in vocational and technical institutions:

> The graduates from the vocational and technical institutions will need to understand how to establish and manage a business effectively. The Working Party noted that this aspect of training was lacking in the majority of training institutions. It also considers it important that they should be equipped with the necessary entrepreneurship skills including the art of communication, the principles of insurance, book-keeping, accounting and marketing, public relations, the concepts of exchange of goods and services and the demand and supply in the market economy. The Working Party, therefore, recommends that:
>
> > *Vocational and training institutions should include the teaching of entrepreneurship skills in their curriculum as an essential component of their training programmes.* (Kenya, 1988b: 41; emphasis in original)

This entrepreneurship education thread was going to be picked up almost immediately and given powerful support in the *Strategy for Small Enterprise Development in Kenya* (Kenya, 1989a), as we saw in Chapter 1. This highly collaborative initiative did clearly draw on some United States entrepreneurship models, but, as already noted, it created a groundswell of a common purpose in identifying the many different things that would have to change in all ministries, in NGOs, and in the banking and other

171

non-financial programmes if Kenya was really to develop an enterprise culture.

The main problems of Non-Financial Promotional Programmes were seen to be a lack of an enterprise culture in society, and an undeveloped entrepreneurship education. Consequently, it was argued that amongst much else entrepreneurship education should be introduced by 'developing an entrepreneurship curriculum for all vocational and technical institutions' (Kenya, 1989a: vii). We shall come in a moment to note how this idea has been followed through, but it needs underlining that these proposals from Kenya are very far from advocating self-employment as a way of urging the poor to stay in the rural areas. Rather, self-employment is frequently linked both to the notion of an enterprise culture and it is associated also with an aspiration for scientific and technological development. This linkage between enterprise and technology is captured in *Education and Manpower Training for the Next Decade and Beyond*:

> The challenges of the growth of the economy and industrialization call for indigenization of technology as a basis for self-reliance. Research will be intensified on indigenous technology and other technologies and their adaption, to meet the needs of the national economy including those of the 'jua kali' industry. (Kenya, 1988b: 5)

In other words, the emphasis within Kenya's encouragement of self-employment is probably much more toward the entrepreneurship ideal than the survival or subsistence forms of work on one's own account. This is also true of the thrust of the Business Education curriculum, which, since the 8-4-4 reforms of 1985, young people will have been following from as early as Standard VI. But the emphasis on entrepreneurial self-employment is likely to be even more significant when it comes to analysing the potential impact of introducing exposure to enterprise in all post-school vocational training institutions. By this point, young people have been selected out of the educational mainstream, if they are in a YP, a TTI or even an IT. The key question, however, for policy makers must be: to what extent does the process of selection out of the formal educational mainstream imply that trainees are really looking for self-employment openings?

This question cannot be easily answered at a general level. In many countries including Kenya, the whole history of certain vocational training institutes (VTIs) has been intimately connected with employment in the modern sector, or in the government's technical ministries. Vocational training institutes such as the TTIs in Kenya have been closely associated with formal sector apprenticeship schemes, and with the donor agencies. In some cases, e.g. in Tanzania, this link to the donor agencies has had the effect of maintaining access to scarce raw materials and modern equipment and even to expatriate staff, and has tended to reinforce the connections with modern sector industry rather than with self-employment. In other situations, where the VTI has long had to rely on local resources, there may be much closer connections with self-employment. This would certainly be the case for many of the youth polytechnics in Kenya.

Re-organizing vocational training institutes (VTIs) for enterprise and self-employment in Kenya

When it comes to determining what can be done about orientation to self-employment and micro-enterprise development in the range of Kenyan VTIs, it must be obvious that there are no panaceas. We shall, however, now look at some of the main suggestions that emerge from experience and research evidence. We shall examine clienteles, the different mixes of vocational and self-employment training, and the kinds of connections possible between the VTIs and the outside world.

New clienteles for enterprise education and self-employment training in VTIs?

In many post-school vocational training systems including Kenya's, the principal source of the trainees are those young people who have come directly from school. Given what we have said from time to time in this book about the importance of employment as an antecedent to starting business on one's own, it may be important for VTIs to rethink their clienteles if self-employment training is really to become one of their main goals. This emphasis upon relevant employment as a precursor to self-employment is reinforced in a recent study from Zimbabwe:

> *Previous experience in related business* – Most of the successful business owners with whom we met had previously worked for companies that made the same or similar products. Most understood the business, its production processes and/or its markets before they started out on their own; they started their own enterprise having already gained experience working for others. Many had previously worked in several different positions in larger firms in the industry, some having reached relatively senior positions with considerable responsibility. They then applied all of the knowledge and experience they had gained, in starting their own companies. (Mead *et al.*, 1993: 12)

The implications of these kinds of findings about the pathways to enterprise are worth thinking through for Kenya. On the one hand, the priority of politicians is often to target the largest possible number of young people with explicit messages about education and training for self-employment. And this certainly accounts for the introduction of the kinds of self-employment orientations we have been examining into the regular school systems at all levels. On the other hand, if the aspiration of government policy is entrepreneurial as opposed to survival self-employment, it must be evident that very few young people, straight from school or VTI, are likely to be able to enter anything remotely like their own micro-enterprise. Rather, Government might want to try and reach those who had already decided to start small businesses themselves, but who might wish to come in as in-service or post-experience candidates for specialist training.

There is, therefore, a real distinction to be made between the idea of offering some kind of enterprise module for all the young trainees in the regular trades offered by the VTIs, on the one hand, and the targeting of managers and owners of small businesses in order to improve the capacity of people who are already in self-employment, on the other. What has happened in many of the VTIs in Latin America in the late 1980s may be instructive. It was not that the enterprises began to ask the VTIs for all their vocational trainees to be given an injection of commerce and enterprise. Rather, it was that the industries realized, as they faced the new, much more competitive demands of industrial restructuring, that they had additional requirements at the management level which VTIs might be able to provide. This has been put well by Ducci in her review of *Vocational Training on the Threshold of the 1990s*:

> What is really new for VTIs regarding small and middle-sized enterprises (SME) takes place when the latter become fully aware that the needs they have detected far exceed those of mere technical training of their workers. In fact, their most urgent needs are related to the economic, financial, administrative, productive, technological and human resources management of these pro-duction units. (Ducci, 1991, Vol. i: 135–6)

It is not clear that Kenya, in adopting the policy of entrepreneurship education for all in the vocational training institutes, has really thought through whether the change in policy does imply a change in the personnel being offered the training. Certainly, apart from a World Bank/Kenya project, little attention has been given yet to schemes that would target experienced jua kali, and encourage them in the evenings to take advantage of specialized courses. And none of the jua kali encountered in our research had any linkage to professional upgrading through VTIs. Many, however, were putting large amounts of their hard-won money into their children's conventional education, but none seemed aware of any night school offerings in a VTI, or of any facility that was targeting the jua kali and encouraging them to hone their skills.

What mixes of vocational and self-employment training?
Intimately connected with the question of clienteles are the different mixes of enterprise and vocational training that are possible in the VTIs. There is clearly a spectrum from a heavy emphasis on vocational skills training with a small component of enterprise training, on the one hand, to a situation where, on the other, the bulk of the training is on business skills and where the vocational training in a particular skill is assumed to be already in place. A full discussion of all the possible permutations is not necessary here. This has been done usefully in guides such as the Commonwealth Secretariat's *Designing Entrepreneurial Skills Development Programmes: Resource book for technical and vocational institutions* (Rao et al., 1990: 90 ff). But it may be useful to tease out some of the implications for institutional change of the principal options.

Minimalist approaches to enterprise education. There are at least two aspects of the minimalist approaches that are perhaps worth bearing in mind for Kenya. First, the enterprise training is kept to a minimum in what is still recognizably a VTI primarily concerned with skill training. Second, the enterprise training is restricted to what can be taught as a subject, and there is no attempt to provide small-scale credit, follow-up, or other services. In the latter approach, the introduction of enterprise training may not be very different from introducing another academic subject. An illustration from Malawi makes the point:

> Malawi has five Technical Colleges ... the curriculum is largely aimed at training for employment, but 'Commerce' is being introduced to assist those with aspirations for self employment. (Malawian Entrepreneurs Development Institute, 1993)

In this kind of initiative, not a great deal changes. The clientele is basically the same, the staff are still trades-oriented; the only difference is that there is a new subject squeezed on to the timetable and a new department. And as far as enterprise exposure is concerned, this is really the lowest common denominator. But this weak version of 'diversification' towards some commerce and enterprise may be all that some governments may wish to undertake.

Maximum approaches. In this perspective the vocational training institute moves to the other pole along the spectrum, with the vocational content being the add-on, and the main business of the institution being the exposure to enterprise. One of the most obvious examples of this trend would appear to be the way that the Vocational Training Institute in Malawi turned from being vocational training for disadvantaged groups to being the Malawian Entrepreneurs Development Institute (MEDI). The move towards entrepreneurship and away from vocational training is neatly captured in the following comment:

> Much progress was made at MEDI during this phase (from 1985), and in 1989 an in-depth evaluation recommended that MEDI should move further from vocational skills training with entrepreneurship towards entrepreneurship development programmes with technical components. (Malawian Entrepreneurs Development Institute, 1993: 9)

However, as institutions seek seriously to become committed to enterprise development, it is no longer a question of mere 'orientation' to self-employment. They may need to consider whether there should be a loan scheme, whether there should be practical experience of enterprise undertaken by the VTI, whether graduates should be assisted with tools, and much else, including extension visits after graduation.

An intriguing example of this move towards more and more elements of small business support is evident in the Kenya Entrepreneurship Education Programme itself. Even though the programme is young (It started in 1990 and the first graduates only left in July 1993), progress has been rapid. The programme claimed in 1994 to have reached more than 40,000 trainees enrolled in 144 different institutions. There have been two graduations of some 4,000 trainees each year. In addition, there are already several small business centres set up at different levels of development in the major VTIs. These in turn have made available services and consultancy to the jua kali entrepreneurs, have encouraged the development of micro-enterprises by students during training, and doubtless have sought to help with ideas of finance (Mburugu, 1993; UNDP/ILO, 1990). This Kenya example is also important evidence of how much needs to be put in place if the subject of enterprise is to have status in VTIs. It illustrates the importance of teacher training and professional development of the field, the requirement that enterprise needs to be both a specialist teacher training field and also a subject to be taken at a more general level by all diploma level teachers. In doing so, it also provides evidence of the importance of an externally aided initiative becoming a regular part of the system. (Originally the donor funding was to terminate in June 1994.)

At the same time, it suggests that the more successful the project, the more it will be under pressure to provide some of the other services associated with small business development. A critical example of this pressure to offer more is mentioned as one of the constraints:

> Lack of readily available funds to finance graduates with viable business proposals could negatively affect the entrepreneurship programme. (Mburugu, 1993: 10)

What can be seen in this Kenya case, (and it is also evident in a paper on enterprise in Kiambu Institute of Science and Technology [Kerre, 1993: 18]), is the logic of seeking fully to institutionalize small enterprise in a former VTI. It cannot be done on the cheap, but also as soon as it is acknowledged that small enterprise is more than just another academic subject, a whole series of further requirements are made of the initiative.

The move to maximum approaches and the change in clienteles

What will be interesting in future to tease out in the Kenya institutions where enterprise education is installed is what happens to the traditional VTI clientele – the young, pre-experience trainees often straight from school – if the institution moves more towards a maximum approach. As one part of the VTI really becomes a small enterprise development centre, does it any longer want to have this kind of regular clientele, or would it not rather begin to have older men and women who have discovered from experience in the field what their business needs are? The evidence from Latin America would suggest that many of the VTIs set up specialist divisions to deal directly with this new clientele of business owners.

But it can be seen that there is indeed a tension between the strategy of making all VTIs conscious of the need to promote small enterprise (which may only be possible through a minimalist approach) and making some VTIs centres of excellence in small enterprise development (a maximum approach). Putting the issue another way, are there limits to what can be done on the small enterprise preparation side if the institution is basically to remain a VTI, focusing on trade and technician training? To what extent, without major institutional restructuring, can the tail of enterprise development expect to wag the dog of regular vocational training?

An even more demanding question in a country such as Kenya that is faced with budget uncertainties in many existing public sector initiatives is the extent to which local funds will be available to continue with what was initially only made possible by external aid (US$1.6 million through ILO/UNDP in the case of the Kenya project).

Orientation to productive self-employment in other Kenyan training institutions

Apart from the enterprise education initiative which illustrates a number of the challenges in re-orienting Kenyan institutions to the demands of self-employment, there have been several other attempts to add an appropriate programme focus to training institutes. In most cases these have identified a particular requirement beyond the technical trade content, and have sought to deliver that in conjunction with the institution.

One example would be the Intermediate Technology Development Group/Voluntary Service Overseas (ITDG/VSO) initiative which has, with British aid, sought to encourage the making of carpentry hand tools. The project has been designed around the assumption that locally made wooden hand tools could find a niche in the jua kali sector because of their lower cost and ease of repair (as compared with imported, metal tools). The manufacture and adoption of these wooden hand tools have been encouraged in a variety of countries, including Kenya, and on paper the rationales are well argued. And yet the project documentation is full of discussion about the acceptability and sustainability of the initiative. At certain points it is almost as if the appropriate strategy had become fixed, from outside the informal sector, and was being pursued regardless of evidence to the contrary. Several examples in the book reporting on the project (Leek *et al.*, 1993) confirm that the capacity to make wooden tools did not outlive the enthusiasm of the VSO volunteers once they had left. And, on the other hand, there seemed little readiness to alter the project priorities when confronted with evidence of dramatic developments in electrically powered jua kali wooden lathes in many of the larger towns. Indeed the project has been further institutionalized by being based in one of the youth polytechnics (YPs) (in Kianjai in Nyambene District), where it is intended to expose YP trainees and jua kali artisans to this particular technology, and to disseminate replicable packages to other polytechnics (ODA, 1993–4, 1994–5). But it is still aid-dependent.

This project has been alluded to because like so many other externally funded projects that have emerged in Kenya it has developed a particular conception of the problem facing the jua kali sector. This can sometimes proceed to take on a life of its own, and in so doing can become dissociated from the changing and very complex order within the informal economy itself.

Another dimension that has been very popular in Kenya has been credit schemes for jua kali. There has been a huge literature on these, and it has been very valuably synthesized by the Kenya Rural Enterprise Programme (Aleke-Dondo, 1991). But here the question is to what extent should credit be associated with a whole range of other support mechanisms, such as business training, skills training, and extension. The Kenya Youth Training and Employment Creation Project (KYTEC) is an example of where credit and business training have become important additional components in what was originally mainly a training programme, in the youth polytechnics. This too, like the hand tool project just alluded to, runs on external money, with credit being guaranteed by the Arab Gulf Fund, and technical assistance from ILO/UNDP. Before its present form, KYTEC was part of the regional Skills Development for Self-Reliance (SDSR) project, and drew its support from SIDA and ILO. At that time it was primarily concerned with the improvement of rural training according to a particular modular formula. Since 1988 despite its name, with the emphasis on training and employment, it will be seen as a vehicle for credit for a small number of youth polytechnic graduates (Aleke-Dondo, 1991: 92–4).

But unlike what are termed the minimalist credit schemes where the administration of the credit is very cheap, with few overheads, and where the credit is not linked with a package of components of business training, and with follow-up visits by the project staff, KYTEC is clearly expensive. As a recent evaluation mission made clear:

> ... if staffing levels are reduced ... the Project will not continue to function in a meaningful way. The time and personnel requirements necessary to implement the Project are large. Total mileage, for example on the three KYTEC vehicles (purchased new) now exceeds 175,000 kms. The distances of the Project sites from Nairobi require many hours on the road. Until that time when the process is able to be managed completely at the District level, it is likely that Project expansion into more Districts and YPs will require more KYTEC staff time. (UNDP, 1992: 5–6)

In many ways KYTEC seems to epitomize the problem of doing something special for the informal sector through the existing training system and training institutions. To do something special is widely assumed to mean having a project. A project, to be successful, needs external money, links to the key ministries and to the donors. It also needs dedicated transport, communication, office space, and, most important of all, committed professionals. KYTEC has been particularly fortunate in recruiting the last, and this results in the KYTEC project becoming visible and even internationally known.

178

The Catch 22 in the project approach with its dependence on external money is that for the first phase of US$2,255,000 (ILO/Kenya Government, 1991) the project has got to establish itself on a national scale, and yet like most projects it suffers from an inherent unsustainability. It is an add-on to the youth polytechnic movement, but an add-on that almost by definition cannot touch more than a tiny handful of youth polytechnic graduates by providing them a loan.

Unlike the Ministry of Education's nationwide introduction of Business Education into primary schools which clearly has been a sustainable locally developed initiative over the last ten years, the three projects we have touched on so far (Enterprise Education; Handtools; and KYTEC) are all running on foreign funds, and therefore their greatest challenge is to acquire some kind of 'rootedness' within the local culture of jua kali development. All too often in the large number of jua kali projects that are connected to the national training system, 'rootedness' or ownership are taken to mean acceptability to the Ministry and to key national decision makers. There is usually very little corresponding interest in securing local sustainability through understanding how the local stakeholders in the youth polytechnics and other institutions can adopt and maintain what was originally a top-down strategy for national replication of a pilot scheme.

Equally, there seems to be insufficient research, amidst the current plethora of externally funded jua kali credit schemes, to discover jua kali attitudes towards credit. Amongst our own sample of jua kali, there is a whole hitherto untapped philosophy about loans. This is very aware of the danger of loans. In the words of one Githiga jua kali, 'Loans can eat your money'. On the other hand, there is also the danger of getting loans that are too small; these can also be counterproductive. Clearly some of this local thinking about needs is essential to sustainabillity.

Self-employment through NGO training schemes

Compared with the jua kali schemes directly supported by multilateral and bilateral agencies, there are a great number of much smaller jua kali training schemes associated with NGOs. It has been customary to assume that NGO training is organized with lower overheads, and succeeds in reaching levels of local disadvantage and poverty that are very difficult for national schemes to penetrate. In terms of our earlier distinction between entrepreneurial self-employment and subsistence self-employment, it is probably also true to say that many NGOs have an almost inbuilt hesitation about initiatives that help the *individual* entrepreneur. Rather there is a tendency with many NGOs to prefer a group-based approach rather than an individualistic approach to income generation. This community perspective, and it is certainly one that seems to run through many NGOs, regardless of whether they are religious or secular in their orientation, is likely to mean that there will be a strong interest in such items as group training or group credit or community cross guarantee schemes for loans.

Another tendency is important enough to re-emphasize; and that is the inclination for NGOs to approach economic development as inseparable from social development, and vice versa. Oxfam has captured particularly strongly the force of this argument about sustainability, which is probably quite widely shared amongst NGOs:

> It will prove difficult if not impossible to achieve social development goals, such as increasing critical awareness among the poor... unless the measures adopted are also economically viable. If this rule is not observed, projects may collapse as soon as foreign funding is withdrawn.
>
> ... A funding agency which subsidises the economic operations of a given scheme too heavily may well sow the seeds of the project's destruction. (Pratt & Boyden, 1985: 180)

Amongst the several hundreds of NGOs in Kenya, it is not of course possible to generalize about the exact number that are specifically involved with the support of training to the informal sector. Many may not even make explicit that they are supporting jua kali, and yet through their frequent income-generation projects, especially for women, they are intimately connected with what is otherwise called the informal economy. Even though we shall not pick out schemes from Kenya in this category, it is worth emphasizing that the record of such projects is very disappointing. Goodale (quoted in McGrath and King, 1995: 87) cites an analysis of some 130 income-generation projects working with women's groups in Africa, where not a single project showed a profit in the year of study (1984/5). More recent projects in Kenya may well have sought to learn from these earlier criticisms.

Even if there has been a tendency to encourage sex-stereotyped women's welfare projects under the umbrella of income generation, there is no doubt that on the positive side NGO projects for the jua kali have been characterized by a very evident sense of commitment to their tasks. This determination by many NGOs to give of their best for the poor, whether in training, technological development, or social welfare has had some paradoxical outcomes. One result of these very high levels of commitment has been that the quality of the training has been frequently very good. Consequently graduates of such NGO training programmes are often sought out by formal sector firms, looking for graduates they can trust (McGrath and King, 1995; King, 1989c).

We would not want to suggest too large a contrast in respect of commitment between the larger donor funded projects for the jua kali and the NGO projects. It must be remembered that most Northern and Southern NGOs working in Kenya are pre-eminently dependent on external funding for their programmes and projects. Indeed many of the larger NGO activities have substantial components of Northern government funding behind them. There is therefore a tendency, despite all that has been said about commitment and dedication to working at the grassroots, for NGOs to lack what Kajese has called a 'rootedness' in the local political, social and financial realities:

... we have to address the issue of the *rootedness* of the African NGO. Who owns an African NGO? Where does its mandate come from? Whose value system does it operate from? Whose guiding vision informs the self-image and mission of an African NGO? The issue of *rootedness* ... is the very essence of what is readily referred to as 'sustainable development'. (Kajese, 1991: 14)

This point is worth underlining in respect of the NGOs' rather recent advocacy of schemes to support jua kali training. How much is their concern with jua kali development a reflection of external, international trends, affecting all the major donors? Does it really have a basis in local funding commitment within local communities and constituencies? At the moment certainly, the jua kali have become one of the new frontiers for the many NGOs in Kenya, but as mentioned above, many NGOs will feel more at home with the lower reaches of the jua kali rather than what have been termed the more 'advanced' jua kali entrepreneurs. In the concluding words of an NGO workshop on the jua kali organized by VSO in Kenya:

> Our major interest would be the lower echelon of the Jua Kali, the starters. Among them are the youth groups/workgroups and the graduates of the youth polytechnics. These deserve our support as they forge ahead themselves, looking for funds, equipment and guidance for their initial take-off into business. (VSO, 1991)

World Bank support to institutional training of Kenyan jua kali

Before leaving this consideration of support to jua kali development through vocational training institutions, it would be important to mention two components of the World Bank's Micro- and Small Enterprise Training and Technology Project (November 1993). One of these, a training voucher programme costing some US$6 million, appears to be based on an earlier NGO scheme organized by the Promotion of Rural Initiatives and Development Enterprises Ltd (PRIDE) and funded by ODA. The latter had been a pilot project in Kenya'a Eldama Ravine area, and had sold coupons which had then been used to buy basic business management training for various training institutions. The mechanism used by PRIDE initially had been to 'sell' the coupons which had a face value of K.Sh.500 each, at just K.Sh.100. The coupons were only available to PRIDE clients who had successfully repaid a loan. On the other side of the equation, training suppliers were invited to present outlines of their proposed training programmes, so that there could be a match made between the demand from these jua kali consumers and the trainers. Over the period of the pilot some 550 clients were actually trained through this system (PRIDE, 1993–4; ODA, 1993–4).

The Bank project is very much more ambitious. Its aim is to distribute a total of 30,000 vouchers (6,000 a year). There would be two different kinds of vouchers, one for management training (worth US$150 per voucher) and the other for skill upgrading (worth US$200 each). It is estimated that a typical skill upgrading course would last some two to six weeks. The mechanism for distributing the 6,000 vouchers per year would apparently be through competitive bids from Jua Kali Associations. In the initial stages, project funds would cover 100 per cent of the cost of the scheme (World Bank, 1993a: 24–6).

There is a strong streak of ideology in the Bank scheme. It quite explicitly draws on the Bank's policy paper, *Vocational and Technical Education and Training*, which argued forcefully for greater encouragement of the private sector in training:

> Training in the private sector – by private employers and in private training institutions – can be the most ˙effective and efficient way to develop the skills of the work force. (World Bank, 1991: 7)

Equally by making the Jua Kali Associations and their individual members the recipients of the vouchers, it seeks to create more of a market in training. Thus, presumably, individuals with vouchers could approach NGOs, private sector or public sector providers of training.

In parallel with this voucher scheme, the Bank would also fund to the tune of US$5.4 million a contract training scheme. This would seek to award on a competitive basis up to 300 training projects a year for five years (at an average cost of US$3,600 per course). Again, like the voucher scheme, there would be strong pressure to encourage private employers to get reimbursement by providing suitable training on site. The courses would need to be relevant to the technical and management skills required by jua kalis (World Bank, 1993a: 27–8).

Taken together, these two Bank projects claim that they will reach up to 60,000 informal sector entrepreneurs and workers, representing about 50 per cent of the total jua kalis in the manufacturing sector.

There are several things that should be said about this quite large chunk of US$11 million coming in support of jua kali training through existing or new institutions. The first is that the sum is large enough that it may well encourage jua kalis and training providers to come forward. Evidence from elsewhere in Africa would indicate that it is, however, extremely difficult to arrange for new training systems to be welded onto the existing provision. In Nigeria's National Open Apprenticeship System, new moneys sought to diversify the quality of training in the 'traditional' system through off-the-job training, and also sought to persuade the masters through cash incentives to take additional apprentices. Both initiatives were to prove highly problematic (Adam, 1993; Boehm, 1994).

Second, as the vouchers are going to be organized through the Jua Kali Associations, and the Jua Kali Federation, which are still extremely weak and in some measure of political competition with other national groupings not registered with MTTAT (see Chapter 1), it may be very difficult to ensure that the 3,000 tickets a year are not seen as something of a political lottery. It seems for instance unlikely that a small rural association such as the Githiga Jua Kali Society would ever be awarded any tickets if they are in competition with large urban based associations in making bids.

Third, there is the challenge to public and private vocational training institutions of mounting courses targeted at the jua kali sector. This, too, is easier said than done. At the moment many of the most formal vocational training institutions offer courses that are closely tied to the specific requirements of formal sector industries, ministries and to formal certification. But arguably such institutions will find it very difficult, as we suggested above, to orient their courses to fundamentally different clienteles. As far as outreach to the lower echelons of the (subsistence) self-employed is concerned, many urban VTIs operate in a culture that little understands the working week, the tools and the technologies of the mass of ordinary self-employed. Youth polytechnics would find it easier to adjust, as they are much closer to the needs of local communities. And as far as re-orientation to the needs of the upper echelons of the self-employed is concerned, it is by no means clear that these very self-reliant micro-entrepreneurs would currently feel themselves unfairly excluded from a very relevant government resource for training. They might well envy the VTIs some of their equipment, but could well regard VTI operations, carried out only during regular office hours, but with low-capacity utilization throughout the year, as inappropriate to their own needs. It has been known for years that in the eyes of these micro-enterprise owners the graduates of such government VTIs would in many cases not be considered suitable for work in their own firms, for the very good reason that they had had no exposure to the culture of work in the 'real world' (King, 1993: 7).

In other words, the World Bank project looks like it will try and put some significant new money into the formal institutional training of jua kali and their representatives. It will also try to do so in ways that encourage more women to enter non-traditional trades, give incentives to more private firms to undertake training, and seek to build up the currently weak capacity both of the new Ministry (MRTT&T)[1] and of the Jua Kali Federation/Jua Kali Associations. Indeed, there are two specific project sub-components in the Bank scheme which are designed to improve the skills in project management of these very bodies that are meant to be the executing agencies of the Bank support to micro and small enterprise training. This staff development turns out to mean some 50 courses of five days' length for most of the key skills required to administer a complex project: project management; procurement and contract administration; financial management; monitoring and evaluation; training materials development; leadership and entrepreneurship development etc etc (World Bank, 1993: 30–2). All these are worthy training goals, but their listing does rather serve to underline the present incapacities of the bodies chosen to execute the project. It seems doubtful that something as slow to form as a management culture can be brought about rapidly through a whole series of short intensive courses. Nor does it seem likely that the project sustainability will be assured by the Jua Kali Associations progressively taking over some of the costs of the voucher scheme and its management, when most of them are not even able regularly to collect their own minimum membership dues.

However, it is much too early to know how this major intervention in the Kenyan training market will work out, but the sums involved are certainly large enough to affect the current training arrangements. If successful they could well do something important not only in the orientation of VTIs towards these new and less conventional clients, but they could also encourage jua kali artisans further to develop their skills through inservice training, off-the-job, which is very uncommon at the moment. The implementation is only just beginning, and the international competitive bidding for parts of the process was only advertised in August 1995 (*Economist*, 12 August 1995).

Vocational training orientation and the culture of business in the different communities

One of the greatest challenges to encouraging an enterprise culture and orientation in all vocational training institutions in some of the ways we have been alluding to is that the outcome of such training for self-employment will depend a great deal upon the existing business cultures and environments in the surrounding community or communities. This contextual factor is of immense importance in Kenya, where there are very powerful traditions of enterprise that have been closely associated with particular communities and particular patterns of trade and commerce. These existing cultures of business must be borne in mind when proposing national schemes for self-employment and micro-enterprise development. Because of these community specializations in trade and commerce, it is by no means clear that the informal sector can be characterized as having 'ease of entry', as was argued by the original Kenya Employment Mission in 1972. In a situation where there is effective domination of the informal sector by particular communities, what is the impact of a national scheme to encourage a greater enterprise orientation? May it not further assist those communities that already have an established position? On the other hand, how acceptable is it for government to seek through positive discrimination to aid those communities that have not had historically powerful traditions of industry and commerce?

This external culture of existing business is noted here because it may make it extremely problematic to disentangle success and failure in institutional initiatives for enterprise education and training. It is not difficult to imagine that some of the graduates of VTIs, after their new orientation to enterprise, will enter a business environment where the family and the community at large can offer connections, credit and confidence, while other graduates may be effectively on their own in struggling to establish themselves. Recent work on small enterprises in Zimbabwe makes it clear that these family connections can be a key characteristic of successful enterprise:

> Families can play an important role in providing an entrepreneur with knowledge about a business as well as access to the markets and capital needed to support a new enterprise. Several of the businesses we visited had been managed by one family for several generations. (Mead, *et al.*, 1993: 12)

This external culture of enterprise is very important in Kenya, and it may become even more evident in the next section of the chapter where the emphasis shifts from the schools and the training institutions to the question of how to improve jua kali training in the enterprise itself. Clearly, unlike school exposure to business education (which is almost universal at least at primary level) and provision through vocational training institutions which is still open to those who are interested and are selected, the targeting of training in the jua kali firms themselves inevitably favours communities that have already developed significant numbers of enterprises.

Enterprise based training for jua kali

Apart from school and vocational training, the jua kali enterprise itself is a key site for skill acquisition, through various kinds of informal apprenticeships. This is sometimes too exact a term for the kind of skill training acquired on the job, when the masters or employers do not necessarily see themselves as involved in an informal training agreement. Nevertheless, whether these are more or less explicit versions of apprenticeship, it is generally admitted that there are more young people acquiring their training on the job, via the urban informal sector enterprises, than there are via the institutional training system of youth polytechnics, technical training institutes etc. which we have just been reviewing. One recent broad estimate is that there were probably some 80,000 informal sector apprentices in the year ending June 1990 as compared with only 55,000 trainees in the formal training system (Yambo, 1991: 12).

It is worth noting, however, that enterprise based training for jua kali does not take place exclusively within the informal sector. A substantial number of jua kali workers and owners acquire their major skills from the formal sector of the economy. Of course, it is not the function nor the intention of the formal sector to provide training for the informal sector. But it is clear in Kenya, as in other countries like Zimbabwe, that significant numbers of formally trained workers have moved and are continuing to transfer to the informal sector. However, it is not so much the initial training in the formal sector that can prove important for a worker that later moves over to self-employment. Arguably much more important is

185

the range of experience obtained over many years in manufacture, design, sourcing of materials, knowledge of clients, marketing etc. We have already argued in our discussion of individual pathways to self-employment in the informal sector that not all formal sector firms have this potential. The formal sector firms with accessible technologies – whether in metal, wood, plastics or textiles – or with schemes for encouraging sub-contracting back to the firm by selected employees, are much more likely to act as sources of experience for eventual informal sector owners than continuous process plants, where the product is inseparable from a very expensive investment in state of the art production lines.

Thus the 'graduates' from the formal sector whom we met in Chapter 3 tended to come from firms like Hartz and Bell engineering, the coffee machinery companies, McCrae's Furniture, or from Avery weighing scales rather than from Colgate (Kenya), Coca Cola (Kenya) or General Motors. And in many cases, they transferred only after many years of acquiring valuable experience.

It is understandably very difficult to develop any policy about the importance of the formal sector as a source of training and experience for the informal sector. Still, it is worth bearing in mind that one factor in the great differences we noted between the micro-enterprises (and their incomes) in Gikomba and those in the tinsmithing concentration of Kamukunji was that a significant number of the jua kali owners we met in Gikomba had had direct experience of working in the formal sector of the economy, while the technologies being employed in Kamukunji had all been learnt directly within the informal sector itself.

One of the principal challenges to the training quality in the informal sector itself is the range of technologies available to any particular micro-enterprise. A good number of the schemes that seek to improve the standard of training in enterprise based training therefore do target either the levels of technology, the range of equipment, or the skill levels of the masters. We shall turn now to look at some of these initiatives for improving enterprise based training. But it may be noted initially that there is a temptation to indulge in technical fixes, which perceive shortcomings of informal sector training in terms of lack of particular inputs e.g. trade theory, or book-keeping. Such interventions can run the risk of seriously altering the social and economic dynamics of the sector.

Amongst interventions which have been tried in different African countries and hold out some hope of positive impact on training are those that seek to strengthen the capacity of informal trade associations. These have been tried in Ghana through the Council of Indigenous Business Associations, and, interestingly, there the associations are based on trades (e.g. Federation of Ghanaian Jewellers) rather than on towns or part of towns as in Kenya. In Uganda, training in intermediate technologies has been available to paid up members of the Uganda Small Scale Industries Association. In Kenya we have noted that the World Bank project seeks to strengthen the capacity of the Jua Kali Associations by linking them selectively into the provision and administration of training vouchers. A number of further examples of the creative use of the informal business associations is evident in Haan's paper 'A role for informal sector associations in technology development and dissemination' (Haan, 1994a).

Technological upgrading for the jua kali

Another set of approaches that has been tried in Kenya focuses on the technological improvement of the jua kali. One of the problems with many of the technological initiatives is that they are, perhaps inevitably, organized around the notion of a short intensive course or demonstration in which the new technologies are introduced and applied to some product – just once. These approaches always seem in very stark contrast to the processes of technological change within the informal sector itself or to when workers embody the technology themselves and carry it with them from the formal sector to their own enterprises.

In a UNIDO/UNDP project for demonstration and training in technology, the site selected by the project for treatment (Kamukunji) is described as being 'highly organized in a most peculiar "disorganized" way'. It is also interesting to note that the process of upgrading the jua kali technology is to be done 'without unduly upsetting their existing entrepreneurship, ingenuity, initiative and social habits'. As to the technology exposure, it 'should not be sophisticated or even standard (such as usual workshop machinery etc). One may think of graduating from manually operated *Jua Kali* to manually operated machine tools and equipment *Jua Kali*. Machines and production techniques should be so designed that new activity will act as a stepping stone to the existing *Jua Kali*' (UNDP, 1990: 4).

What is curious about this conception of the jua kali artisans is that they are seen as needing to go through carefully modulated stages of growth. In order for this to be implemented, it transpires that a whole series of different formal sector institutions are to be involved for technical assistance. But at the same time, it is stressed that the demonstration plant 'should not upset the livelihood of existing *Jua Kalis*'. Indeed it is even emphasized that the trainees 'should not produce any product which will be in competition with the products produced by *Jua Kali* at the present time' (ibid: 8).

While there is certainly value in being cautious about overproducing, through an externally funded and subsidized project, items that may undermine some jua kalis' livelihood, there is an element of overprotection in this concern to guard against jua kali getting access to too modern technology. An awareness of the dynamic of existing technological change within the jua kali sector in Kenya would be a useful antidote to this somewhat anthropological approach to the special character of the jua kali economy.

There are several other examples of technological training to assist the jua kali in Kenya. Several of these are very thoughtful but their great drawback is that they are either linked to one-off injections of expatriate technical assistance, or they are financially unsustainable. Few of them seem to be based on an accurate assessment of cutting edge technological problems in the jua kali sector, nor do they seem sufficiently concerned with designing a mechanism that is affordable and can be incorporated into the current process of technological change.

Conclusions on technological confidence amongst the jua kali and further education and training for self-employment

At the end of *The African Artisan*, we warned against too great a polarization of the informal from the formal. At that time, in the 1970s, there was a widespread international agency retreat from the formal school and from formal industry, and a fascination with the informal and nonformal, both in training and in production. There is again some danger now, as almost every agency and large numbers of NGOs design projects 'for the jua kali', that they become a special case, and that insufficient attention is paid to what are the economic factors that have made them so apparently special and separate from the formal system. We argued back then:

> There are admittedly areas of skill acquisition and of petty production that operate apparently unaffected by the official systems, but it is precisely those elements which would be the hardest to generalise across the nation as some kind of alternative policy objective; their resourcefulness, rapidity of training, technology and low costs are not so much chosen as dictated by necessity. (King, 1977: 196)

This is precisely the problem that is raised by another part of the new World Bank project which seeks to integrate 'indigenous and informal technologies into the trade test system' as an important means of facilitating modernization of the informal sector. 'Reformed trade tests would reflect a broader range of job profiles and technologies found in the informal sector' (World Bank, 1993b: 32). The problem may well be not so much in accrediting different jua kali profiles and informal technologies but rather in recognizing that these apparently separate jua kali processes and improvizations are intimately connected with the absence of very basic machine tools such as lathes, that we noted in Gikomba.

By contrast one of the more positive aspects of the Kenya Government's approach towards education and training for self-employment has been to regard these as a regular part of the national mainstream system. This can be seen in such elements as Business Education being part of the core curriculum of all schools, indicating that this kind of practical information is valuable for all young people. Equally, acknowledging the role of indigenous technology in recent government policy documents is not thought of as a special nod towards primitive technologies in the informal sector. Rather it is seen as essential to national technological development. Some of what we have called in Chapter 3 a second stage of import substitution is relevant here also, since it illustrates a form of technological learning that has broken out of the confines of the Industrial Area and become part of a more widely shared indigenous or, preferably, just local technological confidence.

This last concept, technological confidence, must be at the centre of any strategy for education, training or apprenticeship for micro-enterprise, and it seems to be one of the single most important distinctions between the jua kali of the 1970s and some of those who can be found today, both in the urban areas and in small villages like Githiga. What is intriguing about this confidence – tentative though its character still is – is that it has probably not so far been substantially affected by the changes in the 8-4-4 curriculum in schools. It certainly has not been influenced either by the very recently imported versions of enterprise education that are meant progressively to become part of all vocational training institutions. Rather it is something that has happened in the interface between the formal sector of the economy and its 'graduates' and the rapidly changing jua kali economy. This confidence has emerged, most important of all, without an iota of official help. But it has almost certainly been silently assisted by the very complex cultures of enterprise that are to be found in different Kenyan communities, and including the Indian (or Asian) communities.

The challenge, now that so many government policies are finally on paper in favour of small scale and micro-enterprise, is massively to support this quiet revolution that has already begun to happen, and encourage this technological confidence to move up market, to go to scale, even to contemplate what may now seem a pipedream – the implication of new information technologies for the jua kali sector in Kenya.

It is here particularly that education and further technical knowledge will be inescapably important, and where it will be vital to recall that jua kali development, like the *harambee* movement, is essentially about a way of learning and way of doing. Such matters are not altered overnight, but once this technological confidence within the jua kali economy had begun to be acquired (by processes that we still very inadequately understand over the past two decades) and to be demonstrated, there was at least a chance that it could be built upon through further learning.

There is, admittedly, a learning paradox at the centre of all this. We are obliged to confess that something central to the dynamism, and, more recently, technological confidence of the Kenyan jua kali has not really been connected with any of the policy measures discussed in the hundreds of papers and reports referred to in Chapter 1. We would also accept that it has only very indirectly been influenced by either the pre-8-4-4 or current education and training reforms. Equally there has so far been little contribution to this technological confidence from any of the myriad of micro-credit programmes. The evidence suggests that only a tiny proportion of micro-enterprises have received formal financial assistance or more general business advice (Parker and Torres, 1994: 21–2).

Accordingly, we are left with the policy dilemma that the technological profile of many of the jua kali has certainly changed in the 25 years under review, but the key changes appear to have taken place in an almost silent manner.

Some significant dimension of the changes in some jua kali is attributable to long-term exposure to the relatively small-scale formal industrial sector. The Africanization of skilled positions in many formal sector firms, when Indians left these jobs, produced gradually a whole new generation of artisans who understood high quality furniture production, casting and foundry skills, building management, structural work with steel, some specialized engineering, and a great deal else. In many cases this new generation had been waiting in the wings, and had built up their knowlege gradually over ten or 20 years. Often it has been this group that has moved over from the formal sector to self-employment in the middle to late 1980s.

They have done so at a point where learning on the job the whole range of essential operations had produced technological capacity and confidence, but as the value of real wages in the formal sector fell during the 1980s, many experienced workers in industry began to do the same as their counterparts in other sectors of the economy – take on work on their own account outside working hours. Just as academics were leaving the university for more profitable jobs including self-employment as consultants, so a number of experienced industrial workers also took their skills into self-employment.

This is not to say that all workers leaving the formal sector are likely to swell the ranks of the dynamically self-employed. If, for example, the divestiture of 200 parastatals and the civil service reforms go ahead, the thousands of workers shed in these processes may well be very different from those who have been confident enough to choose self-employment from the security of a formal sector job. Compulsory redundancies following such divestiture may be drawn from the kinds of parastatal firms, government offices and businesses where there have been few opportunities to acquire self-employment related skills. The crucial factor for technological confidence is not the experience of the formal sector *per se* but rather the character and scale of the skills and knowledge that are available in the firm.

Another aspect of this technological confidence which makes the transition to self-employment easier is what might be called their networks of knowledge connecting these new entrepreneurs to markets, to low-cost suppliers, sometimes to their old firms through subcontracts, and to other enterprises. Some of these are as much social as technical or business networks, but they would seem to be a critical dimension of enterprise confidence.

For many of those in self-employment there are few mechanisms for reinforcing these linkages and networks. Jua kali firms have traditionally been excluded from local chambers of commerce, and hence they have turned to join organizations such as the Kenya Small Traders' Society

(KSTS) or the jua kali associations and societies. These latter are still at a very embryonic stage of development, as was seen in Chapter 1, but if they are to be successful they will have to network not just amongst themselves but with the relevant actors in the formal sector of the economy.

Sustaining technological confidence within self-employment

One of the unknown factors about this new technological confidence with its original linkage to formal sector skills and knowledge is how it will develop and be sustained in the economy of scarcity that is the informal sector. Are the machining and finishing standards required in the formal sector lost once workers make the transition and no longer have access to the tools, equipment and quality controls set in the Industrial Area? And are the apprentices the informal sector masters take on inevitably going to be less skilled and experienced than they themselves since the technological environment in these new firms is often very basic? Is there going to be a new role for the formal technical and vocational institutions to service these further education and training needs?

Currently, it must be admitted that most of the formal technical and vocational education and training system is far removed from these further skill needs of the jua kali sector, even if they have set up a few small business centres and have begun to think of offering entrepreneurship education as well as trade skills. Some jua kali artisans do now get access to courses in the three industrial training centres in the evening, and some of these courses are now cross-subsidized from the Industrial Training Levy on formal sector firms. But this is only a small example of linking the resources of the formal VET (vocational education and training) sector with the informal.

The men and women whose pathways to technological confidence we have charted in Chapters 2 to 4 face very different challenges. Some are applying levels of secondary school and university knowledge to self-employment; some are wondering how they can afford secondary education for their own children on the income from self-employment; others are facing on their own the challenge of designing and producing what has never been made before outside the formal factory sector, and others again work such long hours in subsistence self-employment they have little opportunity to think of the luxury of new skills or new products.

The range of what NGOs, foreign donors and the government itself would like to offer to the jua kali is probably wider and more imaginative in Kenya than in many other countries, not just in education and training opportunities, but in credit, technology, management and other areas. Currently, however, the match between jua kali needs and the many possible providers is very poor. It is likely to be the case that only a tiny fraction of the jua kali (the estimated two million of them) know anything about the myriad schemes and projects designed to assist them. If the training system is to become genuinely more responsive to these new clienteles, there will need to be great changes in the mission of the VET system.

But equally the jua kali, either individually or through much more professional societies and associations, will need to stake out what their own missions are, and what role further education and skill play in these. Increasingly it seems likely that further education and training for self-employment will be successful if it is not offered by special organizations in isolation 'for the jua kali', but becomes just one very important part of a national project to advance technological capacity in Kenya. For a glance at this possibility we turn to the final chapter.

Note

1. MTTAT, as explained in Chapter 1, has been merged with another ministry to produce the Ministry of Research, Technical Training and Technology (MRTT&T).

Six

◁◁

Kenya's Jua Kali
in a Wider Context

At the end of this account, it may be appropriate to review some of the wider implications of this particular history of change and development among Kenya's jua kali by drawing out some of the larger issues which have emerged, as well as those which have only been touched upon, and which still need a good deal more research attention. The purpose is to offer some guidance for both research and policy in approaches to the micro-enterprise sector.

The survival of the terms 'formal' and 'informal' in the changing world of work

Twenty-five years after it was first used, the term informal sector is still alive and regularly used by organizations as different as the World Bank, the ILO and NGOs.[1] It is however increasingly common to refer to micro- and small enterprises or in Kenya's case to 'Small enterprise and jua kali development' in preference to using the informal/formal categories. There are good reasons for this, and some of these mark some of the slow changes that have taken place in the conceptualization of these kinds of activities since the early 1970s.

In the early period, the informal sector was thought of as something particularly evident in towns and cities, and this predominantly urban perspective on the informal sector was given increased emphasis by the setting up of a whole programme of work by the ILO's World Employment Programme (WEP) on the urban informal sector. There was still an Urban and Informal Sector unit in WEP in the early 1990s. By contrast, when the informal sector was examined in the rural areas, which happened a good deal less often, it was always conceptualized as 'off-farm' or 'non-farm'.[2]

In other words, the informal sector was set aside from the regular urban (formal) sector and the regular 'enterprise' of running a small farm (cf. Tribe, 1995).

Even in *World Employment 1995: An ILO report*, it is perhaps surprising to see that there is a separate section on 'The urban informal sector' and another one on 'Rural employment', as if these were two fundamentally different kinds of employment environment requiring separate policies (ILO, 1995: 92–5).

In the last decade and a half a number of developments in many African countries have altered this approach. For one thing, the bulk of those who had what used to be thought of as a 'real job' in the formal sector have found that the salary from that alone has not been sufficient to support themselves, let alone their families. Hence, whether they were teachers, lecturers or civil servants, they have undertaken additional income-generation activities outside their original formal sector job. In many cases this second job will bring as much or more income than the first, it may well be assisted by the leverage and influence of the first, and unlike the first it will tend to be untaxed.

In the rural areas, too, there has been some re-analysis of patterns of work. The result, in the case of Kenya, has been to recognize that 78 per cent of employment and of enterprises in the micro and small enterprise (MSE) sector is to be found in rural areas. The huge differences in the estimated size of the MSE sector, computed as recently as 1994, are inseparable from the process of rethinking the nature of rural enterprise. The USAID survey underlined the significance of this shift in estimates:

> This survey's estimates of urban employment in the sector are 33% higher than the Government of Kenya's (GOK), 1991 estimate, while in rural areas this survey's employment estimates are 943% higher than the GOK's 1991 estimate. (Parker & Torres, 1994: 5)

It is interesting that the survey also deliberately avoided any attempt to distinguish between informal and formal sectors but instead talked of micro-enterprises (ten or fewer workers) and small enterprises (11 to 50 workers) across the country. However, it did leave out of its estimates any income-generation activity which was 'in primary agricultural or mineral production' (Parker & Torres, 1994: 4). We now have a situation in which investigators are looking much more at households rather than at jobs, and in doing so are finding that approximately 25 per cent of all households engage in some form of business activity. This varies a great deal from small towns where as many as 59 per cent of all households engage in some small business activity to rural areas where most of the population depend on agriculture and only 23 per cent have business activities.

Arguably, the approach via households could be taken a few stages further. There must be many rural households where a reworking of the traditional distinctions between cash-crop and subsistence agriculture could mean that more attention was given to the multiple occupations of households, and to the mix of activities in the domestic economy. When this is put together with the fact that the one family may well have both an urban and a rural household, and that both partners (and their children) may engage in several different kinds of work, it is probable that more research will need to be done on the multi-faceted work of ordinary rural households and families. Just as we have talked of the subsistence and entrepreneurial self-employed off-farm, so it will be important to be clear what distinguishes an allegedly cash-crop enterprise (which is presumably 'primarily agricultural' in Parker and Torres' terms) from one that is called non-farm.

We can expect any more elaborate analysis of household activities to question our working distinction between subsistence and entrepreneurial self-employment. Many households will probably turn out to have both subsistence and entrepreneurial dimensions, and especially when in practice the micro-enterprise of, for example, the man in town is substantially intertwined with and dependent upon the productivity of the agricultural enterprise of the woman on the family plot.

Greater awareness of differentiation within the micro-enterprise sector

Running through this account is a sense of the huge distinctions between the upper and lower reaches of what are called jua kali in Kenya. We have contrasted the kind of capital stock, income and technology that can be found in Gikomba with that located in Kamukunji, which is immediately nextdoor. But both within Gikomba and Kamukunji there would be great variation. between those working with some security of tenure, permanent premises and machinery on the one hand and those on the other who are on temporary sites, who hire equipment, and have nowhere secure to keep their materials.

In earlier papers (Abuodha & King, 1991; King & Abuodha, 1995), we sought to quantify some of these distinctions, especially between the four trades sampled as part of this research (woodwork, metalwork, tailoring and candlemaking). The largest distinctions were amongst the first three and candlemaking. In respect of many indices, candlemaking proved to be the odd one out. For instance, it had much lower levels of education (only 14 per cent had achieved secondary education as compared with 40 per cent in the other trades). It also had very much lower levels of monthly income, and particularly when contrasted with the metalwork trades. This may appear to be a contradiction since candlemakers are tinsmiths and are therefore a category of metalworkers. In reality if candlemakers had been contrasted with *jiko*-makers (makers of braziers) the contrast might not have been so great, but, in our sample, metalwork covered those such as Thairu in Gikomba and Mutang'ang'i in Githiga, and hence represented what might be called the upper end of the jua kali metalwork spectrum.

Candlemaking also had very much lower levels of initial financial capital, and almost no significant changes in technology in over 20 years.

Although we have emphasized this contrast between these two trades, and between subsistence and entrepreneurial self-employment, we would want to warn against too ready an adoption of the *World Employment 1995*'s distinction between what it calls 'dead-end survival activities' and 'small-scale activities with the potential for growth and technical upgrading' (ILO, 1995: 92). There is a real danger about dichotomizing too statically these two categories and making them sound like fundamentally different modes of production. The evidence from many of the life histories of our jua kali sample would point to the co-existence of survival/subsistence as well as entrepreneurial activities at different stages. Many of our sample who now have established themselves would have looked very much more like subsistence self-employed in the 1970s when they were often engaged in casual (*kibarua*) work. Thus subsistence can often be a stage towards a more enterprise-oriented modality.

Change and development in Kenya's jua kali sector – by chance or design

One of the paradoxes of this particular account of change over time in Kenya is that the often quite significant alterations observed in the lives of specific entrepreneurs seem to have occurred quite independently of those changes which we have also documented over two decades for government policy on jua kali and for national education and training provision. There have been rather substantial changes in these latter two areas, and yet they might well have been taking place on completely parallel tracks for all the direct impact they appear to have had on the workers studied.

This is another of the themes we have traced through this account – that there are now rather extensive literatures on policy development, and on many of the different elements of possible intervention, from credit, to infrastructure, to appropriate technology. There are also a good number of surveys of the MSE sector in Kenya that have looked at different trades, and at MSE in different locations, as well as nationally. But many of these have been concerned to identify what might be called the obstacles to growth, and there is consequently no shortage of tables illustrating jua kali interest in more secure premises, more working capital, easier access to credit, and to business training and higher technical skills. Again, however, it sometimes seems that these wish-lists, faithfully recorded in the jua kali literature, run down a parallel set of tracks from the daily life of the majority of jua kali who have no realistic expectation of receiving any of the items researchers ask them from time to time to prioritize.

In the most recent period, some of this earlier, more static analysis has been replaced, particularly in USAID-funded surveys, by a concern with issues such as 'graduation' – from one category of micro-enterprise to another, or expansion within the present category. The results of such research have pointed to the fact that Kenya's micro-enterprise sector is certainly more dynamic in some respects than that of several other countries:

> Finally, a higher percentage of enterprises in Kenya have added workers than in any of the southern African countries. In sum, it appears that the Kenyan MSE sector has 'grown up' more than its counterparts elsewhere in the continent. (Parker & Torres, 1994: 63)

In some ways this most recent work, looking very carefully at small-scale change over time, is probably more valuable than the more general discussion about Kenya's 'missing middle'. Certainly some of the dynamism with which young people were entering business in Githiga and creating employment would lend credence to these trends. But when it comes to explaining what it is about Kenyan micro-enterprises that may have accounted for this dynamism, there is much less firm evidence to point to. Unlike the early 1970s, there are now sizeable concentrations of micro-enterprises in particular sections of Nairobi and in other towns, with some degree of trade specialization, in garment-making, wood products, metal, tin and much else. There are also the beginnings of more factory-based production in the light industrial area around Komo Rock in Nairobi. But research has scarcely begun to analyse whether there are particular patterns of supportive interaction when micro-enterprises of the same type cluster together (McCormick, 1994b).

The cultural factor in enterprise development

For a number of political reasons, the specifically ethnic factor in enterprise development has been given scant attention in the last 20 years. At the very beginning of our period, we noted that Marris and Somerset's *African Businessmen* (1971) is unique in studies of the MSE sector in Kenya by virtue of its paying very considerable attention to the issue of continuity between the pre-colonial trading traditions of the Kikuyu and the business culture amongst the Kikuyu in the early Independence period.[3] The few other studies that have been concerned with the culture of business have not necessarily advertised the fact. Thus, *The African Artisan* (King, 1977) is arguably as much about the Kikuyu as any other group in Kenya, and the present account, because it is partly revisiting the same artisans as in the early 1970s, is obviously also concerned to a significant extent with Kikuyu jua kali from Central Province.

Only one or two authors have focused explicitly on what may be called the ethnic dimension in enterprise development. Kinuthia Macharia, for instance, has written on 'Social networks: ethnicity and the urban informal sector', and has argued that ethnicity is in some sense the key element in the operation of the social networks pervading the jua kali sector. In contradistinction to the famous ILO Kenya Employment Mission phrase about 'ease of entry' to the informal sector, Macharia argues that ethnicity is a significant factor when it comes to the transfer of skills, the allocation of informal business premises, acquisition of technologies, access to markets and customers. Whole sub-sectors of the informal sector in Nairobi are operated by specific ethnic groups which tend to perpetuate the entry of the same ethnic group members to any space for running a business or a kiosk (Macharia, 1991).

Another dimension of ethnicity which has been given scant attention in the literature on MSE development in Kenya has been the role of the Indian community. Again, Marris and Somerset collected some valuable data of a comparative kind at the very end of the 1960s but since then there have been two really major business revolutions which have been virtually unresearched. One has been the 'graduation' of significant numbers of Indian micro and small enterprises into the formal industrial sector, and the second has been the character and pace of the African replacement of the Indian shopkeeper and the Indian general mechanical workshop in many of the smaller towns as well as in the big cities of Mombasa, Nakuru and Nairobi.

There have been case studies of particular small lines of Indian-to-African skill transfer, for instance in *The African Artisan* (King, 1977), and reference to the politics of the trade licensing act, which sought to restrict certain kinds of commerce to Africans rather than Indians (Leys, 1975). But there has been no full length study of the complex interaction between Indian and African commerce and manufacturing. We have suggested from time to time in this text that the popular view of jua kali (African) enterprise successfully attacking Indian monopolies and putting them out of business is a very partial version of what is a much more complicated set of inter-relations between these two communities, each internally highly diversified.

For every jua kali anecdote about Indians blocking and undermining African business aspirations, there is another emphasizing that without the bulk purchases of jua kali products by the Indian wholesalers, and their immediate payments in cash, there would be much more difficulty in some lines of African production. We have also talked of African jua kali 'graduates' of Indian enterprises. These too are a very significant phenomenon. They are perhaps as significant a 'graduation' phenomenon as any that is sought for by the micro-enterprise policy-making constituency. However, as has been stressed throughout this book, those who have graduated from Indian enterprises to self-employment as engineers, furniture makers, welders, mechanics, founders and a great deal else are in no sense part of a targeted project or programme of training for self-employment. This particular graduation process has happened silently, unplanned, and has been driven entirely by market forces.

A further example of the ethnic factor in enterprise development can be detected in the current debates about the state divesting itself of many of its parastatal enterprises. In a number of countries, hesitations about rapid privatization programmes may be linked to fears about which communities might become even more dominant in the field of business if such public assets were for sale. The existence in both East and West Africa of successful expatriate business communities as well as great differences in business experience and tradition within the local communities have contributed an ethnic dimension to what might otherwise appear as just another element in the many structural adjustment programmes impacting on Africa. In both Kenya and Tanzania, there are potentially ethnic implications of divestment policies (Assunçao, 1993: 11).

There are no rapid solutions for certain ethnic communities in Kenya which may be under-represented both in formal business ventures as well as in the informal economy. When such communities have political control they can seek through policies of positive discrimination to advantage their access to business opportunities. But there is evidence to suggest that growing up in a dynamic family business environment with links to other families is a very powerful first step towards business inclination. It is not one that a modicum of entrepreneurship education and training can readily replace.

Micro-enterprise policies and industrial policies

One of the differences between *The African Artisan* (King, 1977) and *Jua Kali Kenya* is that there has been a huge outpouring of material on informal, micro and small enterprises in the last 20 years. As the bibliography in this volume and the specialist bibliographies within it such as *Jua Kali literature* (K-REP, 1993a) confirm, there are very extensive literatures relating to micro-enterprise in Kenya alone. Whereas in the early 1970s, there was relatively little available. One of the consequences in *The African Artisan* was that discussion of the informal economy was much more closely linked to the analysis of industrial policy and to the changing policies of the formal industrial sector. The same was true of the ILO's Employment Mission to Kenya. Its major chapter on Industry and Construction has a good deal to say about rural industrial development, rural and small-scale industry, and sub-contracting to the informal sector. This essential integration of industrial policy is also reinforced in the chapters on Technology and, further, on the Informal Sector (ILO, 1972).

By contrast in the 1990s, the patterns of scholarly specialization and of the associated literatures are such that whole documents can emerge on the informal sector that make no mention of the formal industrial sector, and equally there are whole books on Kenyan industrialization that may only have two or three lines or possibly just one chapter devoted to the informal sector. This is perhaps understandable in academic terms, but the conceptual separation of Kenya's industrial policy from its micro and small-scale policy development is unfortunate. What is noticeably lacking is a consensus at the highest level in Kenya about an industrialization policy that moves the country ahead to a next and more competitive stage of manufacturing intermediate goods, but at the same time makes the micro-enterprise world an integral part of that industrial project. The result is the lack of an active national policy on industrialization, and the continuing failure to integrate into any such policy the potential both of the Indian industrial sector and the informal economy (Coughlin & Ikiara, 1988; Coughlin & Ikiara, 1991).

We have said sufficient in different chapters of this book to underline the very important close connections between the formal economy and the jua kali economy to be unhappy about policies that target the jua kali sector on its own. We are worried, therefore, at the way that the dogma of macro-economic reform and adjustment is threatening the very survival of substantial segments of even the four largest formal industrial sectors in Sub-Saharan Africa (South Africa, Zimbabwe, Nigeria and Kenya). Specifically in Kenya, we have noted that the informal sector appears to have survived and prospered over many years in an atmosphere of, at most, benign neglect by government. But it has also done so in conjunction with a highly protected formal sector economy.

We remain unconvinced that Kenya's jua kali economy will prosper more, and be able to upskill itself substantially, in the absence of a diversified and growing modern industrial sector. It will be very important, therefore, to monitor the impact both on the formal and on the informal economy of current external conditionalities aimed to reduce protection, liberalize imports, and, hopefully, encourage greater export-oriented growth (King, 1995).

Technological confidence and the technological challenge

Another of the themes in this account has been the unmistakable change for the better that has taken place in the fortunes of many of the jua kali we have revisited, and many others who have reflected on the changes in the last 10–15 years. We have pinpointed changes in machine manufacture, and in what we have termed a second stage of import substitution, in which the particular skill moves out of the enclave of the Industrial Area and becomes part of a more local pattern of engineering knowledge. We have constantly said that this technological confidence has not been the result of a project or a programme of indigenous capacity building. Its developments have been difficult to demarcate (e.g. in exactly what year did the jua kali first develop a mechanized woodworking machine, a maize mill or a zero-grazer?). In other cases, for example with the production of weighing machines and their verification by the Kenya Bureau of Standards, it should be possible to point to particular years when new capacities have been noted. In other cases again, such as our jua kali entrepreneur who 'graduated' successfully to a light industrial area, but did not wish even to be identified, one of the more technologically sophisticated of our study sample is effectively invisible.

The pace of technological change has been quite rapid within the informal sector, and perhaps nowhere more so than in the manufacture of high quality furniture. Equally important, however, has been the quiet extension of the technological frontier as the metal workers learn how to design and make yet another item for the building trade that hitherto was only made in the Industrial Area or was imported. There has been no study of the new ground won on this frontier, but it would certainly be valuable to have a status report on this (Mihyo, 1994: 9; King & Abuodha, 1995).

The limits and fragility of technological confidence

There are several things that need to be said about this newly found technological confidence. It is currently historically connected with the formal industrial sector but its linkages with it are probably weakening. Through this confidence, the informal sector is improvising with the manufacture of a range of products that are of sufficient quality to compete within Kenya, especially with low-income buyers, but are currently less likely to become elements in any export-oriented project except to neighbouring countries. We must be careful, therefore, not to exaggerate the pace and significance of this technological change. Compared with the early 1970s, the metal and woodworking shops are significantly better in terms of what they can now attempt, but the mechanical engineering shops in Gikomba, for example, are still massively under-capitalized in respect of basic metalworking machinery. In late 1994, we have said earlier, there were only two or three metalworking lathes in the whole of the African workshop sector in Gikomba, and this was viewed as one of the more progressive centres of jua kali development in the whole country.

Thus, the African metalworking business has clearly developed compared to where it was in the early 1970s, but the various enterprises whose progress has been documented in these pages have with only one or two exceptions not yet reached the technological capacity of the Indian general engineering workshop of the late colonial period in Kenya. A handful of these workshops which used to dominate Gikomba and nearby areas can still be seen operating on Kombo Munyiri Road, and can still be analysed for comparative purposes.

What should perhaps be underlined, as strategies for encouraging jua kali technological development continue to be debated, is that there is already in Kenya a higher level of engineering capacity in the remaining Indian firms that is underutilized. This is not an argument for failing to support African entrepreneurs, but it is worth noting that it is the overall lack of a positive policy towards existing capacity that keeps Indian firms underutilized:

Without profound changes in the political system it is unlikely that Kenya will move to the second stage of import-substitution industrialization since it is unlikely that the [Asian] foundries and the metal-engineering industries will be revived. (Anyang' Nyong'o, 1988: 41)

Towards a new politics and policy for micro-enterprise in relation to small, medium and large-scale industry

Kenya has distinguished itself in Sub-Saharan Africa by having on the statute books a policy on small-scale and jua kali development, and we have examined the 20 years taken to put it there. But this is not the same as having a policy environment where micro-entrepreneurs have access to support either at the local district or central levels, and where their aspirations for technological growth and transformation are felt to be a significant part of a larger national project. Rather, the most recent analysts of the status of micro-enterprise in government thinking have concluded that the lack of political muscle behind the Small Enterprise Development Unit in the Ministry of Planning and National Development is confirmation 'that the informal sector is still a marginal issue that is being addressed mainly for legitimacy, political stability and aid reasons' (Assunçao, 1993: 6).

This is almost certainly too harsh a comment, but it is not difficult to reach a conclusion that jua kali development in Kenya is less a programme than a series of projects, that many of these are bilateral, multi-lateral, private sector and NGO projects rather than central or local government in origin, and that the jua kali policy, significant though it is in its own right, has much less influence, not only because it has little muscle behind it, but because of the absence of complementary industrial policies and relevant trade policies (Teitel, 1994). We have also noted a disturbing tendency to treat micro-enterprise quite separately from medium and small-scale industry. Again, it is important not to be too judgemental on this lack of integration. There is almost certainly a similar lack of co-ordination in many OECD countries.

For many of the kinds of micro-entrepreneur we have been discussing, there is almost certainly still no sense of even being part of a sector. The information gap about what opportunities do exist is very real. Trade associations (or jua kali societies) are not operating effectively yet, and may not for a long time, as a transparent support group for crucial trade-specific information. The Jua Kali Development Programme of the government which collected information from some tens of thousands of jua kali, on their registration forms, about their readiness to attend courses and seminars, and about their ideas for improving their business, has scarcely had the capacity to issue their Jua Kali Artisan Identification cards, let alone follow up on the thousands of carefully-written ideas and suggestions for business improvement.

Apart from the lack of physical infrastructure for jua kali, there is certainly as large a lack of a knowledge infrastructure. The huge amount of literature that is now locally available on the jua kali in Kenya is not designed for them or by them. There seems to be very little circulating in Swahili or in the main local languages that could be of direct assistance to micro-enterprises. It should not be surprising, therefore, that in a recent contrast between formal and informal firms in Kenya, the informal firms did not even register the fact that 'gaining investment benefits', 'foreign exchange' or 'uncertainty about government policies' were any of their largest problems (RPED, 1994: 38). This is for the very good reason that for most informal firms the very notion of export, foreign exchange and investment benefits are as foreign to them as foreign exchange itself. Apart from this, the majority of the jua kali artisans trade within their own circuits; they have insufficient contact with the formal sector of the economy, and even less with the financial institutions. Certainly, some of the 'social barriers to African entrepreneurship' have been dismantled since Marris wrote about this in the 1960s, but many of them are still in place in 1995 (Marris, 1968; Manji, 1995: 12–13).

Essentially, the jua kali are still much more part of the fragmented world of self-help (*harambee*) than they are of any partnership with government, with the formal private sector or with other sections of a self-confident micro-enterprise constituency. More than 20 years after Keith Hart's article on the informal sector in Ghana (Hart, 1973), the workforce in the informal economies of many countries, including Kenya, is still substantially invisible, in repect of its ambitions, its political alliances, and its associational behaviour. This short book has charted the emergence of both a national as well as an NGO and aid agency concern about micro-enterprise, but almost no item on the shelves upon shelves of literature currently available on Kenya's jua kali is produced by the jua kali themselves. In other words, the consensus about the importance of the jua kali has been achieved without the voice of the jua kali being heard.

We have sought to give some brief insights into this jua kali world that are being missed in so much of the policy literature. We have tried to talk of actual graduates of Indian or of other firms rather than of graduation. We have looked at specific examples of technological change and of technological ambition rather than of models. We have sought to personalize a little the informal sector in Nairobi and in Githiga, and our principal sources of information accordingly have been the jua kali themselves. A great deal more needs to be learnt about their view of micro-enterprise, of their jua kali associations, their ways of raising capital, their attitude to exports, and much else. But in a book that has tried to sketch something of the feeling and the culture of enterprise, it may be appropriate to end with a few words on how the young man on the cover of *The African Artisan* (1977) and who appears, 20 years later, in the pictures on page 63 of *Jua Kali Kenya* (1996) was planning, through a little exercise in community self-help to insert his daughter into something better than subsistence self-employment:

I will not change my view about getting my children into private secondary schools. In fact I cannot support any of my six children at the secondary level, unless I get them into Government secondary school. Since my daughter dropped out in Standard VI, and has repeated three times (she was not so keen on studies!), my wife and I have decided to find money through *harambee*, so as to buy her some few hens to enable her to survive. And for your information, if 200 hens would cost us 58 KShs for a single chick, and we care for them for 3 months, the fourth month they will start laying eggs. Now say cheaply one egg = 3 KSh, then 200 x 3 = 600 KShs. If I can raise 59 x 200 (i.e. about 2,000 KShs), then through my daughter's care I would be getting 18,000 KShs a month. So although she was not good at school this would mean more than mere survival for her. (Nene, 23 January 1995)

The reader will need to judge whether the evidence in this book supports the view taken here that there has been some significant change over 20 years in Kenya. Paradoxically the ILO which did so much to put the informal sector concept on the map in Kenya in the early 1970s appears to have changed its mind over this same period that this book covers. Back in 1972 the ILO argued in the famous Employment Mission to Kenya that 'the bulk of employment in the informal sector, far from being only marginally productive, is economically efficient and profitmaking' (ILO, 1972: 5). Now almost 25 years later, it would seem that for most of Africa the situation is actually more gloomy for the informal sector than in 1972. The ILO's *World Employment 1995* report states baldly, as we mentioned above, that worldwide 'the informal sector typically consists of both dead-end survival activities and small-scale activities with the potential for growth and technical upgrading' (ILO, 1995: 92). Compared to Asia where the sector is allegedly thriving, and Latin America where there is said to be some dynamism in the sector, the diagnosis of Africa is fairly stark and highly generalized. Just one line for a whole continent:

> In Africa informal sectors are still dominated by low-productivity survival activities. (ILO, 1995: 92–3)

This book may act in a small way to challenge present tendencies that increasingly take for granted that Africa is effectively marginal to the global economy. In terms of indicators such as the share of direct foreign investment going to Africa (less than one per cent of the total of US$200 billion annually going to developing countries), it may well appear that many African economies do scarcely participate in the world economy at all, except as aid recipients (ILO, 1995: 98–9).

The jua kali we have studied have little knowledge of the global economy. But many of them have survived and substantially developed without local handouts, and certainly without being part of any aid project. The barriers to their further development are many, and several of these barriers are quite out of their control, like the world prices for primary products such as coffee and tea. Perhaps we should end by looking back at one of the most salient images of all in our study of the Kenyan jua kali – the entire coffee grading assembly sitting rusting in the backyard of one of our Gikomba producers since the coffee farmer who ordered it could not afford to buy it (see fig. 3.2, p. 90). A testimony to the creativity of the jua kali but a reminder that they may be ultimately very dependent on fairer government and world prices for African products.

Notes

1. See, for example, Webster, L. M. and Fidler, F., 1994, *A Review of Informal Sectors in the Sahel*, World Bank; Assunçao, P., 1993, 'Government policies and the urban informal sector in sub-Saharan Africa', Working paper, WEP 2–19/WP 64, ILO; and Haan, H.C., 1994a, 'A role for informal sector associations', Working document no. 1, TOOL, Amsterdam.

2. One of the exceptions to this dearth of literature on the rural is Ng'ethe and Wahome's study (1989).

3. A fascinating account of the construction of Kikuyu ethnicity is contained in John Lonsdale's '"Listen while I read": orality, literacy and Christianity in the young Kenyatta's making of the Kikuyu', paper to the conference on *Ethnicity in Africa*, Centre of African Studies, University of Edinburgh, May 1995.

Bibliography

Abban, C. and J. Quarshie, 1993, 'Integrated Skills Upgrading for Self Employment (NACVET). The Case of Ghana', ILO Expert consultation on training for self-employment through VTIs, Turin.

Abuodha, C., 1990, 'Passive production in small enterprises: the case of low-cost light in Kenya', manuscript, IDS, Nairobi.

Abuodha, C., 1995, 'The role of financial markets in small scale industrial financing in Kenya' in McCormick, D. and Pedersen, P. (eds), 1996, *Small Enterprises: Flexibility and networking in an African context*, Longhorn Kenya, Nairobi.

Abuodha, C. and K. King, 1991, 'The building of an industrial society: change and development in Kenya's informal (jua kali) sector, 1972–1991', IDS Discussion paper No. 292, University of Nairobi, Nairobi.

ACORD, 1991, 'The Kassala Small-Scale Enterprise Project', London.

ACORD, 1992, 'Economic Interest Groups and their Relevance for Women's Development', Research and Policy Programme Occasional paper No. 4, London.

Adam, C. *et al.*, 1992, *Adjusting Privatisation: Case studies from developing countries*, James Currey, London.

Adam, S., 1993, 'Review of the National Open Apprenticeship System (Nigeria)', *Norrag News,* 14: 58–61.

Adam, S., 1995, *Competence Utilisation and Transfer in Informal Sector Production and Service Trades in Ibadan/Nigeria,* Vol. 16, Bremen African Studies, LIT Verlag, Hamburg.

Adams, A.V., *et al.*, 1992, 'The World Bank's policy paper on vocational education and training', *Prospects,* December.

Aleke-Dondo, C., 1989, 'Assisting the informal sector: comparing methodologies and performance', Occasional paper No. 9, K-REP, Nairobi.

Aleke-Dondo, C., 1991, 'Survey and analysis of credit programmes for small and micro-enterprises in Kenya', Research paper No. 2, K-REP, Nairobi.

Allen, C. H., 1972, 'Unions, income and development', *Developmental Trends in Kenya,* Centre of African Studies, Edinburgh University, Edinburgh.

ANC/COSATU, 1993, *A Framework for Lifelong Learning: A unified, multi-path approach to education and training, Draft 1,* Johannesburg.

Annis, S. and J. Franks, 1989, 'The idea, ideology and economics of the informal sector; the case of Peru', *Grassroots Development,* 13/1: 9–22.

Anyang' Nyong'o, P., 1988, 'The possibility and historical limitations of import substitution industrialisation in Kenya' in Coughlin, P. and

Ikiara, G. K. (eds), *Industrialisation in Kenya: in search of a strategy,* Heinemann Kenya, Nairobi; James Currey London.

Anyang' Nyong'o, P. and Coughlin, P. (eds), 1991, *Industrialisation at Bay: African experiences,* African Academy of Sciences, Nairobi.

Appleton, H., 1993, 'Women: invisible technologists', *Appropriate Technology,* 20/2.

ApT, 1991a, 'The establishment of an appropriate technology unit for East Africa: 'Aprotec Services', Proposal to the European Commission, ApT Design and Development, Moreton-in-Marsh, UK.

ApT, 1991b, 'Kenya in-country training programme: jua kali equipment building courses: instructors' report', British Council, ODA Projects Department, London.

ApT, 1993a, 'The Informal Sector: State of the art review', mimeo.

ApT, 1993b, *The Uganda Small Scale Industries Association,* ApT, Moreton-in-Marsh, UK.

Ashe, J., 1985 *The Pisces II Experience: Local efforts in micro-enterprise development vol. 1,* USAID, Washington.

Asian Foundation, 1992, Objectives and other papers, Nairobi.

Assaad, R., 1993, 'Formal and informal institutions in the labour market with applications to the construction sector in Egypt', *World Development,* 21/6: 925–39.

Assunçao, P., 1993, 'Government policies and the urban informal sector in Sub-Saharan Africa: a comparative study on Kenya, Tanzania, Mozambique and Angola', Working paper WEP2–19/WP64, World Employment Programme, ILO, Geneva.

Awashti, D. N., 1993, 'Vocational Training and Self-Employment. The Indian Experience', ILO expert consultation on training for self-employment through VTIs, Turin.

Awashti, D. N., B. P. Murali and B. N. Bhat, 1990, 'Entrepreneurship Development and New Enterprise Creation: Experience of the Enterpreneurship Development Institute of India', ILO SED/17E, Geneva.

Baldemor, R. R., 1993, 'Insights on the TRUGA Project', paper presented at the ILO Meeting of Experts on Community Based Training, Turin.

Ball, C., 1991, *Pathways to Enterprise,* Commonwealth Secretariat, London.

Bannock, G., 1994, 'Deregulation and small and micro-enterprises', Issues paper 3, *Small Enterprise Policy and Implementation Programme,* British Aid to Small Enterprise, ODA, Nairobi..

Benavot, A., 1992, 'Curricular content, educational expansion, and economic growth', in *Comparative Education Review,* 36, No. 2: 150–74.

Bennett, D., 1993, 'Assessing gender in income-generating projects', paper presented at an ODA-sponsored NGO workshop on Gender, Edinburgh, July, 1993.

Berger, M. and M. Buvinic (eds), 1990, *Women's Ventures,* Kumarian, West Hartford, Conn.

Berluti, A., 1985, *Primary Science for Standard Eight,* MacMillan, Kenya.

Berman, B. and Lonsdale, J., 1992, *Unhappy Valley: Clan, class and state in colonial Kenya,* James Currey, London.

Biervliet, W., 1994, 'Training with production', *International Encyclopaedia of Education. Second Edition,* Pergamon, Oxford.

Biggs, T. *et al.,* 1994, 'Africa can compete! Export opportunities and challenges for garments and home products in the US market', Discussion paper, Regional Programme on Enterprise Development, World Bank, Washington.

Birks, S. *et al.,* 1992, 'Skill acquisition and work in micro-enterprises: recent evidence from West Africa', joint study of World Bank, ILO and Development Centre, OECD, draft, World Bank, Washington.

Birks, S., C. Sinclair and F. Fluitman, 1990, 'Education and training for skills and income in the urban informal sector in Sub-Saharan Africa: the case of Ibadan, Nigeria', World Bank, mimeo.

Boeh-Ocansey, O., 1993, 'Education and training needs of the informal sector: Ghana', draft paper for ODA research project on education and training for the informal sector.

Boehm, U., 1993, 'The advantage of statelessness: a vocational training programme for Afghan refugees', mimeo.

Boehm, U., 1994, 'German vocational education and training: national and international dimensions', *International Encyclopaedia of Education. Second Edition,* Pergamon, Oxford.

Boomgard, J. J., 1989, *AID microenterprise stocktaking: synthesis report,* AID evaluation special study No. 65, USAID, Washington.

Bowland, D., 1988, 'Co-ordination of training systems: some basic issues', ILO TPB/DP25, Geneva.

Bowland, D., 1994, 'The International Labour Organisation' in *International Encylcopaedia of Education. Second Edition,* Pergamon, Oxford.

Bown, L., 1993, *Preparing the Future: Women, literacy and development,* Action Aid Development Report No. 4, London.

Bray, M. and K. Lillis, 1988, *Community Financing of Education,* Pergamon, Oxford.

Buchert, L., 1994, *Education in the Development of Tanzania, 1919–1990,* James Currey, London.

Bude, U., 1989, *Developing Instructional Materials for African Primary Schools,* Occasional papers on basic education No. 3, DSE, Bonn.

Burisch, M., 1991, 'Promoting rural industry: the rural industrial development programme in Kenya' in Coughlin, P. and Ikiara, G. K. (eds), *Kenya's Industrialisation Dilemma,* EAEP, Nairobi.

Butt, S. A., 1987, *Primary Business Education. Standard 8,* Booksales, Nairobi.

Buvinic, M., 1986, 'Projects for women in the Third World: explaining their misbehaviour', *World Development,* 14/5: 653–4.

Buvinic, M., 1991, 'Promoting women's enterprises: can Africa learn from Latin America?', paper presented at a conference on Small and Microenterprise Promotion in a Changing Policy Environment: A Special Focus on Africa, The Hague, September–October 1991.

Caillods, F., 1993, 'Reforms in the organisation of vocational education and training: convergences and divergences', Workshop on new trends in training policy, 18–20 October, ILO, Geneva.

Callaway, A., 1964, 'Nigeria's indigenous apprenticeship system', *University of Ife Journal of African Studies,* OUP, Ibadan, Vol. 1, No. 1.

Carnoy, M., 1980, 'Segmented labour markets' in Carnoy, M. *et al.* (eds), *Education, Work and Employment, Volume Two,* IIEP, Paris.

Carnoy, M., 1993, 'Efficiency and equity in vocational education and training policies in a changing international division of labour', Workshop on new trends in training policy, 18–20 October, ILO, Geneva .

Carron, G. and R. A. Carr-Hill, 1991, *Non-Formal Education: Information and Planning Issues,* IIEP research report No. 90, IIEP, Paris.

Chaturvedi, S., 1989, *A Strategy for Self-employment Creation,* ILO Skill Development for Self-Reliance Project, ILO, Nairobi.

Cheru, F., 1990, *The Silent Revolution,* Anvil, Harare.

Child, F. C., 1976, *Employment, Technology and Growth – the Role of the Intermediate Sector in Kenya,* Occasional paper No. 19, Institute for Development Studies, University of Nairobi, Nairobi.

Chisman, D., 1987, *Practical Secondary Education,* Commonwealth Secretariat, London.

Commonwealth Secretariat (a series of leaflets on youth enterprise in the Commonwealth, London).
(1991) 'Jua Kali: Enterprise under the Kenyan sun'.
(1991) 'Siti Hajar: Tailor Made in Malaysia'.
(1992) 'Lonsangano: Women's Enterprise in Rural Zambia'.

Commonwealth Secretariat, 1992, *Entrepreneurial Skills for Young Women: A manual for trainers,* Commonwealth Secretariat, London.

Cooksey, B., *et al.,* 1993, *Parents' Attitudes Towards Education in Rural Tanzania,* Tanzania Development Research Group (TADREG), Report No. 5, Dar es Salaam.

Coombe, C., 1988, *Survey of Vocationally-Oriented Education in the Commonwealth,* Commonwealth Secretariat, London.

Coombs, P., R. Prosser and M. Ahmed, 1973, *New Paths to Learning for Rural Children and Youth,* ICED, New York.

Corvalan, O., 1993, 'Training for Self-Employment Through VTIs: Chilean case study', ILO Expert consultation on training for self-employment through VTIs, Turin.

Corvalan, O., 1994, 'NGOs (Latin America): training for disadvantaged groups', *International Encyclopaedia of Education. Second Edition,* Pergamon, Oxford.

Coughlin, P. and Ikiara, G. K. (eds), 1988, *Industrialisation in Kenya: In search of a strategy,* EAEP, Nairobi; James Currey, London.

Coughlin, P. and Ikiara, G. K. (eds), 1991, *Kenya's Industrialisation Dilemma,* EAEP, Nairobi.

Court, D., 1972, 'Dilemmas of development: the village polytechnic movements as a shadow system of education in Kenya' in *Developmental Trends in Kenya,* Centre of African Studies, University of Edinburgh, Edinburgh.

Court, D., 1991, 'The intellectual context of educational research: reflections from a donor in Africa' in Gmelin, W. and K. King (eds), *Strengthening Analytical and Research Capacities in Education: Lessons from national and donor experiences,* DSE, Bonn.

Court, D., 1995, 'Webs and cobwebs in research linkages: the perspective of a small donor agency' in *Linkages Revisited,* NUFFIC conference, 16–17 March, 1995, The Hague.

Daily Nation, various issues, 1985–6, 1989–90, Nairobi.

D'Souza, K. C. and L. Thomas, 1995, 'Educational training for the informal sector: India' in Leach, F. (ed.), *Education and Training for the Informal Sector,* ODA, London.

Danish Association of Development Researchers, 1987, *The Informal Sector as an Integral Part of the National Economy: Research needs and aid requirements,* Roskilde University Centre, Roskilde.

De Moura Castro, C., 1993, 'Training in East Europe: problem or solution?' in *Norrag News,* No. 14, July.

De Moura Castro, C., 1994, 'Training policies for the end of the century', Washington, processed.

De Moura Castro, C. and D. Bas, n.d., 'La Cuisine du marché: le retour de l'apprentissage traditionel', Training Policies, ILO, Geneva.

De Soto, H., 1989, *The Other Path,* Harper and Row, New York.

Digolo, O. O., 1990, 'A study of the nature, process and problems of training primary school leavers in jua kali workshops in Kenya', Kenya Education Research Awards/IDRC study, University of Nairobi.

Dolman, A. J., 1994, 'Context for small and micro enterprise development in Kenya: framework paper, *Small Enterprise Policy and Implementation Programme,* British Aid to Small Enterprise, ODA, Nairobi.

Dore, R., 1976, *The Diploma Disease,* Unwin.

DSE, 1993, 'Out-of-School Education, Work and Sustainability in the South – Experiences and Strategies', conference, 29 March – 4 April, Berlin.

Ducci, M. A., 1991, *Vocational Training on the Threshold of the 1990s,* World Bank, Washington D.C.

Ducci, M. A., 1994, 'Latin America: National training agencies', *International Encyclopaedia of Education. Second Edition,* Pergamon, Oxford.

East Africa Royal Commission, 1953-1955 Report (EARC), 1955, Cmd. 9475, HMSO, London.

Economic Commission for Latin America and the Caribbean/OREALC, 1992, *Education and Knowledge: Basic pillars of changing production patterns with social equity,* Santiago, Chile.

Economist, 12 August 1995, 'Republic of Kenya, Ministry of Research, Technical Training and Technology, international competitive bidding tender'.

Eisemon, T. O., 1989, 'The impact of primary schooling on agricultural

210

thinking and practices in Kenya and Burundi' in *Studies in Science Education*, 17.

Ellis, P., 1990, *Measures Increasing the Participation of Girls and Women in Technical and Vocational Education and Training: A Caribbean study*, Commonwealth Secretariat, London.

English, E. Philip and G. Hénault (eds), 1995, *Agents of change: Studies on the policy environment for small enterprise in Africa*, IT Publications, London.

Ernst & Young, 1989, *Evaluation of the USAID/Kenya Private Sector Programme. Final Report*, Bureau for Private Enterprise, USAID, Washington.

Federal Republic of Nigeria, Nigerian National Commission for Unesco, 1992, *Development of Education 1990–1992: National report of Nigeria*, International Conference on Education, 43rd session, 1992, Geneva.

Ferej, A., 1993, 'Traditional Apprenticeship', ILO expert consultation on training for self-employment through VTIs, Turin.

Financial Times, 1992, '*Financial Times* survey: Kenya', 8 January.

Fluitman, F., 1994, 'Traditional apprenticeship', *International Encyclopaedia of Education. Second Edition*, Pergamon, Oxford.

Fluitman, F. and A. K. Sangaré, 1989, 'Some recent evidence of informal sector apprenticeship in Abidjan, Cote d'Ivoire' in Fluitman, F. (ed.), *Training for Work in the Informal Sector*, ILO, Geneva.

Fluitman, F. and Oudin, X., 1991, 'Skill acquisition and work in micro-enterprises: evidence from Lomé, Togo', Discussion paper No. 31, Vocational Training Branch, ILO, Geneva.

Foster, P. J., 1968, 'The vocational school fallacy in development planning' in M. Blaug, *Economics of Education. Volume One*, Penguin, Harmondsworth.

Freeman, D. B. and G. B. Norcliffe, 1985, *Rural Enterprise in Kenya*, University of Chicago, Geography Department Research paper No. 214, Chicago.

Friedrich Ebert Foundation, 1990, 'Handbook for credit guarantee associations in Kenya', Friedrich Ebert Foundation, Nairobi.

Frost, D., 1991, 'New approaches to skills training in Nigeria and Trinidad', *Small Enterprise Development*, 2/2: 41–6.

Fungati, M., 1987, 'ZIMFEP's experience in establishing school leaver employment creation programmes in Zimbabwe' in Droogleever-Fortuijn, E., W. Hoppers and M. Morgan, *Paving Pathways to Work*, CESO, The Hague.

Furedi, F, 1989, *The Mau Mau War in Perspective*, James Currey, London.

Gachugi, A. K., 1994, 'Marketing and the development of small and micro-enterprises', Issue paper No. 5, *Small Enterprise Policy and Implementation Programme*, British Aid to Small Enterprise, ODA, Nairobi.

Gallart, M. A., 1994, 'Latin America: articulation of education, training and work', *International Encyclopaedia of Education. Second Edition*, Pergamon, Oxford.

Gatama, W. M., 1986, *Business Education for Primary Schools; Standard Six. Pupils' book*, TransAfrica, Nairobi.

Gibb, A. A., 1988, *Stimulating Entrepreneurship and New Business Development*, ILO, SED/14E, Geneva.

211

Gichira, R., 1987, 'Problems facing entrepreneurs in Kenya', Report for the Ford Foundation, Nairobi.

Gichira, R. and C. Aleke-Dondo, 1988, 'Institutions assisting small scale enterprises in Kenya', Occasional paper, GOK/ILO/UNDP, Centre Project, Nairobi.

Goodale, G., 1989, 'Training for women in the informal sector' in F. Fluitman (ed.), *Training for Work in the Informal Sector*, ILO, Geneva.

Goodale, G., 1990, 'Women and TVET: addressing the challenge', *Norrag News*, December 1990: 13–15.

Grierson, J. P., 1989a, 'Vocational training and self-employment: lessons from the field', Cranfield/ODA, London.

Grierson, J. P., 1989b, 'Cost-covering, production-based vocational training: the case of Nepal's Butwal Technical Institute', *Apsdep Newsletter*, September/October: 10–13.

Grierson, J. P., 1992, 'Assessing appropriate technology in Calcutta's informal sector', *GATE*, 2/92: 14–17.

Grierson, J. P., 1993, 'Self-employment in developing countries: analysing the effectiveness of enterprise-based training approaches', Paper presented at the Development and the Strategies of SMEs in the 1990s Conference, Mikkeli, Finland.

Grierson, J. P., 1994, 'Report on a review of ODA's small enterprise development activities', ODA, London.

Grootings, P., 1994, 'Eastern and Central Europe: vocational education and training in transition', *International Encyclopaedia of Education. Second Edition*, Pergamon, Oxford.

Gupta, S. K., 1990, 'Enterprise development training programmes in India', *Small Enterprise Development*, 1/4: 15–26.

Gustafsson, I., 1987, *Schools and the Transformation of Work*, IIE, Stockholm.

Haan, H. C., 1989, 'Two examples of training projects for the informal sector in Central America' in F. Fluitman (ed.), *Training for Work in the Informal Sector*, ILO, Geneva.

Haan, H. C., 1994a, 'A role for informal sector associations in technology development and dissemination', FIT Working document No. 1, FIT/TOOL/ILO, Amsterdam.

Haan, H. C., 1994b, 'Jua Kali associations in Kenya: what services to provide to the members?', FIT Working Paper No. 10, FIT/TOOL/ILO, Amsterdam.

Hailey, J., 1991, *Small Business Development in the Developing World: An overview of contemporary issues in enterprise development*, Cranfield School of Management, Cranfield.

Hailey, J., 1994, 'Enterprise education: small business training', *International Encyclopaedia of Education. Second Edition*, Pergamon, Oxford.

Hallak, J. and F. Caillods, 1981, *Education, Training and the Traditional Sector*, IIEP, UNESCO, Paris.

Harbison, F. H., 1967, 'The generation of employment in newly developing countries' in J. R. Sheffield (ed.), *Education, Employment and Rural*

Development, East African Publishing House, Nairobi.

Harper, M., 1984, *Small Business in the Third World,* John Wiley and Sons, Chichester.

Harper, M., 1989a, 'The Programme for the Development of Small Enterprises (DESAP) of the Carvajal Foundation, Cali, Colombia' in F. Fluitman (ed.), *Training for Work in the Informal Sector,* ILO, Geneva.

Harper, M., 1989b, 'The Euro-Action Acord programme in Port Sudan, the Sudan' in F. Fluitman (ed.), *Training for Work in the Informal Sector,* ILO, Geneva.

Harper, M., 1992, 'Evaluating enterprise development programmes in India', *Small Enterprise Development,* 3/4: 50–4.

Hart, K., 1973, 'Informal income opportunities and urban employment in Ghana', *Journal of Modern African Studies,* ii, 1: 61–89.

Hart, K., 1992, 'Market and state after the Cold War: the informal economy reconsidered' in R. Dilley (ed.), *Contesting Markets,* Edinburgh University Press, Edinburgh.

HEART TRUST/NTA, 1993, 'Creating a labour force for the twenty-first century', HEART TRUST/NTA, Kingston, Jamaica.

Herz, B., K. Subbarao, M. Habib and L. Raney, 1991, 'Letting girls learn: promising approaches in primary and secondary education', World Bank Discussion Paper 133, Washington.

Hinchliffe, K. *et al.,* 1988, *The Cost Effectiveness of TVET in Botswana,* Ministry of Education, Gaborone.

Honig, B., 1995, 'Education, heterogeneity and the Jamaican informal sector', Comparative and International Education Society Annual Meeting, March 1995, Boston.

Hoppers, W., 1992, 'The Promotion of Self-Employment in Education and Training Institutions: Perspectives in East and Southern Africa', Small Enterprise Development Programme, ILO, Geneva.

Hoppers, W., 1994a, 'Education and productive work', *International Encyclopaedia of Education. Second Edition,* Pergamon, Oxford.

Hoppers, W., 1994b, 'Questioning the school – what room for the local perspective?', NASEDEC Conference on 'Quality of education in the context of culture in developing countries', 13–15 January, Tampere.

Hoppers, W. and D. Komba, 1992, 'Productive work in general education: an analysis of variants', Paper presented at the World Conference on Comparative Education, Prague.

Howarth, R., 1992, 'Women's microenterprise – lessons for enterprise support agencies', Paper presented at the Regional Workshop on the Development of Microenterprises by Women, Ahmedabad.

Ikiara, G. K., 1988, 'The role of government institutions in Kenya's industrialisation' in Coughlin, P. and G. K. Ikiara (eds), *Industrialisation in Kenya: In search of a strategy,* EAEP, Nairobi; James Currey, London.

Ikiara, G. K., 1991a, 'Policy changes and the informal sector: a review' in Coughlin, P and G. K. Ikiara (eds), *Kenya's Industrialisation Dilemma,* EAEP, Nairobi.

Bibliography

Ikiara, G. K., 1991b, 'State intervention in small enterprises: the case of Kenya's Industrial Estates' in Anyang' Nyongo and P.C. Coughlin, (eds), *Industrialisation at Bay: African experiences,* African Academy of Sciences, Nairobi.

ILO, 1972, *Employment, Incomes and Equality: a Strategy for Increasing Productive Employment in Kenya,* ILO, Geneva.

ILO, 1993a, Workshop on new trends in training policy, 18–20 October 1993, Geneva.

ILO, 1993b, Expert consultation on training for self-employment through VTIs, Turin.

ILO, 1995, *World Employment 1995: An ILO report,* ILO, Geneva.

ILO, World Employment Programme, Urbanisation and Employment Programme: series of working papers on the informal sector, various dates, Geneva.

ILO/Kenya Government, 1991, 'Proposal for a Jua Kali training, productivity and employment project', ILO, Geneva.

ILO/SIDA, 1993a, *Skill Development for Self-Reliance: A methodology for training for self-employment,* ILO/SIDA, Geneva/Stockholm.

International Foundation for Education with Production, 1990, *Defusing the Time-Bomb? Education and Employment in Southern Africa,* IFEP, Gaborone.

International Fund for Agricultural Development, 1990, *Kenya: Special programming/general identification mission on small scale enterprises: Vol. 1,* Report No. 0204-KE, Rome.

Iyer, L., 1991, 'Diversification of Women's Occupations Through Training: India', TPB/DP61, ILO, Geneva.

Jackelen, H. R. and E. Rhyne, 1991, 'Towards a more market oriented approach to credit and savings for the poor', *Small Enterprise Development,* 2/4: 4–20.

Jamison, D. T. and L. J. Lau, 1982, *Farmer Education and Farm Efficiency,* Johns Hopkins University Press, Baltimore.

Jeans, A., E. Hyman and M. O'Donnell, 1991, 'Technology – the key to increasing the productivity of microenterprises', *Small Enterprise Development,* 2/2: 14–23.

Joekes, S., 1987, *Women in the World Economy: An INSTRAW report,* OUP, Oxford.

Jones, T. J., 1925, *Education in East Africa,* Phelps Stokes Fund, New York.

Jua Kali Associations, 1992, 'Constitutions of various associations', mimeo.

Jua Kali News, 1995, various issues, Nairobi.

Kahiga, D. K. and N. Lauridsen, 1993, 'Kenya: informal sector (jua kali) development and training project: assistance for training and skill upgrading (draft proposal)', Danida, Nairobi.

Kajese, K., 1991, 'African NGO decolonisation: a critical choice for the 1990s', in *Critical Choices for the NGO Community: African development in the 1990s,* Centre of African Studies, University of Edinburgh, Edinburgh.

Kanawaty, G. and C. De Moura Castro, 1990, 'Towards an employment oriented training policy', ILO TPB/DP60, Geneva.

Karcher, W. *et al.* (eds), 1993, *Zwischen Ökonomie und Sozialer Arbeit: Lernen in informellen Sektor in der dritten Welt*, Iko Verlag, Frankfurt.

Kassam, Y. and M. Kamal, 1992, 'Final report of the evaluation study of the training component of the Bangladesh Rural Development Project', CIDA, Canada.

Keino, I. C. and P. M. Ngau, 1996, 'The social background of women entrepreneurs in Nairobi' in D. McCormick and P. Pedersen (eds), 1996, *Small Enterprises: Flexibility and Networking in an African Context*, Longhorn Kenya, Nairobi.

Kenya Government, 1974, *Development Plan 1974–1978*, Government Printer, Nairobi.

Kenya Government, 1978, *Sessional Paper on Educational Objectives and Policies*, Government Printer, Nairobi.

Kenya Government, 1983, *Development Plan, 1984–1988*, Government Printer, Nairobi.

Kenya Government, Ministry of Education, Science and Technology, 1984a, *8-4-4 System of education*, Government Printer, Nairobi.

Kenya Government, Ministry of Education, Science and Technology, 1984b, *Syllabuses for Kenya Primary Schools: Standards VII and VIII*, Jomo Kenyatta Foundation, Nairobi.

Kenya Government, Ministry of Local Government, 1990, *The informal sector: technical manual. Local authority development programme*, Government Printer, Nairobi.

Kenya Government, 1986, *Economic Management for Renewed Growth. Sessional Paper No. 1 of 1986*, Government Printer, Nairobi.

Kenya Government, 1988a, *Development Plan, 1989–1993*, Government Printer, Nairobi.

Kenya Government, 1988b, *Report of the Presidential Working Party on Education and Manpower Training for the Next Decade and Beyond*, Government Printer, Nairobi.

Kenya Government, 1988c, *Sessional Paper No. 6 of 1988 on Education and Manpower Training for the Next Decade and Beyond*, Government Printer, Nairobi.

Kenya Government, 1989a, *A Strategy for Small Enterprise Development in Kenya: Towards the Year 2000. Part One*, Centre Project, UNDP, GOK, ILO, Nairobi.

Kenya Government, 1989b, *Small Enterprise Development in Kenya: Programme of Action. Part Two*, Centre Project, UNDP, GOK, ILO, Nairobi.

Kenya Government, 1989c, *Small Enterprise Development in Kenya. Project Ideas. Part Three*, Centre Project, UNDP, GOK, ILO, Nairobi.

Kenya Government, 1991a, 'Proposal for a jua kali training, productivity and employment project', prepared with the assistance of ILO, Geneva.

Kenya Government, 1991b, 'Kenya: informal sector (jua kali) development and training project: project preparation facility', draft, Nairobi.

Kenya Government, 1991c, *Development and Employment in Kenya: A Strategy for the transformation of the economy*, Government Printer, Nairobi.

Kenya Government, 1992a, *Sessional Paper No. 2 of 1992 on Small Enterprise and Jua Kali Development in Kenya*, Government Printer, Nairobi.

Kenya Government, 1992b, *Economic Survey, 1992*, Bureau of Statistics, Nairobi.

Kenya Government, Ministry of Planning and National Development, 1994, 'Policy and strategy for small scale and jua kali enterprise development in Kenya: action plan, 1994–1995', draft, Nairobi.

Kenya Industrial Estates (KIE), 1990, *Viwanda (KIE Newsletter) issues 1 and 2*, KIE, Nairobi.

Kenya Industrial Estates (KIE), 1992, 'KIE informal sector loans programmes', KIE, Nairobi, processed.

Kenya Management Assistance Programme (K-MAP), 1993, 'Jua kali Federation works out priorities' in *Small Business Forum* (Nairobi) Vol. 5, No 1.

Kenya Rural Enterprise Programme (K-REP), 1991, *Juhudi: A microenterprise development newsletter*, K-REP, Nairobi.

Kenya Rural Enterprise Programme (K-REP), 1993a, *Jua Kali Literature: An annotated bibliography*, K-REP, Nairobi.

Kenya Rural Enterprise Programme (K-REP), 1993b, *Inventory of Projects and Programmes for Small and Jua Kali Development in Kenya*, K-REP, Nairobi.

Kenya Times, 1985–6.

Kenya Weekly Review special issue on plots scandal, 2 December 1994, Nairobi.

Kerre, B.W., 1993, 'Vocational training for self-employment: a case study of Kiambu Institute of Science and Technology, Kenya', paper presented to ILO Expert Meeting on Training for Self-Employment through VTIs, November–December 1993, Turin.

Kibare, C., 1993, 'Gender considerations under the ILO/KYTEC Project', paper presented at the ILO Meeting of Experts in Community-Based Training for Self-Employment and Income Generation, Turin.

Kilby, P., 1988, 'Breaking the entrepreneurship bottleneck in the late-developing countries: is there a useful role for government?' Draft paper, Wesleyan University.

King, E. M. and M. A. Hill, 1993, *Women's Education in Developing Countries: Barriers, Benefits and Policies*, World Bank, Washington DC.

King, K., 1972, 'Education and development in the Narok District of Kenya', *African Affairs*, Vol. 81, 3: 388–407.

King, K., 1973, 'Jobless in Kenya: the social life of the educated unemployed', unpublished manuscript, 150pp., Centre of African Studies, University of Edinburgh.

King, K., 1975, 'Skill acquisition in the informal sector of an African economy: the Kenya case' in *Journal of Development Studies*, vol. 11, no. 2.

King, K., 1977, *The African Artisan*, Heinemann, London .

King, K., 1980, 'Education and self-employment' in IIEP, *Education, Work and Employment, vol. II,* Paris.

King, K., 1984, 'The end of education for self-reliance in Tanzania?' Occasional paper no. 1, Centre of African Studies, University of Edinburgh.

King, K., 1985, 'The environments of education with production: schools, training institutions and productive enterprises', *Education with Production,* 4/1: 75–91.

King, K., 1987, 'Evaluating the context of diversified secondary education in Tanzania' in J. Lauglo and K. Lillis (eds), *Vocationalising Education,* Pergamon, Oxford.

King, K., 1989a, 'An evaluation of research and policies on informal sector employment in developing countries', PHREE background paper series, 89/12, World Bank, Washington.

King, K., 1989b, 'Primary schooling and developmental knowledge in Africa', *African Futures,* Centre of African Studies, University of Edinburgh, Edinburgh.

King, K., 1989c, 'Training for the urban informal sector in developing countries: policy issues for practitioners' in F. Fluitman (ed.), *Training for Work in the Informal Sector,* ILO, Geneva.

King, K., 1990a, 'Training and structural adjustment: images from Ghana and Nigeria', Occasional paper No. 29, Centre of African Studies, University of Edinburgh, Edinburgh.

King, K., 1990b, 'Education for employment and self-employment interventions in developing countries. Past experience and present prognosis' in International Foundation for Education with Production, *Defusing the Time-Bomb? Education and Employment in Southern Africa,* IFEP, Gaborone.

King, K., 1990c, 'An evaluation of research and policies on informal sector employment in Kenya' in D. Turnham *et al., The Informal Sector Revisited,* OECD, Paris.

King, K., 1991a, 'Training for the Informal Sector', chapter in K. King, *Aid and Education in the Developing World,* Longman, Harlow.

King, K., 1991b, *Aid and Education in the Developing World,* Longman, Harlow.

King, K., 1993, 'Training for self-employment through vocational training institutions: lessons from experience', Paper presented to ILO Expert Meeting on Training for Self-Employment through VTIs, November–December, 1993, Turin.

King, K., 1994, 'Technical and vocational education and training: an overview' in *International Encyclopaedia of Education. Second Edition,* vol. 11, Pergamon, Oxford.

King, K, 1995, 'Revisiting Kenya's informal (jua kali) sector against the background of the formal globalising economy', Third Oxford Conference on 'Globalisation and learning', 21–25 September 1995, New College, Oxford.

King, K., 1996, 'Re-ordering Kenya's informal *Jua Kali* economy in the 1990s: external and internal policy agendas' in D. McCormick and P. Pedersen (eds), *Small Enterprises: Flexibility and networking in an African context*, Longhorn Kenya, Nairobi.

King, K. and C. Abuodha, 1995, 'Education, training and technological development in the informal sector in Kenya' in *Science, Technology and Development* (Cass) Vol. 13, No. 2.

King, T., M. Parnell and R. Carr-Hill, 1992, *The Commercial Culture Gap between British Businessmen and South-East Asia*, School of South-East Asian Studies, University of Hull for the Department of Trade and Industry, Hull.

Kinyanjui, M. N., 1996, 'Entrepreneurial characteristics, motives and small and medium sized enterprises formation and development in Central Kenya' in D. McCormick and P. Pedersen (eds), 1996, *Small Enterprises: Flexibility and networking in an African context*, Longhorn Kenya, Nairobi.

Kivunzyo, K., 1993, 'ILO/Kenya Youth Training and Employment Creation Project', Paper presented at the ILO Meeting of Experts on Community Based Training for Self-Employment and Income Generation, Turin.

Kraak, A., 1991, 'Making the hidden curriculum the formal curriculum: vocational training in South Africa', *Comparative Education Review*, 35/3: 406–29.

Kraak, A., 1993, 'Free or coordinated market? Education and training policy options for a future South Africa', unpublished PhD, University of Western Cape, Cape Town.

La Belle, T., 1982, 'Formal, non-formal and informal education: a holistic perspective on lifelong learning', *International Review of Education*, 28/2.

La Towsky, R. J. and J. P. Grierson, 1992, 'Traditional apprenticeships and enterprise support networks', *Small Enterprise Development*, 3/3: 42–8.

Lauglo, J., 1985, *Practical Subjects in Kenyan Academic Secondary Schools: General report*, Education Division Documents. No. 20, SIDA, Stockholm.

Lauglo, J., 1994, 'Vocational training modes: Sweden, Germany and Japan', *International Encyclopaedia of Education. Second Edition*, Pergamon, Oxford.

Lauglo, J. and A. Närman, 1988, 'Diversified secondary education in Kenya: the status of practical subjects and their uses after school' in Lauglo, J. and K. Lillis (eds), *Vocationalizing Education*, Pergamon, Oxford.

Lauglo, J. and K. Lillis, 1988, ' "Vocationalization" in International Perspective' in J. Lauglo and K. Lillis, *Vocationalizing Education*, Pergamon, Oxford.

Lavrijsen, L., 1991, *Enterprise Education and Self-Employment Promotion*, FACET BV Apeldoorn, The Netherlands.

Layton, D., 1994, 'Technology: educational programs' in *International Encyclopedia of Education. Second Edition*, Pergamon, Oxford.

Leach, F. (ed.), 1995, *Education and Training for the Informal Sector: Case studies*, ODA Occasional publication, Serial No. 11, Vol. II, ODA, London.

Leek, J. *et al.*, 1993, *Made in Africa: Learning from carpentry hand-tool projects*, VSO/IT Publications, London.

Levitsky, J., 1992, 'Private sector membership associations and support for small and medium enterprises', *Small Enterprise Development*, 3/1: 22–33.

Leys, C., 1972, 'The limits of African capitalism: the formation of the monopolistic petty-bourgeoisie in Kenya', in *Developmental Trends in Kenya*, Centre of African Studies, University of Edinburgh, Edinburgh.

Leys, C., 1975, *Underdevelopment in Kenya: The political economy of neo-colonialism, 1964-1971*, James Currey, London.

Leys, C., 1996, *The Rise and Fall of Development Theory*, James Currey, London.

Liedholm, C., 1990, 'The dynamics of small-scale industry in Africa and the role of policy', Occasional paper, GEMINI Project, USAID, Washington.

Liedholm, C. and D. Mead, 1986, 'Small scale enterprises in developing countries: a review of the state of the art', International Development Working paper No. 30, Michigan State University, East Lansing.

Liedholm, C. and D. Mead, 1993, 'The structure and growth of microenterprises in Southern and Eastern Africa: evidence from recent surveys', GEMINI/USAID, Bethesda, Maryland.

Lohmar-Kuhnle, C., 1992, *Occupation-Oriented Training and Education for Target Groups from the Informal Sector*, BMZ, Bonn.

Lonsdale, J, 1995, ' "Listen while I read": orality, literacy and Christianity in the young Kenyatta's making of the Kikuyu', paper to the conference on Ethnicity in Africa, Centre of African Studies, University of Edinburgh, May 1995.

MacGaffey, J. *et al.*, 1991, *The Real Economy of Zaire: The contribution of smuggling and other unofficial activities to national wealth*, James Currey, London.

Macharia, K., 1991, 'Social networks: ethnicity and the informal sector in Nairobi', Harvard University, Boston.

Macharia, K., 1995, 'The Jua Kali sector in Kenya: its contribution to development', Sociology Department, Harvard University, processed.

Mahabir, D., 1993, *Servol Pre-School and Adolescent Training Programmes in Trinidad and Tobago*, IIEP, Paris.

Mahajan, V. and T. W. Dichter, 1990, 'A contingency approach to small business and microenterprise development', *Small Enterprise Development*, 1/1: 4–16.

Makau, B. M., 1985, 'Educational planning and development in Kenya: the 8-4-4 school curriculum and its implications for self-employment', Working paper No. 433, Institute for Development Studies, University of Nairobi, Nairobi.

Malawian Entrepreneurs Development Institute (MEDI), 1993, 'Training for self-employment through VTIs: lessons from experience', MEDI for Expert meeting on training for self-employment through VTIs, ILO, Turin.

Maldonado, C., 1987, *Petits producteurs urbains d'Afrique francophone*, ILO, Geneva.

Maldonado, C., 1989, 'Self-training in theory and practice' in F. Fluitman, (ed.), *Training for Work in the Informal Sector,* ILO, Geneva.

Maliyamkono, T. L. and M.S.D. Bagachwa, 1990, *The Second Economy in Tanzania,* James Currey, London.

Manji, Z., 1995, 'Minding your own business: an investigation into the main problems and constraints faced by small and medium sized enterprises in Nairobi', BA dissertation, University of Edinburgh, 1995.

Manu, G. and A. A. Gibb, 1990, 'The design of extension and related support services for small-scale enterprise', *International Small Business Journal,* 8/3.

Maravanyika, O. E., 1989, 'The new vocationalism, entrepreneurial skills development and a search for a worthwhile work-oriented curriculum', *Bulletin of the Associate College Centre,* 25/1: 23–32.

Marris, P., 1968, 'The social barriers to African entrepreneurship', *The Journal of Development Studies,* Vol. 5, No. 1.

Marris, P. and A. Somerset, 1971, *African Businessmen,* East African Publishing House, Nairobi.

Mashek, R. W., 1992, 'The Don Bosco way to train disadvantaged youth', ILO TPB/DP92, Geneva.

Mason, G., 1994, 'Vocational education and training: Anglo-German comparisons', *International Encyclopaedia of Education. Second Edition,* Pergamon, Oxford.

Matrix Consultants, 1990, *Infrastructure Needs Assessment for the Informal Sector: Phase 1 Report,* Nairobi.

Mbilinyi, M. and P. Mbughuni (eds), 1991, *Education in Tanzania with a Gender Perspective: Summary report,* SIDA Education Division, Documents 53, Stockholm.

Mburugu, J. B., 1993, 'Self-employment and entrepreneurship in vocational training institutions in Kenya', paper to expert meeting on Training for self-employment through VTIs, November/December, 1993, Turin.

McCormick, D., 1991, 'Manufacturing in miniature', unpublished manuscript.

McCormick, D., 1993, 'Risk and firm growth: the dilemma of Nairobi's small-scale manufacturers', Institute for Development Studies, Discussion paper No. 291, University of Nairobi, Nairobi.

McCormick, D. with M. N. Kinyanjui, 1994a, 'Financing, human resources, environment, and markets of African small enterprise: a literature review', prepared for the International Centre for Economic Growth, Nairobi.

McCormick, D., 1994b, 'Industrial district or garment ghetto? The case of Nairobi's mini-manufacturers', paper to workshop on Industrialisation, organisation, innovation and institutions in the South', Vienna, Austria, 17–18 November.

McCormick, D., 1994c, 'Women in business: class and Nairobi's small and medium-sized producers' in K. Sheldon (ed.), *Courtyards, Markets, City Streets: Urban women in Africa,* Westview Press, Boulder.

Bibliography

McCormick, D. and P. Pedersen (eds), 1996, *Small Enterprises: Flexibility and networking in an African context,* Longhorn Kenya, Nairobi.

McGrath, S. A., 1993, 'Changing the subject', Occasional paper No. 44, Centre of African Studies, University of Edinburgh, Edinburgh.

McGrath, S. A., 1996, 'Learning to work? Changing discourses on education and training in South Africa, 1976–1996', unpublished PhD dissertation, University of Edinburgh.

McGrath, S. and K. King with F. Leach and R. Carr-Hill, 1995, *Education and Training for the Informal Sector,* ODA Occasional publication, Serial No. 11, vol. I, ODA, London.

McLaughlin, S. D., 1979, *The Wayside Mechanic,* Centre for International Education, Massachusetts.

McPherson, M. A., 1991, 'Micro and small-scale enterprises in Zimbabwe: results of a country-wide survey', GEMINI/USAID, Bethesda, Maryland.

Mead, D. C. and P. Kunjeku, 1993, *Business Linkages and Enterprise Development in Zimbabwe,* CZI, Harare.

Mead, D. C., H. O. Mukwenha, and L. Reed, 1993, 'Growth and transformation among small enterprises in Zimbabwe', GEMINI/USAID, Bethesda, Maryland.

Messina, G., 1993, 'Education and training needs of the informal sector: Chile', in F. Leach (ed.), *Education and Training for the Informal Sector,* vol. 2, Serial No. 11, ODA, London.

Mihyo, P. B., 1994, 'Technology policy and small and micro enterprises: preliminary findings, observations and recommendations on technical change, training, and small and micro enterprises', Issues paper No. 4, *Small Enterprise Policy and Implementation Programme,* British Aid to Small Enterprise, ODA, Nairobi.

Mikkelsen, B., 1987, 'Formation of an industrial labour force in Kenya: experiences of labour training in the metal manufacturing industries', IDS Occasional paper No. 49, University of Nairobi, Nairobi.

Molyneux, M., 1985, 'Mobilisation without emancipation? Women's interests, state and revolution in Nicaragua', *Feminist Studies,* 11/2.

Monji, R., 1993, 'The skills development for self-reliance methodology: RYTE experience', paper presented at the ILO Meeting of Experts on Community Based Training for Self-Employment and Income Generation, Turin.

Montrichard, R., 1987, 'Beyond skills training: the work of Servol in Trinidad' in E. Droogleever-Fortuijn, W. Hoppers and M. Morgan, *Paving Pathways to Work,* CESO, The Hague.

Moser, C., 1989, 'Gender planning in the Third World: Meeting Practical and Strategic Gender Needs', *World Development,* 17/11: 1799–825.

Mosse, J. C., 1993, *Half the World, Half a Chance,* Oxfam, Oxford.

Mothobi, B., 1978, *Training for Development,* ARTCA, Salisbury/Harare.

Mutua, A. K. and C. Aleke-Dondo, 1990, 'The informal financial markets in Kenya', K-REP Research Paper, No. 4, Nairobi.

Bibliography

Närman, A., 1988, *Practical Subjects in Kenyan Academic Secondary Schools: Tracer Study II*, SIDA Education Division, Documents 39, Stockholm.

Ndua, N. and Ng'ethe, N., 1984, 'Education, training and welfare in the informal sector: a study of carpentry and metal work in the Eastlands of Nairobi, Kenya', (Report for Undugu Society of Kenya), Institute for Development Studies, University of Nairobi.

Nelson, R., 1993, 'Guidelines for reorienting vocational training to self-employment', paper to ILO expert meeting on Training for self-employment through VTIs, Turin .

NEPI, 1992, *Human Resources Development*, Oxford University Press, Cape Town.

Netherlands, Ministry of Foreign Affairs, c.1992, *Small-scale Enterprise*, Policy Document No. 3, Development Cooperation Information Department, The Hague.

Ng'ethe, N. and J.G. Wahome, 1989, 'The rural informal sector in Kenya: a study of micro-enterprises in Nyeri, Meru, Uasin Gishu and Siaya Districts', IDS Occasional paper No. 54, University of Nairobi, Nairobi.

Nkinyangi, J. and S. Shaeffer (eds), 1983, *Educational Research Environments in the Developing World*, IDRC, Ottawa.

Norrag News, Nos 7 & 8, Centre of African Studies, University of Edinburgh.

Obura, A., 1993a, 'Education as support or hindrance of small and intermediate size enterprise in Africa', African Centre for Technology Studies, Nairobi.

Obura, A., *et al.*, 1993b, 'Process and product of science and technology learning in primary schools in Kenya', Project report, African Centre for Technology Studies, Nairobi.

ODA, 1990, *Into the Nineties: An education policy for British aid*, ODA, London.

ODA, 1994a, *Education Policy Paper: Aid to education in 1993 and beyond*, ODA, London.

ODA, 1994b, *'Report of the Small Enterprise Policy Implementation Programme (SEPIP) Mission*, ODA, Nairobi.

ODA, 1991–2; 1993–4, 1994–5, 'Small Enterprise Development Programme' Annual Reports, British Aid to Small Enterprise, ODA, Nairobi.

ODA, 1995, *Small Enterprise Development Strategy Report*, ODA, London.

Odurkene, J. N., 1985, 'Indigenous apprenticeship and on-the-job training practices in Uganda', Makerere University, Kampala, processsed.

Oehring, E., 1990, 'FUNDES – an attempt to establish loan guarantee schemes through private foundations in Latin America', *Small Enterprise Development*, 1/2: 27–33.

Oketch, H. O., 1995, 'Education and training needs of the informal sector: Kenya' in F. Leach (ed.), *Education and Training for the Informal Sector* Vol. II, Serial No. 11, ODA, London .

Oketch, H. O. and J. Parker, 1991, 'Furniture making in Kibera', K-REP Research paper No. 6, K-REP, Nairobi.

Oketch, H. O., *et al.*, 1991, 'Microenterprise credit, employment, incomes

222

and output: some evidence from Kenya', K-REP Research paper Series, No. 8, K-REP, Nairobi.

Ongile, G. and D. McCormick, 1996, 'Growth and flexibility: case studies from Nairobi's garment industry' in D. McCormick and P. Pedersen, (eds), 1996, *Small Enterprises: Flexibility and networking in an African context,* Longhorn Kenya, Nairobi.

Orsini, D. (ed.), 1989, 'Report on the East and Southern African Regional Conference on the informal sector: issues in policy reform and programmes', Africa Bureau, USAID, Labat-Anderson, Arlington.

Oxfam, 1992, *Income Generating Projects: A view from the grassroots,* Oxford.

Pantin, G., 1984, *The Servol Village,* Bernard van Leer Foundation, The Hague.

Parker, J and C. Aleke-Dondo, 1991, 'Kenya: Kibera's small enterprise sector: baseline survey report', GEMINI Working paper No. 17, Bethesda, Maryland.

Parker, J. C. and T. R. Torres, 1994, 'Micro and small enterprise in Kenya: results of the 1993 national baseline survey', USAID/GEMINI, Bethesda, Maryland.

Peace, G. and D. Hulme, 1993, 'Children and income-generating programmes: a report for SCF (UK)', Institute for Development Policy and Management, Manchester.

Peters-Berries, C., 1993a, 'Putting development policies into practice: the problems of implementing policy reforms in Africa', WEP 2–19/WP 63, working paper, Urban and Informal Sector Programme, World Employment Programme, ILO, Geneva.

Peters-Berries, C., 1993, 'The urban informal sector in Zimbabwe', working paper, WEP2–19/WP 61, World Employment Programme, ILO, Geneva.

Powell, J., 1991, 'Kumasi University's involvement in grassroots industrial development', *Small Enterprise Development,* 2/2: 35–43.

Pratt B. and J. Boyden (eds), 1985, *The Field Directors' Handbook: An OXFAM Manual for Development Workers.* Oxfam, OUP, Oxford.

Pratt, V., 1993, 'Experiences of Kenya Management Assistance Programme (K-MAP) as a practical link between large and small enterprises', symposium on Beyond subcontracting: assessing linkages between large and small enterprises, Royal Tropical Institute, 28–29 June, Amsterdam.

PRIDE, 1990, 'The PRIDE Micro-Credit Scheme', Programme of Rural Initiatives and Development Enterprises Ltd (PRIDE), Nairobi.

PRIDE, 1993–4, 'Evaluation of PRIDE coupon training project', Programme of Rural Initiatives and Development Enterprises Ltd (PRIDE), Nairobi.

PRODDER Newsletter, August 1994, special issue on 'Small business development: the entrepreneurial challenge', Braamfontein, South Africa.

Psacharopoulos, G. and W. Loxley, 1985, *Diversified Education: Evidence from*

223

Colombia and Tanzania, Johns Hopkins University Press, Baltimore.

Ramirez, J., 1993a, 'The Role of NGOs in Vocational Training for Self-Employment: Some Aspects of the Colombian Experience', ILO Expert consultation on training for self-employment through VTIs, Turin.

Ramirez, J., 1993b, 'The experiences in vocational training for self-employment in the Servicio Nacional de Apprendizaje (SENA) of Colombia', ILO Expert consultation on Training for self-employment through VTIs, Turin.

Rao, T. V. and C. Wright, 1991, *Entrepreneurial Skills Development Programmes in Fifteen Commonwealth Countries,* Commonwealth Secretariat, London.

Rao, T. V., C. Wright and H. Mukherjee, 1990, *Designing Entrepreneurial Skills Development Programmes: Resource book for technical and vocational institutions,* Commonwealth Secretariat, London.

Regional Programme on Enterprise Development (RPED), 1993, 'Economic development and the manufacturing sector in Kenya', Country background papers, Department of Economics, Nairobi and Department of Economics, Gothenburg.

Regional Programme on Enterprise Development (RPED), 1994, 'Limitations and reward in Kenya's manufacturing sector: a study of enterprise development', Country study series, Department of Economics, Nairobi and Department of Economics, Gothenburg.

Republic of Ghana, 1992, *Ghana's Country Paper on Development of Education, 1990-1992,* International conference on Education Geneva.

Republic of Uganda, Ministry of Planning and Economic Development, 1992, *Review of Government Policy as it Affects Small-scale Enterprises,* ApT Design and Development, UK.

Riddell, R. C. (ed.), 1990, *Manufacturing Africa: Performance and prospects of seven countries in Sub-Saharan Africa,* James Currey, London.

Riedmiller, S., 1994, 'Primary School Agriculture in Africa', *International Encyclopaedia of Education. Second Edition,* Pergamon, Oxford.

Riedmiller, S. and G. G. Mades, 1991, *Primary School Agriculture in Sub-Saharan Africa: Policies and Practices,* GTZ, Eschborn.

Robinson, M., 1991, 'Evaluating the impact of NGOs in rural poverty alleviation: India country study', ODI working paper No. 49, London.

Robson, M., 1992, 'Introducing technology through science education: a case study from Zimbabwe', *Science, Technology and Development,* 10/2: 203–21.

Ryan, T. C. I., 1987, 'The macro-economic context for education and manpower training for the next decade', paper to Seminar on Future Strategies and Options, Eldoret, 4–8 May 1987, Kenya.

Sako, M., 1994, 'Japan: vocational education and training', *International Encyclopaedia of Education. Second Edition,* Pergamon, Oxford.

Salleh Hj Din, M. and A. A. Gibb, 1990, 'Universities, Small Businesses and enterprise education – towards a holistic approach', *Small Enterprise Development,* 1/4: 27–36.

Shaeffer, S. (ed.), 1992, *Collaborating for Educational Change: The role of teachers, parents and community in school improvement,* IIEP, Paris.

Schmelkes, S. (ed.), 1990, *Post-alfabetizacion y trabajo en America Latina,* CREFAL UNESCO-OREALC, Patzcuaro, Mexico.

Sealy, C.G.W., 1993, 'Enhancing traditional apprenticeships in East Africa', ApT Design and Development, Moreton-in-Marsh, UK.

Sheffield, J. and V. Diejomah, 1972, *Non-Formal Education in African Development,* Afro-American Institute, New York.

Sheffield, J. R. (ed.), 1967, *Education, Employment and Rural Development,* East African Publishing House, Nairobi.

Standard, various issues, 1988–90, Nairobi.

Steele, D., 1972, 'Hindrances to the programme to encourage the rise of African entrepreneurship in Kenya resulting from the theory of the dual economy' in *Developmental Trends in Kenya,* Centre of African Studies, University of Edinburgh, Edinburgh.

Stevens, J., 1990, 'Mombasa Jua Kali Association: statistical data and recommendations for the jua kali development in Mombasa', Nairobi, processed.

Streeten, P., 1991, 'The judo trick – or crowding in', *Small Enterprise Development,* 2/2: 24–34.

Sutherland, M. B., 1991, 'Women and education: progress and problems', *Prospects,* 21/2: 145–55.

Swainson, N., 1991, 'Formalising the informal: training for the informal sector in South Africa', NEPI Working Paper, Educational Policy Unit, Witwatersrand.

Teitel, S., 1994, 'Technology and skills in Kenya manufacturing', draft, Case study series, Regional Programme on Enterprise Development, World Bank, Washington.

Theocharides, S. and A. Tolentino, 1991, *Integrated Strategies for Small Enterprise Development: A policy paper,* ILO SED/19/E, Geneva.

Thomas, L., 1993, 'The education and training needs of the informal sector: four case studies from India', draft paper for ODA research project on education and training for the informal sector.

Tolentino, A. and S. Theocharides, 1992, 'Strengthening Small Enterprises', ILO SED/21E, Geneva.

Tribe, M., 1995, 'Rural small-scale industrial development in Ghana: an exploration of issues', in *Science, Technology and Development,* Vol. 13. No. 1: 55–62.

Turnham, D., *et al.* (eds), 1990, *The Informal Sector Revisited,* OECD Development Centre, Paris.

UNDP, 1990, 'Demonstration and training for jua kalis', Project Document, DP/KEN/90/009, Nairobi.

UNDP, 1992, 'Kenya Youth Training and Employment Creation Project (KYTEC): Report of the Evaluation Mission', UNDP, Nairobi.

UNDP/ILO, 1990, 'Promoting entrepreneurship education in technical training institutions: project document', Project of the Government of Kenya, Nairobi.

Bibliography

Undugu Society of Kenya, 1986, *Annual Report,* Undugu, Nairobi.

Undugu, 1994, *Survival: The Undugu Society of Kenya's integrated approach to urban development, including 1992–3 Biennial Report,* Nairobi.

UNESCO, 1991, *World Education Report,* Geneva.

UNESCO, 1993, *UNESCO: Worldwide action in education,* Paris.

USAID, 1983, Rural private enterprise, Project paper: 615-0220, 11.6.83, USAID, Washington.

USAID/Kenya, 1985, *Private Enterprise Strategy Statement,* Edition 2, 13 September 1985, Nairobi.

USAID/Kenya, 1988, 'Evaluation of the Kenya Commercial Bank informal sector jua kali loan programme: a pilot scheme', Evaluation report No. 1, USAID, Kenya.

Utria, B. and B. Salomé, 1994, 'Informal sector: vocational education and training', *International Encyclopaedia of Education. Second Edition,* Pergamon, Oxford.

Van Rensburg, P., 1978, *The Serowe Brigades,* Macmillan, Basingstoke.

van der Wees, C. and H. Romijn, 1987, 'Entrepreneurship and small enterprise development for women in developing countries: an agenda of unanswered questions', Management Development Branch, Discussion paper, SED/13/E, ILO, Geneva.

Von Pischke, J. D., 1992, 'The exit problem in credit projects', *Small Enterprise Development,* 3/4: 25–33.

VSO Kenya, 1991, 'Report on jua kali sector workshop organised by VSO Kenya', 15–17 April 1991, Nairobi.

Waithaka, J. M., 1987, *Business Education for Standard Six: Pupil's book,* Kenya Literature Bureau, Nairobi.

Walsh, M., 1991, 'Informal sector apprenticeship in Mombasa and Dar es Salaam', a study by ILO/SDSR Project, Nairobi.

Walsh, M., 1992, 'Education, training and the informal sector in Kenya', Discussion paper no. 33, Vocational Training Branch, ILO, Geneva.

Walsh, M., K. Kane and C. Nelson, 1991, 'A case for business training with women's groups', *Small Enterprise Development,* 2/1: 13–19.

Webster, L., 1990, 'Fifteen years of World Bank lending for small and medium enterprises', *Small Enterprise Development,* 1/1: 17–25.

Webster, L.M. and P. Fidler (eds), 1994, *A Review of Informal Sectors in the Sahel,* Private Sector Development Department, World Bank, Washington.

Webster, L.M., R. Riopelle, and A-M. Chidzero, 1994, *World Bank Lending for Small Enterprises, 1989–1993,* Private Sector Development Department, World Bank, Washington.

Wilson, S. and Adams, A. V., 1994, 'Self-employment for the unemployed: experience in OECD and transitional economies', World Bank discussion papers, No. 263, World Bank, Washington.

World Bank, 1987, *Kenya Industrial Sector Policies for Investment and Export Growth,* Report No. 6711 KE., Vol. 1, World Bank, Washington.

World Bank, 1988, *Education in Sub-Saharan Africa,* World Bank, Washington DC.

World Bank, 1990, 'Africa. Regional programme on enterprise development: research & development programme proposal', Technical Department, Africa Region, World Bank, Washington.

World Bank, 1990, 'A poverty profile for Ghana, 1987–1988', by E. O Boateng *et al.*, Social Dimensions of Adjustment in Sub-Saharan Africa, SDA working paper No. 5, World Bank, Washington.

World Bank, 1991, *Vocational and Technical Education and Training*, World Bank, Washington.

World Bank, 1993a, 'Economic development and the manufacturing sector in Kenya', Country background papers, Regional Programme on Enterprise Development, Department of Economics, University of Nairobi and Department of Economics, University of Gothenburg.

World Bank, 1993b, 'Informal sector training and technology development project: Kenya pre-appraisal mission: aide memoire', World Bank, Washington.

World Bank, 1993c, *Republic of Kenya: Micro-and small enterprise training and technology project*, Staff Appraisal Report, Population and Human Resources Division, World Bank, Washington.

World Bank, 1995a, 'A continent in transition: Sub-Saharan Africa in the mid-1990s', draft, Africa Region, World Bank, Washington.

World Bank, 1995b, *Priorities and Strategies for Education: A World Bank review*, World Bank, Washington.

World Bank, Regional Programme on Enterprise Development, 1993, 'Technology and enterprise development in Ghana', Africa Technical Department, World Bank, Washington.

World Conference on Education for All, 1990, *World Declaration on Education for All and Framework for Action to Meet Basic Learning Needs*, New York.

Wright, D., 1989, 'Proposals for British aid to small-scale enterprise development in Kenya', ODA, London.

Wright, D., 1990, 'A study of the employment effects and other benefits of collaboration between multinational enterprises and small-scale enterprises', Multinational Enterprises Programme paper No. 60, ILO, Geneva.

Yambo, M., 1988, 'Reconnaissance of jua kali support activities in Kenya', report for DANIDA, Nairobi.

Yambo, M., 1991, 'Training needs assessment of the Kenyan informal sector', report to Kenya Industrial Estates *et al.*, Nairobi.

Young, A., 1989, 'Evaluation of the USAID/Kenya private sector programme: annexes, vol. 2', Bureau for Private Enterprise, USAID, Washington.

Young, B., 1992, 'Science and technology education: the response of the aid donors' in K. King, and D. Layton (eds), *Education in Science and Technology: Innovations and implications for the developing world*, special issue of *Science, Technology and Development* 10/2.

227

Index

229

233